AREAS "A" – Lands lost in the Winter War

A

1 – LAUTTASAARI
2 – KAUNISSAARI
3 – SUURSAARI
4 – KARELIAN ISTHMUS
5 – HANKO
6 – PORKKALA
7 – KOTKA

8 – SORTAVALA
9 – LAPPEENRANTA
10 – SAVONLINNA
11 – SUOMUSSALMI
12 – JUNTUSRANTA
13 – KRÄKSHÄR
14 – UTO

Lion Among Roses

David Bradley

Lion Among Roses:

A Memoir of Finland

Holt, Rinehart and Winston
New York   Chicago
San Francisco

Published, March, 1965
Second Printing, September, 1965

Designer: Ernst Reichl
81055-0215
Printed in the United States of America

ACKNOWLEDGMENTS For permission to quote from various sources,
thanks are due to the following:
Cassel & Co., Ltd., and the estate of Baron Gustaf Mannerheim for
Memoirs of Field Marshall Mannerheim.
Holt, Rinehart and Winston, Inc. The lines from "The Gift Outright,"
"Desert Places," "New Hampshire," and "Mending Wall" from *Complete Poems of Robert Frost.* Copyright 1923, 1930, 1939, by Holt,
Rinehart and Winston, Inc. Copyright 1936, 1942, 1951, © 1958 by
Robert Frost. Copyright © 1964 by Lesley Frost Ballantine. Reprinted
by permission of Holt, Rinehart and Winston, Inc.
Alfred A. Knopf, Inc. Reprinted by permission of Alfred A. Knopf, Inc.,
from *Meek Heritage* by F. E. Sillanpää, translated from the Finnish by
Alexander Matson. Copyright 1938 by Alfred A. Knopf, Inc.
G. P. Putnam's Sons. *The Unknown Soldier* by Väinö Linna. Copyright
© 1956 by Väinö Linna.
The Viking Press, Inc. The lines from "Chart 1203" and "Adam" from
Letter From a Distant Land by Philip Booth. Copyright © 1955, 1956
by Philip Booth. Reprinted by permission of the Viking Press, Inc.
Special thanks are given to Professor Irma Rantavaara and Lektori
Philip Binham, both of Helsinki, for their willing help and criticism. So,
too, to the Baker Library at Dartmouth College for providing a quiet
place in which to work.

To Ben, who fought them,
and Bron, who loved them.

Contents

Part Three

Part One

A country unique, admired,
pitied but never envied.
—Patrick O'Donovan

Edge of Land

The shape of the map outlines a man standing on an ill-balanced world. He faces half west. His right arm and hand are raised as if in salutation to the west, and at his back is Russia. The world he stands on is old, rocky, ice-worn, buried in forests and tortured with lakes. The man looks stocky and clothed for cold weather. He stands alone.

We had hoped, flying out of Stockholm, to catch some glimpse of this man's world, but the Caravelle, climbing steeply through broken layers of clouds, emerged in the high cold air of 34,000 feet where all but the sun is frozen still and no one really knows his own whereabouts any more.

The sun that evening, already set, rose again at an enormous distance beyond the ranges of clouds heaped up over the border of Norway and Sweden. That the sun should rise for the second time in one day, and this time in the far west, did not interest the children at all. They gave but a glance around at the pale sky, glad to be finished with the jolting press of clouds, and settled back with their books. Elisabeth was asleep with the baby, Steve, curled against her. Three hours of night was all we'd had over the great Atlantic; after that, hours in the London airport, then Hamburg, Copenhagen, Stockholm. An eighteen-hour flight was an abrupt way to begin two years in a land which chose to name itself in celebration of its swamps—Suomi (Fen-land).

The plane left the Swedish channels rapidly behind, passing over green blotches of islands and foam-etched skerries to the deep water of the Baltic. Soon we should be able to make out the Åland Islands below, see the patterned lights of Marie-hamn, count a few of the thousands of islands that stretch like steppingstones a hundred miles to the east where they make onto the mainland; we might even catch the flashing seaward signals of Utö (Out-island), the furthermost light on the southern coast of Finland. But clouds like panes of frosted glass slid under us and our airship was left to cruise by other invisible markers.

Once before, as a newspaperman during Finland's Winter War, I had made this trip—at that time in a Junker trimotor, a cold box of corrugated metal held together by rivets and an envelope of noise. The pilot had flown under a murky ceiling only a few hundred feet above the marbled ice floes marching down from the Gulf of Bothnia. There were reports of Russian aircraft operating overhead. Inside our snowy ship were a dozen British volunteers and some Canadian Finns coming over to join the defenders, all nonchalant warriors—and the rest were native types, military and diplomatic, returning from Sweden after another unsuccessful appeal for help. They seemed utterly impassive, almost asleep, flying in clouds between Baltic ice and Russian fighters. They were going home to a country so deeply involved in war that even their utmost efforts might earn them no more than death or deportation.

It seemed a lonely land then. It always has been.

When Russia attacked in November, 1939, almost no one outside of Finland expected the country to stand more than a week or two. "Poor little Finland" and "Brave little Finland" were the phrases we wrote in newspaper articles, trying to hide our shame and helplessness in heroic words. Yet the Finnish army held out for three and a half months and forced a negotiated peace. Within a year and a quarter it was Finland (forty times smaller) which went to war with Russia.

The Winter War came too early to be a turning point in the darkness of that greater conflict just beginning in Europe. But it was a fixed bright beacon. The Battle of Britain, El Alamein, Stalingrad, the Coral Sea, and Normandy were long to come—yet men in those times could take heart in the knowledge of what boys had done on the Karelian Isthmus.

4

Now, in 1960, twenty-one years later, I was returning. Americans need to see their country now and then from the outside. America is not just a rich bitch of a nation worried about her necklaces, though she often seems just that to those who read her weekly magazines but do not know her. She would need defending and explaining. I thought I could explain her best through teaching the works of her writers, poets, musicians. I did not fear what others might say about us. There was nothing anyone from the outside might say—good or bad—that was as true as what our own people, out of love and bitterness, had already written about us.

If that were the only objective, one might as well teach anywhere in the world. But I wanted Finland. Finns were strange people. I had known a few, miners and ski jumpers from upper Michigan. In street clothes they appeared to be average stocky fellows, though they talked a queer brand of English and nothing would make them change their ways. But see them out on their skis, stretched out over a big hill straining for a broken record (or a broken jaw) and you knew you were dealing with fanatics. Some sort of exultation carried them beyond the bounds of rationality—yet they survived, to go back up and ride the hill again.

And I had seen Finns in the Winter War. This was, in fact, a people who had fought forty wars against Russians, losing them all; still they survived. There must be some explanation. The Winter War had shown that in modern times a peaceable people need not cower, that right makes uncommon might. Now under the shadow of the atom, which makes all nations small nations, these simple ideas must still prevail. "My country—right or wrong" was of no use to anyone any more. Instinctively, as one who has lost something, I wanted to go back to Finland, taking my wife and five children. I didn't know what it was, exactly, that I was seeking, but I knew we were right in going there.

We could have gone to Norway. Norway would certainly have been more comfortable, for it is a happy friendly land. But Finland would be more interesting. In Finland one meets face to face both East and West. Finns are themselves an Eastern people, hailing from regions near the upper Volga. At

5

some time prior to the birth of Christ these people, like their cousins in Estonia and distant relatives in Hungary, had migrated west. But living more than a thousand years beside the Baltic had changed them. They were half westernized. Moreover for many centuries their cold brushy swampy land has been both bridge and barricade for the trampling of empires: Swedish kings, Russian Czars (both old and new style), even the British and Germans have waded through Finland, though few of them wanted to stay there.

Out of a confused and tortured past, startlingly in our day, these people revolted against both East and West and set up a republic of their own. Strangely, too, they have kept that republic in spite of invasion, subversion, a civil war, a huge Communist movement, a Fascist uprising; they have kept it in spite of the Great Depression and a recent World War which brought them two defeats by Russia.

So they stand, still balanced between East and West, one of the few countries where neutrality is a fact rather than a worn-out epithet. One would be hard put to find a comparable record of survival.

All this we knew, coming to Finland, and not much more. We thought in all the traditional clichés: land of Paavo Nurmi, Mannerheim, Sibelius; land of reindeer, steam baths, and the payers of debts.

Our companions in the Caravelle were mainly home-coming Finns—businessmen, government officials, vacationers, some with their wives. Stocky and middle-aged they slumped down solidly into their seats and stared blankly from the oval windows. The men wore dark suits, Homburgs, heavy black overcoats. Beside them sat their wives, newly coiffeured in the latest Italian mode, a little tightly tailored, a little short of breath. There were no Paavo Nurmis in this plane.

Our small band contrasted sharply with these well-dressed people. The children ranged in age from sixteen years to eight months. Four, for comfort's sake, were wearing sneakers; the girls' print dresses had lost something of their newness from being slept in overnight; and here and there Steve's bottle had added something. However, if this invasion by one family of Americans interested or horrified our companions at all they gave not the least sign of it.

6

Taciturn and inscrutable they seemed, like their migratory Asiatic ancestors. Long before Christ, somewhere north of what is now Kiev, Finnlike tribes met and mixed with Russians. This early contact seems to have been both happy and fruitful. The Russians called them "the strange people" or "the unusual people," not in a derogatory sense but out of admiration. The Russians wisely took the women for wives, but wanted nothing of the language. Thus that talented and energetic people who came to be known as the Great Russians owes something to a strain of Finnish blood.

Finns moved on into the region of Estonia, and then, in the first millennium after Christ, crossed the Baltic islands into the land of swamps. There they found Lapps (referred to as Finns by Tacitus) and probably some early Swedish tribesmen. Hunting north, settling north themselves over the centuries, they became the western Finns. Later other bands migrated from Estonia around the eastern shore of the Gulf, through the swamps that were to become St. Petersburg, into the wilderness of lakes and forests lying to the west of Lake Ladoga: these were the Karelians. Until the Swedes came in the twelfth century, bringing Christianity and a better sword, the various tribes fought and plundered each other.

Looking south from our plane, I thought I could make out the curving shape of a dim shore that might be Estonia, or what used to be called Estonia. But I couldn't be sure; night comes on fast in late August. Estonia was one of those small countries created, perhaps too artificially, out of the universal tribal desire for independence and the special muddle of the First World War. In a Second World War, along with Latvia, Lithuania, Czechoslovakia and many others, it had been swallowed up again. Ask for these small countries now and all you're likely to get are ghostly voices off the steppes of the latest greatest imperialism.

I watched the coastline for a while, looking down from that unreal sky-perch; slowly the shape changed, separated, greyed away into obscurity and I knew I was only looking at a layer of clouds. Hard to say where Estonia and Latvia had gotten to.

When the sun went down again, we flew in a diffusion of lavender light. But night was rising out of the east; it seemed to well up blue and thick from the whole continent. I bumped

7

Ben's arm so that he might have a last look. Sharp stars were already piercing the sky.

"Hey, Ben, look."

"What?" The seven-year-old was deep in a Classic Comics' version of Robinson Crusoe.

"What do you think's down there?"

Ben jammed a finger into the text so as not to lose his place by so much as a word.

"Nothing. Clouds."

"The big guy's down there."

"What big guy?"

"Russia."

Ben examined the darkness, unimpressed. "Okay," he said, turning back at once to Robinson Crusoe. The question of what to do after seeing a cannibal's print in the sand was real and immediate, and of a size the imagination could grasp. But Russia . . .

Soon after, the plane began slanting down in a long shuddering power glide; the clouds came licking up like the frozen surf of a ghost sea; somewhere within the opaque mass the plane upended in a singing arc and almost before the mists gave way we saw the blue lights riding beside us and felt the big thing touch.

Kim, Wendy, Ben, Bronwen, Steven—jackets, books, handbags, diapers—brief case, tickets, money, passports. Outside the plane the air was balmy and the land a wonderfully certain thing underfoot. We were herded into one end of a long barracks building—for Helsinki is probably the only Western capital which hasn't yet built a chrome-glass Wurlitzer airport—and there, in due course, we stood before a passport official in a glass box.

"Americans? All?"

"Yes. Seven of us."

He took the green books and read them back and forth with some puzzlement.

"Seven? Here is only five passes."

I tried to explain that two passports carried two children each, but he ignored me and went to reading the stamped matter, upside down, sideways, with a happy curiosity which did not seem to require comprehension. Then with sudden decisiveness he turned to a fresh page in each book and stamped it vigorously.

"You see, it is here your work permit. Good. You must report to police where you live."

"Tonight?" I asked. "We'll be in a hotel tonight."

"Oh, not that. But later, when you will know where you will live. You have seven children?"

"Five."

He shook his head sympathetically. "In any case—welcome."

We thanked the official and pushed through the door into Finland.

Old Friends

We had come in the dark out of farmlands and copses, suddenly, into the city. First we saw apartment houses with shops on the ground floor—oranges, bread, eyeglasses, shoes, flowers, milk—then, as the sound of the tires turned to a rumble over cobblestones, all at once we were among big buildings of old red granite and modern cement and glass structures, all with their night lights burning. Scarcely a person was abroad on the streets. Helsinki, ghostly in the pale glare of mercury lamps, looked like a city abandoned with its machinery left running.

But in the morning the city was reoccupied. The glint of sun from red-tile roofs across the street and the senseless pushing and flapping of pigeons outside on the window ledge woke me. We had two rooms on the top floor of the Helsinki Hotel, very modern, clean rooms, which would serve as our temporary home. I lay in my bed wondering where we should begin. Schools, transportation, proximity to shops, playgrounds, doctors—all of these would be considerations, but all were secondary to the main question: Where, in a big city of two strange languages, did one begin?

I knew only five people in Finland. Early in the summer I had written them asking for advice and help in finding an apartment. Two had replied that nothing could be done until we arrived; the other three, I supposed, were still pondering how to frame an answer. Now in late August just a week remained before the opening of the public schools.

While I was mulling over these questions, running feet came

pounding down the hall and Ben and Bronwen banged through the door.

"Hey, I know one word already. Guess what? . . . *Hissi.* Know what a *hissi* is? An elevator!" Ben was hitching up his pajama bottoms as he followed the shining Bronwen into the room. "It's great," she said.

"Me and Bron were having a race."

"And I can run it myself."

"Don't you guys know Steve's asleep?" I asked.

"No he isn't," Ben replied. "I beat her. I ran up the stairs and just made it."

"Didn't the hotel man say anything?"

"Nope." Bronwen shrugged. "He just looked at us. But anyways, he's got another elevator he can use."

"Get dressed," I said. Life in Helsinki had begun. There was no turning back now.

After breakfast, I looked up the telephone numbers of our five friends. Seeing their names in the book—people I had not seen, in some cases, for twenty years—gave me a jolt of reality which neither the airport nor the hotel had produced. The desk clerk took the numbers and had the telephone operator call them all, one after another. There were no responses.

"I am sorry," said the clerk sympathetically, "but just now, you know, in summer, all people are in the country. You could, of course, try at the University. But it is locked."

I told the clerk we would try the numbers later, then went out to have a look around. I had seen this city first during the bitter winter of 1940, at the end of the Winter War and beginning of the peace. Some places I remembered, and certain faces. I remembered particularly the stunned, shocked expression on everyone's face the morning of the announcement that peace had been concluded with Russia: "Stop fighting? Why? We are not beaten." Some people even thought it was treason to accept the peace. Only later came understanding of the desperate condition at the front which had forced Mannerheim to make terms.

In those days most of us newsmen worked at the Kämp Hotel, a quaint baroque mansion on North Esplanade. It was always full of people who seemed to know everything that was going to happen all over Europe, though none of them guessed the invasion of Norway before it came. Inside the Kämp, war was conducted with Victorian grace; there was plenty of liquor, smoke, speculation, wisdom, advice, and heroism. Probably half the spies in Finland were registered at the Kämp. It was hard, though, to get any facts about the war in Karelia. The government offices handed us bulletins, translated into four languages, and we, mixing these with liberal dashes of rumor, passed them on for news. Outside, the windows were boarded up and banked with sandbags; inside, long black velvet curtains were pulled shut. We lived in a world all our own, far from the war, and when the war was over, everyone scattered. I remember that feeling too: the war finished; the glamour all gone out of Helsinki; only the Finns left to start cleaning up the mess.

Outside the Helsinki Hotel the air was sweet and cool, blowing in from the sea; the sun was bright but thin, having an end-of-summer feeling in the shadows. Crowds of people were moving in the streets, seemingly unconscious of the cars that tried to force a passage among them, or of the sputtering motor bikes and their red-faced frustrated riders. Helsinki without sandbags and boards looked clean, wide, polished, shining with glass. The restaurant where I had taken my meals was gone; in its place stood a tall modern co-operative department store. Up the hill but a block or two the great white and green Lutheran Cathedral looked down over Alexander's Square and the government buildings. Across a corner of the square was the University, and behind it a new glass frame, the Porthania annex to the University. Both were closed and locked.

Retracing my steps against the tide of people I found the city's most notable landmark: the railway station, with the bus platforms and the National Theater close by. Although I had seen this station many times before, its peculiar scalloped arches, rounded buttresses, and high rounded clock tower, all built of red granite blocks and beaded with ancient tribal designs, struck me anew as something too beautiful to be sheer design; luck in a sense of proportion must have had something to do with it.

Eliel Saarinen designed the railway station years ago. Though often called an example of modern architecture, owing to its frank simplicity, it seems rather to step back into furthest history and take for its model the plain ice-cut rounded contours of Finland's granite knolls and seaward bluffs. More modern buildings, taller and glassier, rise up all around the station, but they are unexciting by comparison. In its way the railroad building stands as an everyday monument to that Finnish national movement which brought such great music, art, and literature at the end of the last century, and which gave form and spirit to Finnish independence.

Lenin left for St. Petersburg from this station in a shrouded carriage one night in 1917. Presidents and Ministers of the Republic have beaten a path across its floors, summoned to Russia for innumerable conferences and crises. I remembered the station in winter, blacked out and bulking huge in falling snow, the dark air pierced by the sharp whistles of birch-burning locomotives. Inside, the halls had been draped with smoke; everywhere soldiers had been sitting on their gear waiting to move east; even wounded men still in bandages were returning to the front.

Now there were happy people heading toward a vacation in the country, others coming to Helsinki for shopping, business, pleasure. Tourists too: Swedes, Germans in leather pants; groups of Russians, festooned with cameras.

Among all the flux of people around the railway square there was one man entirely alone. He sat askew in his chair, brows knitted, face a little sad, thinking. This was Alexis Kivi (or Aaltonen's granite study of the man), Finland's great novelist and playwright. In the smooth grey stone even the pale fever of the tubercular was recorded.

Finnish writing begins with Alexis Kivi in much the same way that American writing begins with Mark Twain. The two were contemporaries. *The Seven Brothers* and *Huckleberry Finn* were published in the same decade, and in many ways the books and the men are remarkably similar. Both writers broke so completely with an overelegant tradition that the tradition ceased to exist. Both gave tongue to backwoods men and boys.

Neither overlooked brutality or stupidity or failed to ease us toward the truth with humor and sympathy.

Finns turn automatically to *The Seven Brothers* for a mirror of themselves: "Read this," they say, "if you want to understand us." *The Seven Brothers* is much more than just a native country story extolling wit and perseverance through many funny episodes; here you meet the whole strange tribe: the boastful pigheaded Finns; the strong taciturn Finns; the peacemakers; the forest lovers; the religious Finns (with a dash of mysticism and two dashes of alcohol); the tellers of tall stories; the fast-talking, needling wily ones. Moreover, the brothers, striving to hack a place for themselves in a harsh environment and among unyielding neighbors, recapitulate the struggle of the race to leave their bogs and superstitions and gain a culture, self-respect, and independence.

I was glad to see Kivi again. I would need him in teaching. Different as America and Finland now seem to be, there are many striking similarities both in history and in literature. Twain and Kivi could form the abutments of a solid bridge of understanding between the two countries.

Following the incoming throngs, I crossed the traffic in front of the station, walked through the glass arcades, visited the two great book stores, then turned down side streets where the wealth of an artistic nation was poured out for display. I tipped the cap of youth to one shop in particular, where over a window of neckties a weathered brass sign read: PAAVO NURMI. Then to the Esplanade: a quiet park, lined with trees and flower beds, which runs from the Swedish Theater down to South Harbor.

Helsinki looked blooming and prosperous. A city now of half a million, it is growing and changing rapidly. Exuberant, unfinished, it lacks the magnificence of Stockholm or Paris, as it lacks the sadness of a greatness that is past. At its center Helsinki still retains the intimate feeling of a town. One may cross the main business and shopping area in ten minutes of steady walking; there are the two National Theaters (Finnish and Swedish) and many lesser ones, the principal restaurants, the large department stores, the hundreds of specialty shops, and, down by the sea, the great outdoor morning market.

Grandmothers hauling children out of the flower beds, men of affairs sunning themselves on park benches, soldiers whistling and jibing at girls in short dresses, old women and young boys licking ice-cream cones—this was the look of the Esplanade under a summer sun. There, too (in bronze), was Runeberg, national poet. And overlooking the market from a fountain of seals and fish, *Havis Amanda*, brash and beautiful in her nakedness, the sea wind always in her hair.

Suddenly I felt at home. It didn't matter that all the words I heard conveyed no meaning. It didn't matter that the only people I recognized were statues. Helsinki looked like a fine place to live in and I knew we would make out.

One thing of value, at least, remained from my days at the Kämp Hotel—the friendship of a small sharp-faced black-haired man named Ole Reuter. A teacher of English, he had been employed during the war in a government information bureau set up to help foreign journalists. Ole and I had kept track of each other. Now he was Professor Reuter, chairman of the English Department at the University of Helsinki. He was responsible for our coming. Once, during a sabbatical of research in America, he had visited us and proposed that I come to Finland to teach. The salary would not be large he said, but added, "at least you will not have to set up a tent in the Esplanade."

I told him that while the idea sounded interesting, it was also crazy: I knew no Finnish, and as for the ocean of English literature, any man going there puts to sea in his own small boat.

Ole Reuter smiled at this, looking sideways at me: "My dear fellow, I have to make the assumption, I am willing to make the assumption, that you probably know more English at least than our Finnish students . . ."

Some weeks later I wrote him in Washington that we liked his proposal and would make arrangements to come to Finland whenever he gave the signal. Three and a half years later Ole Reuter replied: "My colleagues welcome you, but they think with your big family it is quite impossible."

Decisiveness was in order. I wrote back: "We are steadily losing ground here, Ole. Elisabeth has had another one since. Expect us in late August."

First you build a sauna. After that, when there is time, a house.

ℌome

We never knew for sure how we came to get an apartment. Perhaps it was Li Enbom telephoning all over the city, perhaps it was the newspaper advertisement. Once the negotiations were under way, the Finns seemed as confused as we were, and it is my personal opinion that we were given a home intended for someone else, though we did not actually read in the paper that our landlord, Mr. Kurikka, had taken his jumpy salesman out to the city dump and shot him.

Our choices were not many—only two, in fact. A summer villa was available twenty miles to the east of the city on the shore of a cove, facing a stony point and an island-studded bay of the Baltic. But it was a home fit for President Kekkonen himself—a modern house, a wide lawn, and, down by the water, a sauna built of hand-hewn logs. The villa would have aged ten years with our troops quartered there for a season. We had to let it go.

A few days after our arrival Li Enbom drove into town from her summer place to see if she could help us. A fine-looking blonde-haired woman of middle height, Li breezed into the hotel with eye shadow enough for the Queen of Sweden and a stride suited to an inspector general. The bell-boys went into a panic of action at her request to see all the daily newspapers; a moment later, after kisses all around, flowers for Elisabeth and candy for the children, Li was seated at the phone in our bedroom, scanning the directory with one eye and the For Rent columns with the other.

16

In an hour and a half Li called all the Swedish Finns in Helsinki, insisting that they do something for the Americans who had come "bringing such terrible masses of children."

"You know," Li said, dialing furiously, "housing in this city is quite impossible. After the war we could build nothing. All must go to the Russians to pay the war debts. Now it is worse. Everyone wants to live in Helsinki. Why? The weather is terrible, the worst in Finland, so all wish to come here."

The upshot of these phone calls was inconclusive. While the Swedish community was thrown into a convulsion, no one was willing to vacate his own apartment for the invading Americans. Li dumped all the papers into a wastebasket; there was only one way to find a home, she said, and that was to place an advertisement in the *Helsingin Sanomat*. One happy event however followed Li's prodigious efforts: the finding of a bed. Somewhere, in one of the furniture stores, Li was told by a friend, was a double bed—"the American kind."

Li was embarrassed to bring the matter up: "Perhaps, considering all things, you should sleep the Finnish way—in two beds."

"Twin beds!" shouted Elisabeth. "In this cold country?"

"Well, I only thought—come on then, we must find it."

The American bed must have been famous among furniture dealers in Helsinki, for Li inquired only at two stores before she was hot on the trail. She ran it down that afternoon, finding it, with the help of a salesman, dismantled and packed away behind cartons of furniture at the end of an underground storeroom. The salesman, a slender stooped fellow with a mournful expression, pried out the pieces of the bed and assembled them. It was merely a wooden frame with four legs, having a mahogany headboard, a hard box of springs, and, over this, a thin cotton-batting mattress.

"Well," said the salesman, surveying the unique piece, "in any case it is a bed."

"It cannot cost so much," Li said. "No one wants a thing like that."

"It was ordered by an American . . ."

"Then it is not for sale?"

"The American never came back," the thin man replied,

struggling with a moral problem. "But—that is three years ago. I suppose he comes not for it now."

Thus we acquired our first piece of a home in Finland. For the next three days we had no further clues to follow. Our advertisment appeared in the *Helsingin Sanomat;* we received a number of telephone calls at the hotel, but nothing came of them. The children, meanwhile, went off to the island zoo, to the fair grounds and Olympic pool, to parks and movies. Once they took a boat trip around Helsinki's famous archipelago. The boat broke down and the engineer, cussing mightily and spitting tobacco juice, explained to the passengers that the engine had not been working right since the Russians had it in 1917.

Then one morning a note was left for us at the hotel suggesting that we go to the Cité Notariata. No one at the hotel knew what the Cité was, but the clerk assured us that at least it was not the police station. The Cité Notariata was located on the second floor of a dingy stone building in the old part of the city. We entered through swinging doors, and when our eyes became accommodated to the penumbra within, we could make out a long barricade of wood and four tables beyond. The tables were buried in loose paper. No one could work at them; nor could anyone see to read there, for the windows were encrusted with a century of dirt and in the middle of the high dark ceiling a single bulb glowed like an exhausted firefly. Several old people and two families were seated along the wall, waiting. Behind the barricade fevered denizens were rushing back and forth brandishing paper. Over in a corner sat a man shouting Finnish into a telephone with the wrath of one falsely accused of stealing horses.

"Let's get out of here," Elisabeth whispered harshly.

"But it may be a real-estate office," I said.

"I know that, and it looks as crooked as they come."

Finally one of the young men motioned us forward.

"We believe you have an apartment to rent," I said.

"*Mitä?*" he snapped.

"An apartment. Home—*Koti*—rent."

With a dazed look the young man rushed from the room. A second young man approached; I repeated the question.

"One moment," he said in English, bowing apologetically. "I am sorry but I do not speak English." He too vanished.

The room and all its occupants were silent now. Our simple colloquy seemed to have paralyzed even the horse thief. What happened to the staff of the Cité was never clear. A frightened secretary from some other office beckoned us through the swinging doors, a middle-aged man who claimed to be in the wood-export business conducted us downstairs, and a nervous blond youth ushered us into a taxi. From that moment on everything happened with cinematic swiftness. The taxi driver withdrew his head into his coat collar and aimed the car down the nearest street. Buildings flashed by, trolley cars and trucks loomed up in front of us and evaporated, shocked faces surged by on either side. We looped over a railroad track and saw harbor warehouses on one side, a Moslem graveyard on the other.

"Are you interested in religion?" the export man asked, pulling contentedly on a cigar.

Down a long avenue we saw a great factory with the sign ALKO displayed on top. "*Voi Voi*," said the youth in front. "The men are lucky who can work in there."

"It is the State Alcohol Monopol," explained the older man. The young man combed his yellow hair with his fingers and told us with a melancholy smirk that he had just lost his automobile permit because he "loved too much the bottle."

Up on a high wooden bridge over an arm of the sea, the planks rumbling from the weight of oncoming buses; then down. "The bridge is so old," our philosophic friend said, "even the engineers don't dare look underneath. . . . But, in any case, it has not fallen yet." Then we were in an island suburb where, among the stucco apartment buildings and glass-fronted ground-floor shops, the taxi driver whirled us this way and that until he came to a street called Kuikkarinne (Ducks' Slope) that ran directly down to the sea. Stopping in a spray of gravel he indicated a row house, seven two-story apartments side by side, with entries at the back. "Here," the driver said. Now the blond salesman (whose suit and grey shirt looked like an unmade bed) was all a shooting of cuffs and a flourishing of keys. We entered what seemed to be a small basketball court: solid cement and plaster walls, a gleaming wood floor smelling of varnish, and a high reverberating echo always hovering in the air. Downstairs 30′ x 13′, including the stairway and a minute kitchen; 30′ x 13′ upstairs, for three bedrooms, two closets, and a bath. Under the building was storage, parking, a sauna, and a laundry.

"You see," smiled the older man, "very modern and spacious, finished only yesterday." That statement was probably true. Outside the living room window were heaps of rubble, twisted iron bars, broken plaster-covered boards, glass. But beyond this: a stretch of sandy beach where people were sitting and children playing, and then a bay, yachts, and two islands.

I think Elisabeth's mind was made up from the very beginning. I had hoped to find an old house with a little less spaciousness and more elbow room, someplace where we wouldn't have to step out into the hall to brush our teeth, but in matters of this kind a woman's instinct is infallible. If she wants to live in a piano box in a tree, it is sure that there she will make her best home. All the rest is unimportant. Besides, logic was on Elisabeth's side: this apartment at least existed; it was empty; school would begin in two days; and the price was within our means.

Our jumpy blond friend was hovering around with a printed form in one hand and a dripping pen in the other. However there were a few questions yet to be answered. "What about schools?" Elisabeth asked.

Neither the wood exporter nor the salesman knew anything about the schools, but here the taxi driver, who had followed us around, taking a great interest in the proceedings, volunteered, "Yes, good schools. Four schools. Two Finnish and two Swedish, but one is not built yet."

And the neighborhood?

"Good," the wood man said. "All good Finnish people. In former times up on the hill had the Communists a school. . . ."

"Communists?"

"Yes. A school to train agitators . . . but they are good people, too. They will not bother."

The next question was more serious: the contract. The

paper that the salesman waved before us was densely packed with long unintelligible words—more than enough words for a Treaty of Mutual Assistance—and the only symbols I could make out were the blanks left for the date and signatures.

"We must have a lawyer," I said.

"A lawyer. For what?" asked the older man.

"I will not sign something I cannot read."

An argument then ensued between the taxi driver and the salesman, one shrugging his shoulders, the other shouting that Mr. Kurikka, who owned the apartment, already had twenty people who wanted to rent it. But at last the wood exporter prevailed upon them to return with us to the city where we could find a lawyer.

All of us (except the taxi man) marched into the offices of a Harvard-trained barrister whose name I happened to know. This man soon allayed our fears, the contract was a standard one, good for one year from the date of signing and renewable on notice. We signed two copies, the blond agent counter-signed, then the lawyer witnessed the contract. The agent, receiving his fee according to Finnish custom, was all good will again. He took his copy and studied it with the air of a man proud of having dealt a good stroke for international amity.

Then suddenly he jumped to his feet, choking and pointing to the paper: "Bradley? Is that the name? Is the name that stands there Bradley?"

"Bradley, yes," said the lawyer.

"But . . ." The poor man gave a moan and, muttering something that sounded like Sat-on-a-Percolator, dashed from the room.

The lawyer shrugged. "He thought you were someone else. . . . However, a contract is a contract. The place is yours."

We never heard any more from the blond man.

As we were leaving the building our sylvan philosopher took from an inner pocket of his coat a thirty-page document which he pressed into my hand. It was written in English, single-spaced, and there was not a paragraph break in the first four pages. The title read: *Some Considerations about the*

Need for a Universal Religion for the Salvation of Mankind in the Atomic Age.

"Please," he said, giving a ceremonious bow. "Perhaps someday I will come to your apartment, then we can talk about such things."

Next day we moved out of the Helsinki Hotel to Ducks' Slope No. 2 on the island of Lauttasaari. The famous American-style bed arrived on a truck. Thus the three girls could sleep on the mattress, Ben on some coats, Elisabeth and I on the box springs, and Steve on the floor in one of the closets. We would have to sleep in our clothes, using coats for covers, until our shipment of household things arrived from Hoboken.

The children all ran off to the beach to swim while I hiked up to a corner store for milk, bread, cheese, and chocolate. Kim bought some candles and several bottles of carbonated juice. At supper we sat with our backs to the plaster walls. The ceiling boomed back everything we said.

"Are we camping?" asked Bronwen. "Isn't it the beautifulest place?"

Two sailboats were ghosting into the bay on a dying breeze. Later Kim lit the candles and propped them in the empty juice bottles. The warm lights cast a confusion of shadows on the walls. This was a beautiful place. We felt very lucky.

"Missä . . . ?"
"Mitä?"
"Missä, where . . .?"
"Mitä?"
"Missä. . . . Aw, skip it."

School

They were sleeping like the slaughtered, four of them on the floor half covered by rumpled coats: Kim, Wendy, Bronwen, radiating from our cotton mattress; Ben curled up on the linoleum, his head under a radiator.

"Come on. Rise and shine. School today."

Sun was flooding in through the big windows. Outside the children's rooms was a balcony running the width of our apartment. It gave fine view out over the beach and the bay to an arm of the land beyond, now dark in the shade of spruce.

"What time i

"Seven."

"Do I have to go school?"

Downstairs Elisabeth was getting breakfast ready. It would have to be a cold breakfast of Kellogg's Corn Flakes (manufactured in Finland), bread, butter, milk—for while we had a stove we did not yet have any pots or saucepans. Like new moths fresh from their cocoons the children began to crawl stiffly around, harvesting a sock here, a shoe there, from the contents of suitcases spilled on the floor. Even the minimum organization of one child to each corner had already broken down; chaos would rule until we could get these small rooms furnished.

Kim came down first, for she had farthest to go. If she felt anxiety over beginning in a new school in a new language, she was determined not to show it. Both Kim and Wendy were

23

entered in Swedish-speaking schools. (It had taken the kindly intervention of a Deputy Minister of Education to place them, for the "bulge" of postwar children had hit Finnish schools.) Kim had spent two years on her own in Norway and already spoke Norwegian. She should not have great difficulty in learning Swedish, though she had first insisted she wanted to go to a Finnish school so she wouldn't ruin her Norwegian. But she would be a junior now in high school and the Minister persuaded her she would lose a whole year of other work simply learning enough Finnish to understand. Wendy didn't care either way; her attitude was "How do I know whether I can speak Swedish or Finnish? I haven't tried yet."

Kim ate quickly and left at once to catch a bus into town. From there she would have to transfer and make a long journey out to the north to reach her Svenska Samskola (co-educational school). The entire trip would take her forty-five minutes, twice a day.

" 'Bye," she said, giving a little smile and a wave. She was a shy one. In the sun outside her hair looked like carded brass.

Wendy next, skipping downstairs and eating breakfast while she pulled on her coat.

"Daddy, do you think I should cut off all my hair?"

"No."

"I knew you wouldn't," she giggled. "But all the kids here wear short hair."

"Don't talk the teacher to death the first day, Wendy."

"I'll try not to. 'Bye."

Wendy was going to a Svenska Flika Skola (Swedish Girls School) over on Bulevardi Street. We didn't worry about her. Flika sounded about right. Never was there, with brighter plumage, a harder hammerhead.

"Two down, two to go," sighed Elisabeth. By this time Steve was yelling to be released from his closet, Bronwen, age six, was yelling that she hadn't a thing to wear, and Ben was yelling that his shoes had been stolen. Ben had always hated school. . . . Having already endured two years of incarceration, he had concluded that school was nothing less than a conspiracy against him. His highest academic goal was to set a world's record by being expelled before noon on the first day, and he had agreed to try the Lauttasaari folk school only because he had seen boys playing soccer in the playfield.

It was Bronwen who nearly caused a revolt that day. She stood at the top of the stairs shivering in her white slip, her large eyes leaking water:

"Mummie . . . Mother . . . Motherrrrrrrrr!"

"What is it, Bronwen? Hurry. We'll be late."

"I don't . . ."

"What?"

"No."

"Are you sick?"

"NO!"

"Then for heaven's sake what's the matter?"

"Clothes."

"But I laid out your best new dress."

"I know . . ." Tears were splashing onto the varnished floor.

"Bronwen!"

"Well . . . Finnish kids don't wear . . . stuff like that."

There was no choice, however. We promised to take her shopping as soon as she was out of school and get her a proper Finnish outfit—garters, mud-colored cotton stockings, dresses, the works—if she would go along and get through this one day.

Ben understood: "Don't worry, Bron. If someone says something . . ."

"But they'll laugh at me . . ."

"If anyone laughs, I'll pop him one."

So they went at last. When the bells of a church began ringing from the woods below Windmill Hill, we saw the streams of children flowing toward school. Elisabeth went off with Ben and Bron. She wanted to see that they were placed in the right grades. The school was a Finnish elementary, or folk, school, one of two on the island. Though it was only two years old, it was already so full that classes had to be conducted in morning and afternoon shifts.

School was across a main street and through the woods. As long as we could, Steve and I watched the little delegation going up the sidewalk under the stucco four-story apartments, then we went down on the beach to sit in the sun. The first day of school would be sudden and total immersion. I tried to guess what a child would think having to sit in a room full of people where not one sound in four hours would convey any meaning. What would he do? I could not even imagine the experience, for I had the adult's well-developed protective responses, but the child would face his uncertainties as naked as Adam.

September 2. Summer was still the ease of things beside the Baltic: the sky soft blue, pale gulls flickering over the islands, and the yachts in the bay hauling and slacking their reflections. This could have been a stretch of Maine coast except that there were no stacked lobster pots, and no tidemarks darkening the pilings of wharves. As in Maine the water was cold even at the end of summer, though it lacked the salt and the iodine smell of rockweed. Out among the far islands two coasting schooners, sand luggers, were sliding downwind. Beach, water, islands in summer—skiing right here in winter—it seemed unlikely that we could have found a better location near Helsinki. The kids would make friends, and begin to learn the language.

When Elisabeth returned from school her eyes were too bright and her smile pasted to her lips:

"Bronnie's all set anyway. She's in with a nice young teacher, Mrs. Laitinen, who has a girl just starting school. But Ben, nobody knew what to do about him. The principal didn't know what to do."

"Did anybody speak English?"

"Mrs. Laitinen came with me to help. By age Ben ought to be in the third grade, but really he ought to be in the first. They put him in third because the teacher is a man."

"Well, it might work."

Then she began to cry. "He looked so lost. You should have seen the look on his face. As if we'd stuck him in a mad house and he didn't know why."

"Oh, he'll make out," I said.

"I hope so. I gave him a dictionary, anyway."

We put Steve in a collapsible stroller, walked up to the main street, and boarded a No. 23 bus for town. We needed to supply an entire household. Our home would have to be a small harbor of refuge for the weeks just ahead; we had no idea what kind of storms would come, but lights must be burning and the stove ready with food.

Shopping for lamps, glasses, dishes, and cutlery proved to be less easy than we had imagined, not because things were unavailable but because there was so much, all so well designed. The most ordinary things, like glass tumblers, had been touched with grace and color; they would be art objects elsewhere in the world. I resolved to hold my tongue. With two people judging nothing would ever be decided. But the resolution didn't last. After the first half hour Finnish designers had their way with us and we bought twice the glass we would need, just for the pleasure of looking at it.

Buying beds raised a different problem. The two small rooms on the seaward side of our apartment measured exactly 6′ x 13′. Each room must house two beds, a desk, bureau, and book shelves. Twin beds, side by side, would take up the whole space clear across. Bunk beds would serve all right, but a fall from the top bunk onto linoleum-covered cement might crack a head. After prospecting through several furniture stores, we discovered what seemed to be the perfect solution: one large bed with a smaller one on wheels that could roll away under the first. We ordered two sets immediately.

"Very well," the salesman said, "in two months you get them."

"In two months?"

"Yes. It can be six weeks."

"But the children are sleeping on the floor!"

The salesman, wanting to help us but scarcely able to keep his amusement from showing, explained that in Finland furniture is not made up in bulk and stocked in warehouses. The home market was too small for that. New designs and models are brought out as samples and the plant awaits orders before going into production. He would, he said, be glad to sell us the set of beds we were looking at, but they were the only sample he had. Then he asked us where we lived.

"Lauttasaari."

"Ah-ha. You can of course . . . one moment, I write for you a name." He scribbled a name and address on a scrap of paper.

27

"So. Here is a very good carpenter. Two months is too long for children. But to him you take the plans, and in one week you get the beds. All right?"

This was a queer business, a salesman telling us how not to buy his furniture, but I wasn't going to argue. We bought four spongy plastic mattresses of a size to fit the beds. They would be delivered that afternoon. Then we walked Steve down through the gardens of the Esplanade to the waterside market where half the mothers of Helsinki seem to do their morning shopping. Stalls and tables of flowers occupied the square around the fountain of *Havis Amanda*. On the great cobblestone plaza beyond were hundreds of other stalls, four deep along the stone quay. Fish first, next to the boats; vegetables in the second tier, then fruit, then flowers; the rows in the far distance displayed brooms, baskets, hardware, bath towels, table mats, toys, work clothing, gym suits, even gaudy homemade oil paintings. Such a harvest of things at the open market, and such a gallery of faces: Mongol, Tartar, neckless Russians, blond Swedes, sharp-faced Lapps, English, German, scowling black-eyed Gypsies, painted upper class faces, broad peasant faces, and the composed strong faces of Finnish Finns.

We walked with the crowd, looking, tasting, buying. When our arms were full, we bought market bags and kept on. Lettuce, cucumbers, peas, broccoli. There were tables piled high with varieties of mushrooms. Others heaped with red lingonberries raked that morning from the forests, like the world's treasure of rubies. Down by the water a score of double-ended wooden fishing boats were tied up stern first to the quay. Some were loaded with apples, some with potatoes, and in other boats the men ran their fingers through boxes of quicksilver Baltic herring.

When our bags were full, we bought ice-cream cones for lunch, and watched to see the market vanish. At twelve-thirty the canvas awnings began to come down, then the frames of the stalls. Some of the stalls were on wheels, others were packed into small trucks and vans. By one o'clock the plaza was empty except for the men sweeping up the refuse, and the hosing and brushing trucks scouring the cobblestones.

Then we walked back through the Esplanade to the bus

station by the Swedish Theater, for we wanted to be home before school let out.

Wendy was already at home getting ready for swimming. She had had no key with which to let herself in but Mrs. Nordgren, our next-door neighbor, had taken Wendy upstairs in her own apartment and shown her where to crawl across from one balcony to the other. Wendy went off to the beach with her hair piled up and bobbing on her head, straight back, straight walk. At eleven, she had already given up running as something only kids did. We watched her march down to the water's edge and begin the tiptoe act of immersion. There were boys and girls around. We could see them watching her. But Wendy did not look to right or left, even at the boys riding bicycles through the shallows off the beach. She was going wading and it didn't bother her if the whole world was watching.

And then we heard running feet coming up the gravel driveway behind the house, the door crashed open and Ben was taking the stairs three steps at a time:

"Gangway, gangway." The toilet door slammed.

"Man," he said as he came out, "what a crazy place! No bathrooms in Finnish schools."

"Of course there are bathrooms," Elisabeth said.

"Nope. I looked all over."

Just then Bronwen appeared, running, her face a mask of tragedy. Vaulting up the steps she, too, disappeared into the bathroom.

"Why didn't you look up the word in the dictionary, Ben?"

"Dictionary! What's the good of that?" Ben said, laughing. "Alls I found was a lot of stupid words."

When Bronwen appeared at the head of the stairs, Ben went up and patted her on the shoulder. "You couldn't find it either, eh, Bronnie?"

"No."

"But couldn't you ask the teacher?" Elisabeth asked. Bron shook her head, crying and laughing at the same time.

"Or draw a picture?"

"No." She squeaked. "Why did that woman have to holler at me?"

"What woman?"

"A big fat woman."

"The teacher?"

"No. A fat woman hollered her head off at me and chased me with a stick and I hate Finland."

Eventually, over bread and butter and jam, the story came out: Bron had needed the bathroom. Too ashamed to say anything to Mrs. Laitinen, she had let herself out of the room into a long empty corridor, where, fearful of being seen, she had run from door to door finding nothing. Then she had gone outside to look for a bosky dingo. There being none, and her business of some urgency, she had cut across the road to a grove of trees. Here, just as she was settling down in the comfort of brush, she was hailed by a woman from a nearby apartment house. This one, getting no reply, had come thundering through the weeds brandishing a broomstick. Escape was into the forest for Bron and she might never have returned to school except that school was directly away from the woman. The woman couldn't run very well, but stood bellowing and whacking at the brush. When this tale had been unfolded, Bron began to smile again. Soon after, she and Ben were in their swimming suits and headed for the beach.

We had survived our first academic crisis.

Academic Formalities

With the children settled in school and our basketball court looking daily more like a home, I could spend some time preparing my courses. Or so I thought. I had been scheduled to teach at three institutions: the KKK (Kauppakorkeakoulu, or Business School), the Technical Institute, and the University of Helsinki. But only the first, the KKK, seemed to know anything about it. The schedules and hours had all been made out and posted: I would teach thirteen hours a week of conversational and business English, and one seminar course in essay writing.

At the Technical Institute, down by West Harbor across from the shipbuilding works and the Koff brewery, the school secretary said she had heard nothing about me. However, it didn't matter, she went on, as though this were the normal way, for during the first four weeks of the fall term the students would be taking examinations; after that someone would get in touch with me and set up a program.

At the University, the secretary (there was only one for all departments) remembered that Professor Reuter had said, before leaving for the summer, that "a new American" would be giving one seminar course, perhaps two. Did I know what my seminar would cover? No, I said. Did she? No, but in any case I could work that out with Professor Reuter when he returned. And when would he return? She smiled. Surely not before the last moment.

Wandering around the old University building, I ran into

two Fulbright teachers who were as bemused as myself. One was a lecturer in American Literature, the other in American History. They hadn't been able to find out what they would be teaching, or when, or where, but after the miasmas of American college committees, they were basking in the open spaces of academic Finland.

We walked over to the main library, opposite the Lutheran Cathedral, to examine the English collections, then over to the new Porthania building. Here were two new collections of English books, one given by the British, and one by the Americans out of the famous War Debt payments. Both were excellent undergraduate libraries having all the classical titles, critical works, and current journals that anyone could want. In addition, the library had a wide selection of tape recordings and LP records, ranging from drama and poetry to spirituals and frontier ballads. With such resources at hand almost any teaching program could be fitted into the University's mysterious and perhaps nonexistent schedule.

For want of anything better to do, the three of us left Porthania and walked down the street to a little *Kahvila* where we stopped for a cup of coffee. The girl behind the counter took our orders and then we went to one of the small marble-topped tables and sat down. One other person was in the café at the time, a drooping figure of a man asleep before a half-empty cup of coffee.

My companions had been hearing stories about Finns. One story concerned a farmer who had gone into the wilderness in order to be free. But one day he heard that another man had moved into the territory twenty miles away; then and there the old settler had taken out his sheath knife and gone to chase the intruder out. The rest of the yarns were much like this. Folk tales. I had heard several of them twenty years before. Finns tell them, with a completely straight face, to all new-comers, as though they expected to be believed, as though they believed the stories themselves. And the funny thing was my two companions—after meeting a few non-talking Finns—half believed these stories themselves.

"Are they really so antisocial?" the historian wanted to know.

"The word they use is 'shy,' " I said, feeling like an old hand. "It's not the right word, though. It's extreme reticence, caution, mixed with a fierce sense of privacy."

"Well," said the English teacher, "I don't know what you'd call it, but I was told not to expect any questions or discussion in class. Never."

Just then the girl came with coffee which she placed on the table with sugar and milk. After she had taken our money and brought the change, she stood by the table and asked, in good English: "Excuse me, but are you the new Fulbrighters?"

"Yes," I said. "Two of us are."

"In English?"

"One English, one history."

"Then one thing I must ask—please do not teach that *Mobby Dick*."

"You did not like that book?"

"Oh no! For three months last year we had to read that book. Not only had we to know all the words in the book, but all meanings for all words, all symbolisms, and all the meanings which are between words. Oh, that horrible *Mob-by Dick!*"

It was not a book to teach foreign students beginning in American Literature. The girl stayed awhile and discussed, very intelligently, some of the other books she had read. I could almost hear the shuffling of papers as the English teacher began to revise his lecture notes. When the girl finished and made a motion to go, I indicated the sleeping man at the next table. "What's the matter with your friend?"

"Him? Full."

She looked at the old fellow without changing her expression. The man had slumped farther down in his chair, so that his old grey hat almost rested on the collar of his tattered brown coat.

"Is he all right?"

"Oh, yes. You know, last night—a little too much."

The girl returned to the counter and the English teacher remarked that there was one student he'd like to have in class. Maybe students were not so different here as people liked to tell.

"Well," said the history teacher doubtfully, "I'll tell you a

33

queer one that was told to me by my predecessor. He said to be sure I got myself *presented* to the head of the Department of History."

"Presented?"

"Yes, formally presented."

"What for? Can't you just go and talk to the man?"

"Apparently not."

"I don't believe it," I said. "Finns aren't that difficult to meet."

"He said, until I was formally presented to the professor no one in the department would speak to me. Not a word. It's some sort of a code, I suppose. The hitch is," he continued, ruefully, "I don't know a soul here. Who's to present me? And how do I get presented to him?"

At that moment a shadow passed the window of the *Kahvila* and a tall uniformed policeman stepped in at the door. He and the waitress said a few words—they seemed to be joking about the condition of our sleeping neighbor.

Then the policeman went to the table and touched the man on the shoulder. "*Herra*," he said, "*Herra!*" in a soft voice.

The man continued to sleep and the girl began to snicker.

"*HERRA!* Wake up," the cop said, shaking the man's coat.

The man suddenly woke up, looking wide-eyed straight into the face of the officer. "What is it?"

"Home."

"What?"

"Go home now."

"Oh, yes, yes." The old man pulled his coat about him, fumbling at the buttons. Then with the help of the policeman, he got to his feet, looking around at us all with great dignity. "Yes, yes, home. Good." Then he took one staggering step, his hat fell off on the floor, and reaching for it he fell back into the chair again. Over his bony face and large ears a fringe of thin grey hair straggled down. The cop stooped to retrieve the fallen felt hat, which he replaced on the head of the old man, who by this time was deep in sleep again.

"*Voi voi*," sighed the cop, shaking his head. "You know him?"

"No," said the girl.

"Perhaps, then, another cup of coffee."

34

When we left the *Kahvila* the policeman and the girl from the University were still joking and puzzling over what to do with the old man.

"Don't tell me," said the historian, as we walked down the road, "that Finland isn't a queer place."

One evening a week later, when the University term was about to begin, I managed to get my boss on the telephone. With Professor Reuter I needed no formal introduction; during the war, when we were working together on a number of research projects for the newspapers, he had proposed that we "go on a first-name basis." That request was the ultimate symbol of acceptance and friendship in Finland, given in sincerity and forever.

Ole and his family had just returned from their summer place on an island near Turku. All were well; they were glad to hear that at last we were in Finland. Ole's voice sounded exactly as it had twenty years before: cultivated, precise, very British.

We talked for a while about the seminar I was to teach. I told him I wanted to teach not books, *per se*, or writers, but rather to take my class through American history, using our best writers as guides and commentators along the way. He thought for a moment, then said that he saw no reason why it could not be done. Where would I begin?

With the colonial period, I said; after all, like the Finns, we'd been subjects of an empire, too, for a while; we had had to fight a revolution to get free, and after that a civil war. We, too, had had to pioneer the land, fight against a brutal primitive capitalism, create social legislation, and fight two World Wars. It seemed to me a natural way to interest Finns in the study of America—our two peoples had been through so many things in common.

"Most of your writers are writers of protest," Ole pointed out. "They have been against history."

"Most good writers are," I said. "If you don't have a literature of protest, you don't have a literature at all, only propaganda." I could point out to him that his own writers, from Kivi and Minna Canth on down to Sillanpää and Väinö Linna were vigorous protesters.

Ole explained that the main purpose of the seminars (he

35

called them "proseminars") was to teach as much as possible of the art of essay writing, a subject not well taught in the secondary schools. With that proviso, I was free to order the books and conduct my course in any way I liked.

This settled, I asked him about the acedemic procession. I had heard that on the opening day of the University all the teachers, in academic robes, paraded up to the Lutheran Cathedral for the invocation. I had brought no robes or swallow-tailed coats, I told him. If I had to walk in such a procession I would have to find some proper garments.

At this Ole said with half a chuckle: "My dear fellow, you don't *have* to walk in that procession. . . . You would not be permitted to walk in it. Only members of the faculty may march. The faculty would have to vote to accept you, and . . ."

"And?"

"They haven't voted yet. As a matter of fact, they don't even know you are here."

When Ole Reuter was having a good time with words, he tended to lapse into an Oxford accent that was tinged with mockery.

"Let me get this straight," I said, trying not to sound annoyed. "Here I am in Finland, with a wife and five kids, and so far as the University is concerned I have no job."

"Technically that is right."

"Well, that's news."

"Oh," he laughed, "don't worry, I will put you up at the first meeting. The Faculty will vote. Eventually you will get a note from the Chancellor . . ."

It all happened exactly as Professor Reuter said. When, toward the end of November, I received a letter signed by Mr. Linkomies appointing me for one term as a temporary instructor in English, I had already been teaching for two months.

Business School

In contrast to the ways of the University, the Business School (KKK) would have served as a model of efficient direction for any industrial machine. Students and faculty assembled on the morning of the opening day; at exactly ten o'clock the convocation began, the Rector's oration took its scheduled hour and a half, classes began promptly at noon, and by evening the cafeteria had been converted to a temple of culinary art for the all-night welcoming party.

I knew only one person on the faculty of the KKK, and she only by name: Irma Rantavaara, Chairman of the English Department. At her suggestion we had met the day before to go over the texts and books. They were not inspiring, she admitted; the book on Business English was known as "the blue horror," but the terms and procedures defined therein would be bread and butter to Finns in the future.

The Finnish Business School had been in operation for forty-nine years. (There was a Swedish Business School just across the road for Swedish-speaking Finns.) It had started with only three faculty members; now the teachers numbered nearly a hundred. Nevertheless the school had maintained a close family spirit over the years, which was exceptional in institutions of higher education. The standards and admission requirements of the KKK were already higher than those of the University, and the range of courses and electives was very wide; some of the students would become secretaries and office managers, others would get important administrative jobs in business or in government, and a few, academically inclined, could go on with their studies and complete a Ph.D.

"We must trade if we would eat," Irma said. "Many people don't seem to know it, even politicians don't know it, but we cannot shut ourselves up in this little country any more. We cannot be self-supporting even if we wanted to. A fourth of our income must be earned abroad." Irma was a striking woman, taller than most of her race, black-haired, black-eyed, always animated. In English she talked so fast that the words came leaping over each other. (Irma's Finnish, when she was on a tear, swarmed in the air like night rocketry at the Lahti Ski Championships.) "A fourth! Think of it. In America, only six per cent. . . . So, even if you must suffer the blue horror—that awful book—you will see you have a very important job to do here."

Irma introduced me to the Rector of the school, Mr. Kalle Kauppi. This gentle man was one of the country's leading authorities in business law, but there was nothing stiff or juridical about him. He asked about the family, smiled when he heard of our difficulties in finding beds, offered to get some cot beds from the army if we needed them. I had expected something more solemn in my "formal presentation," but Rector Kauppi's warm smile and the plain word "welcome" was the sum of the ceremony.

Next morning the faculty collected in the teachers' lounge preparatory to marching to the auditorium. I found myself among scores of people dressed in academic finery. The women wore dark long dresses and the men heavily striped trousers and black mourning coats. All around were strange faces and the machine-gun rattle of Finnish. Old friends were meeting for the first time since the beginning of summer. Irma Rantavaara came at once to take me through a bewildering number of introductions. Then Rector Kauppi came through the crowd—I think he made a special point of coming—to hold out his hand and give me welcome again. The Rector was wearing a long crimson and black cape, and he carried a purple-banded top hat in a special way across his wrist. "Sometimes, you will see, we Finns like to dress up," he said, amused by the role he was acting and enjoying it the more on that account.

When the procession began to form, Irma took me to the section of language teachers and there introduced me to a short black-haired man who was dressed much like myself in a plain dark suit.

"This is Philip Binham," she said, "our British-language specialist."

"Ahhh!" Philip smiled. "Is this the ex-colonial? The Yank, should I say? Welcome to the KKK."

"You can comfort each other," Irma said, "whenever Finns are behaving deplorably like Finns."

Philip had a ready smile and a shock of wavy hair, combed sideways and always unruly. He would have been recognizably British anywhere in the world. As we got into line he said, "You're not required to put yourself through this, you know. Beyond the call of duty, and all that."

"This opening performance?"

"I warn you, there is nothing a Finn loves so much as to have a captive audience . . ."

"I'd like to see it once, anyway," I said.

"Once is usually enough . . . oh, well, forward then. Ours not to question why."

With the Rector at the head, followed by fine-looking older men who were members of the Board of Overseers, the procession wound down the hall and into a magnificent wood-paneled auditorium; we moved between rows of silent students and under the balcony which was also filled with students. When everyone was seated, the Rector, still carrying his top hat across his wrist, in the dead silence of the room, mounted the stage, took a manuscript from his coat pocket, brushed the paper smooth on the podium, then adjusted his glasses and launched forth.

After the first words of welcome there was little that I could understand. I settled down in my chair to listen to the sounds of oratorical Finnish, the long cadences, the endlessly elaborated sentences, always strangely dying away, so that the final two or three words were spoken in a whisper and the whisper sucked in with the next breath. As time went on and the speech went on, I fancied I was listening to an ocean where long swells were moving ashore in pomp and majesty, only to die among bays of reeds. So far as I could tell, the speech was entirely serious. No smiles appeared, Rector Kauppi showed not the least emotion, one or two of the older men went quietly asleep, and the rest sat wrapped in meditations. The students, too, behind and above us seemed stonily attentive.

After three-quarters of an hour I whispered to Philip, "How long, O Lord, how long . . . ?"

"It's a very good speech," Philip answered under his breath, "and he is just getting into it."

Afterward, during the all-night party in the school's cafeteria, I found that Rector Kauppi could make a speech full of humor and ironical twists. So could the others, members of the board or faculty, who were given the job of proposing toasts. But then we were finding our way through a six-course banquet; each course had its special wines, its toastmaster, and was supposed to last at least an hour. Philip had brought his Finnish wife, Marja. It was hard to guess Marja's age: at one moment you saw the shyness and eagerness of a girl, then the next you could see Marja manning a barricade ready to meet a battalion. I was filled with envy to hear Philip spouting Finnish, though he said it had taken him five years to learn the rudiments of the language. I was at a point where I could start a conversation, but had no idea what happened to it after that.

"The trick," volunteered Philip, "is to talk fast. The less you know, the faster you talk; that's Finnish."

"Philip!" Marja broke in, a warning glitter in her eye.

Philip had a simple Anglo-Saxon constitution. After midnight he began to fade, while Marja burned steadily brighter and refused to hear of going home. At three o'clock in the morning when coffee and brandy had given way to Scotch and soda, and this to talk about scrambled eggs, I excused myself, thanked my hosts and went home. It was an excellent party, but I could see the Finns were just getting into it.

Teaching began at eight fifteen in the morning. At precisely quarter past the hour, somewhat sandy of eye and limp of knee, and with a queer sense that this was what we had traveled five thousand miles for, I stood before the door of my classroom and wondered what I would say. I braced myself with Ole Reuter's words: ". . . you probably know more English at least than our Finnish students," and pushed the door open. The class, boys and girls, all strangers, well-dressed strangers, rose as one body and stood at attention.

"Good morning," I said. "Please sit down."

No one said a word. The students stood there until I took a seat, then they subsided into their own. They had packed themselves against the back wall, as far away as they could get, so that I looked across a dozen empty rows from my desk.

"Do you always stand up when a teacher comes in?" I asked.

A slight inclination of heads.

"It would not happen in America."

Blank stare.

"But I think it is a nice thing to do. Teachers deserve respect. Let us hope so anyway."

No response.

"I wonder if I have the right room. Is this the class in conversational English?"

An affirmative nod.

"Good, then, today we will begin to talk English. But it will be American English. . . . The wrong kind of English."

Blank faces.

"By that I mean, most of your work and all of your examinations will be in British English. Therefore, whenever you have a choice, you will use the British expression."

I wondered whether my American accent was too much for the students.

"Can you understand me?"

No reply.

"Way back there against the wall, can you hear me?"

A slow smile, then one voice said, from deep in the last row: "We hear."

Girls' hair, such hairdos! I wanted to go down and touch them. There were Yak-dos, and things like inverted artichokes, and the wild-animal-in-the-undergrowth look that is the major art of modern Paris, and something whirled up and stuck on the head like circus candy. Yet under these bizarre getups shone open, guileless faces, and the hint of a smile, as though to say, "I know my hair's absurd, but it's fun, and I can change it tomorrow."

So began my instruction in conversational English. I drew

them a map of America and told them where I came from, what it looked like, how the lakes and birches looked rather like the Finland I had seen. No response or questions. I told them of how I had built a sauna, and how it had burned down one evening, leaving us all dancing naked in the snow. Not a smile. I asked them about the coming Patterson-Johansson heavyweight championships and found only that the boys favored the Swede while the girls unanimously hoped Patterson would win. I asked them about Kennedy and Nixon; they had no opinions. Finally, all invention gone, I retreated at last into the roll call.

"Passi?"

"Here."

"Calonius?" (A Swedish Finn.)

"Here."

"Virkkala?"

"Here."

"Selinheimo?"

"Present." (Obviously a joker.)

The roll call was something my class was sure about and responded to at once, but further questions brought no more than monosyllabic answers. Yet there was no hostility in these faces, or curiosity, or interest, or resentment, or anything I could be sure of, save a kind of uneasiness which reddened into blushes if I looked too long at any one person.

"Juhani Savuaho?"

"Here."

"What does your name mean, Juhani?"

"It means . . . nothing."

"But *Savu?*"

Juhani was beginning to squirm. "Smoke."

"And *Aho?* I have seen that word somewhere."

"Perhaps . . . one can say . . ." A committee was formed in the back row which consulted in rapid-fire but soundless whispers.

Finally the reluctant Mr. Savuaho looked up and gave the consensus: "It can be . . . where, in the forest . . . some trees . . . are put away."

"Cut down? A clearing, then?"

"Perhaps."

"So your name means Smoke Clearing, or Smoky Clearing?"

"I'm sorry, but it means . . . nothing."

When the bell clanged the end of the period, I'm sure all of us were relieved. The class stood at attention again, moving no muscle until I had left. Then came the "Academic Quarter," that blessed fifteen minutes between classes.

Later in the morning Philip came into the teachers' lounge: "Hello, chum. You look stricken. Been working?"

"I've had a three-hour monologue with myself."

"It shakes you, doesn't it?" He smiled. But this was normal, he said. Even the native teachers fared no better. The fault lay in the lower schools, he thought—"a bloody awful system, run by absolute Tartars."

As we picked up our books for another class he gave me a good tip: "Remember, you can't assume nothing goes in. You will be surprised. Even though a Finn would rather die than speak, months later out will come something on an examination paper that is absolutely perfect. So . . . it is worth having a go at it."

From the start the names of my students intrigued me: they were all picture names: Virtanen (the man from the place where the stream flows); Lehtonen (the fellow from the grove of trees); Kallio (rocky cliff); Aalto (the wave); Hämäläinen (the man from the district of Häme); Mattila (the man from Matti's place).

I began to understand something of the Finnish tongue, to see a little of what Irma meant when she said that Finnish was "a precise language, of hard, solid words, a language of metaphor, and therefore of poetry."

The prettiest name I ever came across belonged to one of the prettiest girls: Tuulikki Tiirikkala. In Finnish the words look well and sound well. They suited the cool pertness of a rather sophisticated young lady. Tuulikki is an ancient tribal name (a *Kalevala* name) deriving from *tuuli*: the wind. Transmuted into English nothing remains. "Little Breeze" is no equivalent, and "Little daughter of the zephyr" might exist on the shore of Gitche Gumee but not in Helsinki. Add to this the last name "Skeleton Key," or better "The Little Breeze

43

from the Picklock's place" and you have the kind of horrible joke that language plays on translators.

Sometimes at noon I would go down to the cafeteria for a bite of lunch. Often Irma was there. She always took the most frugal noon meals, a bowl of oatmeal, or spinach soup, or a dish of plain boiled rice sprinkled with cinnamon and sugar, but these she ate with great relish.

Irma had many funny stories about Americans who had tried to teach Finns. Her favorite concerned a happy-go-lucky young man from the Midwest who after months of silent toil had gone into his class with: "Awright. I know you can speak so I'm just going to sit here and wait until somebody speaks." He made himself comfortable, read the paper, waited and waited, and no one in forty-five minutes said a word.

"I suppose," Irma laughed, "the students thought he had gone crazy, but they were much too polite to say anything." Irma understood the value of the work at KKK. She had the hard courses—translations, business-letter writing, grammar, yet she always glowed with teaching.

The school was burdened now with many new tasks essential to the nation. Finland had emerged from the postwar period a country heavily committed to foreign trade: it must now not only modernize its concepts of economics and its methods of business, but also train the linguists, the traders, the diplomats on whom the country's future would depend. Thus graduates of the KKK had to know six languages, four fluently. After Finnish and Swedish (which every Finn was supposed to know), English was the next language of importance. English was beginning to be taught in elementary schools. After English came German, Russian, and French—all essential to the interlocking balances of exports and imports.

Even with these standard language courses given at the Business School—in addition to all the rest of the curriculum—the numbers of men and women who could go out to occupy essential frontier posts were far below the needs. One day I found Irma sputtering about a newspaper article which described how great opportunities for new business and trade were being lost every year in South America, Africa, and the Far East, because

44

businessmen didn't know any Spanish and Portuguese, and too few knew enough French.

"Always we lose to the Swedes," Irma said. "We have so much to do to catch up. The opportunities come and the Swedes have the people already trained in the lauguages—and the Danes, and the Swiss, and the Dutch."

Irma was incensed, too, at the time lost by the students merely because of their reticence.

"Why is it? No one else in the world believes you have to speak a language perfectly before you can speak at all. The French would not speak English perfectly on pain of the guillotine. But Finns . . . oh, sometimes you can hear the wheels grinding in their heads."

The tables around us were full of boys and girls gesticulating and laughing together.

"At least," I said, "down here they don't want for words."

Irma softened. "Poor children, they have to sit in class forty-four hours a week. You must understand that, and not be discouraged."

Irma was, I suppose, about forty years old, one of the generation that came to maturity during the last wars. Out of luck with love, or owing to the high Finnish casualties, she never married. Instead she had thrown herself into studying and teaching. A Ph.D. in English, now with a wide range in the literature of many languages, Irma was obviously made for bigger things than teaching grammar and business writing. But whatever she did she did with intense conviction.

"When they were young boys and girls, mere babies," Irma said, looking around at the students, "just after the war, we had almost nothing to eat, only frozen potatoes; imagine grey, mushy potatoes. And we never knew from day to day whether the tanks would be in Helsinki next morning. . . . But look at them now! Perhaps a little starvation now and then is a good thing. Aren't they beautiful creatures?"

Day of Rest

Dear Granpa,
    How are you? I am fine. I go to a Finnish skool. I go to first grade. I have a teacher and she speaks a little english. But they got skool here on Saturdays and that's bad for me anyways.

Ben had never written a letter before in his life. It was hard work deciding what to say. The smudges on the paper were from dirty fingers, not tears; he had been down on the beach climbing trees. He had been down on the beach for more than an hour watching the kids play soccer. He had hung around, here and there, shagged balls for the goalie, yelled when yelling was needed, looked in vain for classmates from school. He had watched the motorboats going out to the islands on fishing expeditions, and a young boy on the end of the wharf trying to cast his line against the wind. Then he had watched the soccer some more, thrown rocks, climbed trees, and come home.

Other Sundays had been the same. The promises of his parents that he would pick up friends on the beach had come to nothing. In school he had been sent down from third grade to first because someone thought he would learn Finnish quicker if he could be in with children just beginning their ABC's. He had said he didn't want to be in with all those little kids, but no one listened. Even his Finnish tutor didn't stick up for him. Now he wanted to write a letter. . . .

46

What was really in Ben's heart we could only guess at. But there was a beach full of people sunning themselves, there were balls flying and the shrill sounds of debate—and here was Ben hunched over his labor, a small apelike figure cramped to the most ancient problem of the race:

I hope you had a good trip. We have a beautiful view and see boats bobbing up and down. I hope you will be standing on our dor step next summer.

Love from Ben
Sometimes called Hacker McGracker

Three weeks had brought changes to Ducks' Slope No. 2. We had a second-hand table, six chairs, a broken down high chair, and a wrecked but repairable crib for Steve which filled one of the closets upstairs. The roll-away beds had come from the carpenter's shop. Desks and bureaus next. Downstairs in the living room I was drilling the flinty cement walls with a star drill in order eventually to put up bookshelves. Elisabeth had hemmed and put up curtains. Now, with the warning that fall would soon sweep all fresh vegetables and berries from the open market, she was cooking vats of lingonberry preserves in the kitchen. Home was beginning to look fairly normal.

Necessarily Sunday was a day of chores, for this was our day to use the laundry and steam bath. (The apartment house was run co-operatively, all home owners participating in decisions. Mr. Nordgren, our next-door neighbor, was serving his year as "house man," paying the bills, arranging for repairs, and so on. For the next three months Sunday would be our day among the machinery.)

Kim and Wendy had the duty downstairs. The washing machine had been manufactured in the Tampere locomotive works. It resembled the boiler of a switching engine with everything hooked up except the drive wheels. You stuffed in a load of laundry, sprinkled in a cup of powdered soap, clamped the cast iron door shut, slammed the throttle to full ahead and then retired down the hall for fear the thing would tear up its floor-bolts and get loose in the room. Fifteen minutes later you came back, pulled on rubber boots, opened the door, threw the

47

clutch into reverse, and waded ashore in a millrace of soapy water. Then the process was repeated for rinsing.

When the girls were done with the work, lugging armloads of diapers and a week's worth of dresses and shirts, we went out into the vacant lot behind the apartment to find a drying place. September's sun was beginning to lose its heat, it brightened but could not warm; however, a breeze was blowing. In a little clearing that would catch the afternoon sun, near to the fence of a private home, we rigged some lines between trees and set out the wash like flags of truce in our futile war with dirt.

After lunch Ben started for the beach again, this time armed with a fishing pole that Mr. Nordgren had lent him. He had bread, too, for bait: it worked for ducks, perhaps it would for fish. The rest of the family were busy, and with Steve napping, Elizabeth and I could continue our weekly explorations of the island. Lauttasaari was always exciting to walk through. Every week, it seemed, we saw changes in the community: a reef of rock opened up for a building here, the staging coming down on a new apartment there. The urge to build—stifled for so many years by the war debt to Russia—seemed to be almost an obsession among Finns.

Lauttasaari is a heart-shaped island, three to four miles across, lying almost at the mouth of Helsinki's West Harbor. The bay on which we lived and the two rounded promontories on either side face south and west, exposed to the prevailing winds, though the Baltic's steep seas are broken up by chains of islands outside. Two major hills rise at either end of the island, both glaciated terraces of granite and a scattering of stubborn pine. Both hills are preserved as parks. On the crest of the eastern hill stands the island's famous seaward landmark, a graceful spreading mushroom of cement, two hundred feet high, which is the island's water tower.

Fifteen years ago, Lauttasaari (Ferry Island) was the quiet home of a score or two of fishing families, and of a few wealthy Swedish-Finns who had their summer villas here. Now all that was changed. Among the many satellite suburbs of the capital, Lauttasaari was one of the largest. Although 23,000 people were said to live here, there was land enough

48

remaining for a few thousand more. Some industries had moved in, there were many home industries (shoemaking, upholstering, et cetera), but most of the island was residential land or parks.

Here and there one could find the old original houses, high, square, board-and-batten structures, painted yellow and faded to nondescript mustard. They added a sense of time to the straight-edged modernity of the new buildings. (At one place on the island a broad new street had a pie-shaped wedge cut into it in order to accommodate the back corner of an old fisherman's home—there was time, there was room for people still. The road could be straightened out later.)

Curiously, we could almost date the new buildings by their façades: earliest the plain grey stucco, drab but durable and inexpensive; then the brick-faced walls, now and then offset to catch more winter sunlight; then, with increasing affluence, wood, copper, stainless steel, glass brick, in many combinations to vary the color and the texture. Whatever the structure, from the plain five-story balcony apartments to the most radical private homes, we could see that magical change of pace— the shift of a wall, a complement of color—which is the difference between drafting and design.

Design was everywhere, however, from the layout of the whole island to the arrangement of flowers or fruits in shop windows. Design—imagination tempered by taste—seems to be a kind of sixth sense of these Finns.

Necessarily, most of the buildings were apartment houses. City-planning authorities deem land near the Capitol too valuable to be squandered in single dwellings. People moving to the city seem to be content to live in beehive arrangements. The decision is made easier for them by the fact that most Finns, rich or poor, have camps by lake or sea for summer vacations and winter weekends.

In spite of the fact that Lauttasaari was compactly built, there was no sense of congestion. Adequate land had been set aside for the schools and churches; playfields were being built according to a master plan; children's play areas, and grassy parks for older people were under construction; one track oval and sports field was already in full operation, and a second one planned; beyond this, the city authorities had set aside a dozen park areas for walking and skiing which could not be built upon.

To my American eyes Lauttasaari seemed nothing short of a miracle. Fancier developments—like the garden city of Tapiola—might receive the publicity, but our island was a good average and sufficient example of Finnish city planning. While most of the construction was by "private enterprise," subsidized housing protected the lower-income groups, and strict control of all building was exercised by a Central Planning Board that had the power to match its visions, and uncommon good sense into the bargain: trees had not been sacrificed to bulldozers, children had not been sacrificed to cement. Americans, so much richer than Finns in standards of living, were so much poorer in city life.

We climbed up Windmill Hill, where the famous school for Communist agitators was said to be located, but saw nothing more alarming than a bunch of small boys smirking over their cigarettes. Then down to the western point of the island, a park of about half a square mile set aside for the cottages of police and disabled soldiers. Several hundred families lived there during the summer. The individual plots contained no more than a few trees and a minute rock garden, the cabins were scarcely more than playhouses—yet the people we saw looked happy. (You can tell a family's contentment best in the face of the mother.)

Down by the shore of the point of land we came upon a number of artillery bunkers and machine-gun nests remaining from the last war. Most of the islands near Helsinki had been fortified and held by small detachments of men against a possible invasion of Russian troops crossing from Estonia. Whether over the ice in winter, or by landing boats in summer, the attacks would have had to be met by desperate men, too few in number, who knew they would have little chance to retreat and no chance for reinforcement. The whole defense of Finland had had to be based upon desperate men few in number. That war still seems possible to imagine but impossible to believe.

Now, however, war seemed very far away. The sea bore

sails, children rode bicycles down the sides of the bunkers, and the apron of rock had become a Finnish Laundromat. A handsome woman, barely disguised by a bikini, had spread a rug out on the smooth rock where she could kneel and scrub it with soap and a brush. Two small children, like bear cubs, scrambled around her. Now and then a wave would lick one into the sea; the woman would fetch him out and go on with her scrubbing. When the rug was clean she waded out to hold it for a rinsing, then spread it on the rocks above the wash of waves to dry.

"That's what you would like, isn't it?" Elisabeth said sweetly. "To get me to a place where I have to wade around in the ocean to do the laundry."

It was a crude way of putting the case, but at least it could be said that the ocean would not break down every week. Yet I think Elisabeth shared my enthusiasm for some of the things we saw: the acceptance of social planning, the determination to save parks and play space, the strong family unity of Finns, their contentment. These were values we could see and hoped the children would somehow acquire.

Coming home from our excursion, we found Kim in a rage. Not a rag remained out in the clearing where we had set up our laundry lines, the rope was down, and the red-faced girl was lugging the wash upstairs to the balcony:

"Don't ask me what it's all about," she glared. "I'm not a crazy Finn."

"What? What happened?"

"Oh, some dopey man over there."

"What man?"

"Next door, in that house. People in Norway don't go around hollering at everybody. He came over and cussed me out for hanging up the laundry. But it wasn't in his yard. He spoke Swedish. I said the junk had to dry and he kept yelling that he didn't spend all that money to buy a house in Lauttasaari to have to look at laundry all day and then he untied the ropes and everything fell down and he walked off."

"Let's go and talk with him," Elisabeth said.

"He said it's against the law to hang laundry out in the

51

woods. It has to be on a balcony or on a line." Kim snapped. "Besides he has two big dogs."

"Well . . ." Elisabeth sighed, picking up some diapers, "Live and learn."

Ben was still down on the beach. From the balcony we could see him sitting there. He was not fishing any more, but piling up sand castles. I went down to sit with him. The air was getting cold as evening came on. Most of the rowboats and motorboats were back, tied up at the wharf. Three small jumblies in a waterlogged rowboat were trying to pole or paddle offshore, but the wind was setting them steadily into the reeds. Nearby, the soccer teams were being decimated by supper calls. Now and then a sharp high command would come from a balcony overhead and some Pekka or Timo would turn in his tracks, without a word or argument, and go home.

We sat there. After a while Ben said, in his soft voice, "Why did we come here? Did we have to?"

"We'll get a soccer ball for you tomorrow, McGracker." No reasons I could give would make sense to the boy. I could not say I hoped living in Finland would make him a better American—he was 100-per-cent American already. I couldn't argue that it was good for us all to learn how America looked from the outside. The wires of loneliness and wanting produce the deep chords of life: you have somehow to be put on a stretch —like a guitar string—before any vibrations come. But no grownup can instruct a seven-year-old in loneliness.

"What do the kids do at recess?" I asked.

"Not much."

"Play games?"

"Oh—run around, push everybody, you know—hack off."

"Is it fun?"

"It isn't great."

Customs

In those first weeks we were trying to live like Finns but understanding very little. Why, for example, were apartments kept gleaming and spotless, and children expected to play outdoors whatever the weather? The two were connected, of course, but since when did furniture require more solicitude than children? Why, for example, were small children so inordinately quiet at home, hiding behind their mother's skirts with mouths full of fingers, and yet on the beach so forceful and shrill in argument?

There was certainly little togetherness practiced by Finn father on Finn son. The old man might go off fishing with some friends, or happily enough entirely alone; the boy meanwhile joined his embattled playmates on the sand. No one seemed to know where the youngsters played, or to care. It was part of the domestic plan for children to be dumped outdoors to fend for themselves. If three urchins should decide to pole a collection of old planks out to sea, the only certain thing was that no one would ever come down to call them back.

There was always a good deal of fighting going on along the beach. Fighting went on under the sun, in pitch-darkness, in rain or sleet. It went on regardless of sizes or numbers. A small hardhead might struggle against six larger boys, gaining only mouthfuls of sand for his effort, but never letting up in his determination to destroy them—and never crying.

Steve, I suppose, took most naturally to being a Finn. At Mrs. Nordgren's suggestion, he was attending morning and

53

afternoon sessions at a Finnish nursery school. This institution was located in an empty lot not far from our home. For walls it had a snow-fence, for play facilities it had trees, rocks, and sand; for a ceiling it had *le temps du jour*, and for a teacher a big motherly woman of about sixty-five, dressed in a heavy overcoat and a knitted bucket of a hat, who had been certified by inclination and duly licensed by the city. Her school was a park, and she was called a *Park Auntie*.

Tuition was $7 a month and school kept whatever the weather. The only equipment required of each scholar was a handkerchief. In rain or slush or sleet the children, aged six months to five years, came in plastic coveralls and rubber boots; in snow they wore heavier clothing and felt boots. All children brought shovels; if they could not yet walk, they could certainly excavate. Steve was soon absorbed in such practical work, a shovel after all was only a better spoon. Every morning he joined the stolid small citizens in the park where they practiced give and take and learned the art of self-defense by beating each other on the head with shovels.

Thanks to the Park Aunties, mothers were free to take part-time work in the city, or attend lectures at the University, or to make the marketing rounds which take so much of a Finnish woman's time.

On one such free morning Elisabeth and I went down to South Harbor where, we had heard, our shipment of books and winter clothing had arrived from Hoboken. One expects only the worst when going through Customs—endless delays, irrational red tape, and assessments from which there is never any appeal. But it did not turn out quite that way. We first had to find, among the scores of warehouses, the one where our two cartons and two small trunks were located. Then we had to find a man inside a wire cage who understood what was written on the notice I had received. So much we managed to do. The man stamped our notice and a longshoreman brought our gear. Then an inspector opened it, studied the contents thoughtfully, discussed something with an assistant, and finally called in the head inspector to survey the stuff. The head inspector, a tall aloof Swedish gentleman, gave our coats and

54

sweaters a practiced glance, then, as though knowing exactly where everything was, he reached into the bottom of the trunk and fetched out a quart bottle of capsules.

"What is this?"

"Vitamins."

The inspector unscrewed the cover of the jar and cautiously tested the smell within. Then he poured out some of the brownish capsules into his palm.

"Is it to sell?" he asked. "Here are very many."

I explained that we had five children who would eat vitamins once a day over the winter.

"Children will eat them?" He looked at me pityingly. The capsules were tubular and large enough to choke a horse. "For health?"

By this time half a dozen men had collected around our belongings, obviously enjoying the novel things that strangers bring into Finland. The inspector next produced several cans of coffee and some small jars of baby food. The coffee we expected to have to pay duty on, for coffee carries a 100-per-cent tax in Finland. The inspector counted the cans, then turned his attention to the small glass jars of puréed spinach, meat, puréed prunes and some other evil gooey yellow substance which was labeled egg yolk. He passed the jars around among his friends who looked at them curiously and shook their heads.

"Americans eat this?" he asked, incredulous.

"Babies do."

He grimaced and replaced the coffee and the jars neatly under the winter clothing.

"You are diplomatic?" he asked, poising his piece of chalk over our effects.

"No. I am a teacher at the University."

"Ah! Fulbrighter?"

I knew the Fulbright teachers and scholars had some sort of import privileges, but I could not claim them for myself.

"No, I am a teacher only."

The chief inspector meditated for a while. I could see he was trying to give me some sort of break, but with a dozen cans of coffee in the trunk the law was being stretched pretty hard. Suddenly he brightened: "Very good. Soon it is Christmas, no? All right, for the coffee—happy Christmas to all."

Then he chalked his curlicue sign on the boxes and walked away. The assistant inspector shrugged, the inspector shrugged and grinned, and we made off with the puréed swag.

Next came the business of getting a telephone. The clerk at the office where we called said that telephones were so scarce in Helsinki that she could not tell when we might get one. (The instruments are bought outright in Finland; people sell them as they wish or use them for collateral in getting loans.) But as we were leaving the clerk said, hastily scribbling down an address, that while it was "not exactly according to the law," we might possibly rent a telephone.

So we traced the address to an obscure stone archway and a courtyard filled with barrels of trash. There in a dingy second-floor office some kind of a transaction was made with two people who looked as though they'd been trained in a speakeasy. Some money passed—perhaps it was illegal—and we received a piece of paper which even our neighbor, Mr. Nordgren, could not decipher.

"How is it," Elisabeth said, having decided we'd been swindled, "your friends always send us to the crummiest places?"

But the telephone arrived and was installed. There followed a two-day running altercation with people who kept calling up on urgent business, and who upon hearing our English, sighed, apologized, cursed, hung up, and then called again. We had no idea what the trouble was about until Mirjam Nordgren came to answer the phone and discovered that we had been given the same number as some "very big judge" in the city. Judge, speak-easies, illegal phones, desperate callers—we felt on slippery ground with the law for a while, but nothing came of it except that we got another telephone number.

Then the Germans came. One morning a small station wagon, with an engine that sounded as though it had been made from a coffee can, backed up to the door of the apartment next to ours. Three people got out. They looked very un-Finnish, for the woman was plainly dressed and the two men were in trench coats and soft hats. They went to work at once to unload a small household from the back of the car into the apartment, which for weeks had been unoccupied. When this was done, the two men jumped into the car and putted off.

Later in the morning the woman came to our door and rang the bell. She was short, plump, rather pretty but without any makeup whatever. She talked in a thick German accent: she did not wish to bother, but did we by chance have an iron she could use to press a few blouses? Elisabeth fixed her up with an iron and a place to work on the dining table. When our visitor had finished her work she asked whether our apartment was the same as hers. Elisabeth took her around to show the place off. The two apartments were mirror images of each other except that the other one had a fireplace in it which the children had discovered by peeping around when the place was not in use.

Our new neighbor came from Berlin. I asked her how things were in Berlin and she replied:

"Good, good. Always better." Then she thanked us for the use of the iron and went off to her home.

That same morning Eric Nordgren come to our door dressed in a Persian dressing gown and leather slippers.

"Big day for me," he said. (He liked to show off his American English, learned by listening and talking on his ham radio set.) "Today is my fiftieth birthday. . . . My picture stands in all the papers this morning. I'm not supposed to know, but I tell you anyway. You must come—all must come. My wife, she is making a big blow up this afternoon."

We were, of course, glad to accept. The Nordgrens were our best friends in Lauttasaari. Eric had filled out my forms for the police, and my tax blanks, and Mirjam had run a hostelry for wandering Bradleys. The children were forever forgetting to wear their house keys around their necks so that scarcely a day passed but one or another had to crawl across from the Nordgren balcony to our own in order to get in. The trips got to be so commonplace that Mirjam took to serving cold drinks. She liked Ben especially; he told her all about the horrid trials of the young scholar in Finland. (Mirjam's own two boys were of high-school age and no longer communicative.)

That the Nordgren fiftieth celebration was a big affair we could tell from the numbers of couples all dressed in black and furs who passed our door that afternoon. When Ben and Bron came home from school, we polished them up, got them into their Sunday best, and sent them off to buy some flowers. Then we presented ourselves at the Nordgren door and rang the bell. Mirjam answered the ring—a dozen people were standing in the living room—and then Mirjam, laughing, backed rapidly inside: No, no, we could not shake hands until we were inside. Did we not know that it was bad luck to shake hands through a door? Ben bowed like a cadet over her hand, and Bron curtsied. Then Ben brought the hubbub in the room to a stop with a loud yell:

"Yaay! Lookit that cake."

A magnificent cake stood in the center of the dining table, covered with sugared fruit and whipped cream. Around it there were sandwiches, and cookies, and half a dozen spiced cakes; also glass plates and coffee cups and saucers.

"Some cake, eh, Ben?" Eric smiled, coming to welcome us. "But I tell you I waited a long time for it."

Eric was the man of the day. All afternoon and long into the evening friends, relatives, and members of his office staff came bringing presents and prepared with speeches. The living room fountained flowers and the silver and glass gifts could scarcely find room between the good things to eat. Eric's two boys, Pauli and Jon, served as waiters, silent and formal, while Eric welcomed the guests and made speeches in return.

At one point he brought out a decanter full of homemade rice wine. He was very proud of it—it was good wine, and a good threat to the State Alko Monopoly not to let their prices get too high. Having the boys fill glasses for all the guests, he gave us all a toast of welcome and received toasts in return.

"Watch out," he said, raising his glass to Elisabeth, "it's strong stuff."

Contrary to what we had always heard, Finnish-Finns and Swedish-Finns mixed here without the least embarrassment. One heard Swedish and Finnish spoken on all sides. Either the

58

old mores were passing away, or Eric himself set a special tone. He was himself a Swedish-Finn, and Mirjam a honey-haired Karelian. Mirjam suffered from her English, though it was much better than she supposed, and Eric blandly brushed all linguistic problems aside, saying, "I don't have to study English. I just make it up as I go along."

Once when there was a lull in the proceedings, when one group from the office had gone and before another arrived, Eric turned to me and said, "I see the new neighbors have come."

"They are from Berlin," I replied.

"Yes . . ." he said, "from East Berlin."

"East Berlin? Then they are Communists."

"Have they kids to play with?" Bron asked.

"What will they do?" I asked.

Eric shrugged. "They run a library or something. Something to do with trade with East Germany; there comes a trade mission I think. But the library, you know, all that will be propaganda."

"Probably they are spies?" I said, thinking myself very quick.

"Spies?" he said, surprised. "Of course. What else?"

Ben who had been keeping close to the cake table, quietly stuffing himself, now pricked up his ears. He came over to Mr. Nordgren and took him confidentially by the arm: "You want me to blast 'em out of there?"

"Blast 'em? Who, Ben?"

"Those guys."

"But why?"

"You said they were spies."

"Oh, we have hundreds of spies in Finland."

"Well"—Ben hated to give up his plan—"I could climb up there and put a bomb down their chimney, that would be a neat trick . . . someday, if you want me to, Mr. Nordgren."

But Eric thought that would be unnecessary. The police would keep an eye on them. They were used to having spies around.

"Besides"—Eric laughed—"what is there to see here? Nothing. We are afraid of no one."

59

Strange to say, that first meeting with the East German *Hausfrau* next door was almost all we saw of our three new neighbors. Once in a while we saw them walking down the street—always together, never alone. Who was married to whom, or what sort of design for living they had, communal or otherwise, we could never make out. They bought a second heavy-duty lock for their door, and they soon had all the windows blocked with Venetian blinds. No one ever came to their door and sometimes they were away for weeks at a time. Their lives must have been very lonely. The children called them The Spooks.

Perhaps we, too, were considered spies. As we learned much later, the police knew a lot more about what we were doing than I did. For the time, though, I was much too busy to think about such details. When in addition to the Business School, the Tech School and University classes got under way, I found myself teaching downtown most of the day. The old Tech School buildings were down by the shore of West Harbor where Bulevardi runs into the sea. The harbor was full of activity—one sensed here the vitality of this great import harbor of Finland. Ships changed berths almost daily, the great gantry cranes were swinging over gaping holds, small switching engines puffed white smoke at a grey sky. Out toward the end of the harbor was a long wharf which carried a mountain range of Polish coal for the coming winter; at the head were the Wärtsilä ship-building works where pale green flares of arc welding flickered like heat lightning day and night among the gigantic forms of new steel ships. (A tremendous green and black hull was going together inside the locked fences of the plant. I learned that this would be the hull of a new atomic-powered icebreaker for Soviet Russia.) Export and import: around West Harbor I could see at a glance the truth of Irma's words "We must trade if we would eat."

This was a new Finland growing up. The expanding metal industries—ship building, wire rope, machinery, instruments, copper, etc.—owed much of their impetus to trade with Russia and the Eastern satellites. Finland couldn't compete with larger richer countries for the Western markets, but trade with the East had brought a steady and important income to

this little country. Finland was going through a second industrial revolution. In a generation it had left its rural past
behind and was moving rapidly toward a modern technological
society that would have one foot in the East and one in the
West. Independence was shifting toward interdependence. I
couldn't begin to understand all the changes that this fact
would bring to social and political life of Finland, but at the
Tech School, at least, I had the feeling of being in touch with
the country's future.

Sometimes my classes in town were very early and I had to
leave home when it was still dark. Buses were always jammed
at rush hour, men and women hurled themselves aboard in
order to get a last remaining seat, the rest of us were packed in
to the gasping point, and then the doors were closed. At later
stations along the line we could see the static fury of waiting
in the faces of people outside. There was no room for them.
Inside there was no sound, except for the " 'sss" of the uniformed ticket-taker in her box by the rear door. This was
conversation reduced to the vanishing point, for her sibilant
" 'sss" was the final sound of the word *Kiitos,* Thanks. So much
had to be said for politeness' sake, but anything more would
have been unseemly loquaciousness.

Rarely did any man offer his seat to a woman, or speak to
the man sitting alongside of him. Each person stared glumly at
the steamy windows, the deisel snorted, the brakes screeched,
the traffic hurled itself toward the bottleneck of the Lauttasaari bridge. Often at first I wondered about my companions:
what were they brooding about so grimly? But later I could
see they were only hibernating. Talking was the kind of thing
that Swedes did, but in Finland a man's privacy was inviolable.

In spite of the impenetrable silence of those bus rides, I
found early morning in Lauttasaari exciting. Here I saw a
Finland buried in darkness, a Finland no tourist would see.
However early I got up, and however drizzly the weather, the
laboring people were always ahead of me. They were busy
whacking up the frames of new buildings, or laying stone
borders for a road, or bringing fill for a new playfield in
wooden carts pulled by chestnut horses. Sometimes pairs of
chimney sweeps, clad in black tights, rattled by on bicycles,

lugging ropes and brushes over their shoulders. And always there was a migration of strange vehicles down the highway; motorized wheel chairs, three-legged cars, bicycles, motorcycles.

At such times I was conscious of how middle class we Americans were. For the rest of the day I could imagine that the Finland we saw, the people we met, were representative of this country. But in the early mornings I knew that there was a vast population of Finns, much more than a majority, whom we would never meet or know about.

Oh, this horrible weather! It goes on and on.
Now you see why we are a melancholy and
phlegmatic race.

—Irma

𝔉all

The change came with the first cold night of drizzle out of the
east on what was called the Siberian Wind, and after that no
one thought of summer any more. Alders and birch felt the
change and their leaves began to stiffen and turn. Summer
birds vanished overnight, except for the harbor mallards squatting on the sand. Sailboats took wing for quieter coves and
boatyards. Then the plump winter birds came to sit stolidly in
rows on the branches outside our kitchen windows: we saw
them in the grey mornings hustling their feet to balance
against the ruffling gusts.

Always there was the sense of light draining away from our
continent. Snow was reported falling in Lapland. The fjells
would be empty of reindeer. The brief blazing *Ruska Aika*
(Russet Time) when the blueberries spread the hills with a
mash of summer wine would long be gone to dregs; soon
would come the time when the sun, withdrawn below the
horizon, would raise but a noonday dusk over the waiting
land.

At Tornio, Kemi, Oulu along the northern curve of the
Gulf of Bothnia where winter ice forms thickest, the icebreakers would already be plowing lanes to the sea through the
brittle panes. Farmers would be sitting around their kitchen
fires, belaboring their wives with good advice and waiting for
the forest work to begin; and wives would curse the sullen sun
which, after three days, still left their Monday wash as stiff as
sheet metal.

But we, beside the eastern Baltic—the Gulf of Finland—for three months, or four, had neither fall nor winter, only varying forms of wet. There were weeks when we saw no sun; when the cold disc did appear over the trees across the bay, it only rolled up to a low zenith and then sank slowly into the mists beyond the seaward islands. Day by day the light dimmed. Day by day, by seven minutes each day, the sun left us and the change was so great that one could see it each morning and evening.

Yet not all weather was bad. Finns have a word for it—*intiaanikesä*—and, indeed, we had a few days of Indian Summer. The birches all at once shivered into gold, the reeds along the shallow shores turned to stiff golden brushes; then in a few days the color slipped away; almost before we knew it the crest of fall had come and passed.

During that brief splendor Ole Reuter asked me to go on a moose-hunting expedition with him at his ancestral island home in southwest Finland. The Reuters, of German and Swedish stock, had once been landed gentry there. But times had changed: the many crises through which the country had gone since Independence, in 1917, had pretty well wiped out the estate. Other men owned the land. Now Ole retained but a small piece of shore, a cabin, a sauna, a wharf and boat, and (according to ancient perquisites) an annual claim to moose meat.

At best the claim was only theoretical. No moose was ever in any danger from us. We tramped around in the damp and heavy star moss of the forest; we sat on stumps in swamps and waited for the footfalls of the heavy-horned animals; we climbed rocky knolls to look out over the peaceful fields to where birches burned like torches against the spruce—then we came home and killed a couple of bottles of cognac. Two weeks later Ole's neighbors went out and shot three moose. They shipped some of the meat to Helsinki for us, delighting, I am sure, in the incompetence of professors. But the meat was good—a happy remembrance of feudal times.

After Indian Summer the steady drizzle was upon us. This melancholy time was probably hardest for the children to bear. They had to go to school in the dark, leaping the black pools in the road, and after school there was not light enough

64

to play games on the beach. Sundays too—the only free day of the week—might offer no more than a lashing rainstorm or a walk under dripping spruce.

Sometimes we went down to watch the men getting their rowboats or motorboats ashore. They pulled them into the shallows beside the wharf and laid out planks and birch rollers by means of which the boats could be dragged up into a grove of trees where they were overturned on horses and left for the winter. Each man did his own work without help or comment from his neighbors. One day we saw a man drive down to the beach in a truck. He had an inboard powerboat lying on its side in the cove. He stretched a hawser from his craft to the truck and then simply drove off down the road. The boat plowed ashore, the propeller snapped off, the rudder hung off to one side like a broken flipper—then the man coiled his rope and, without so much as a "Perrrrkele!" drove off in his truck.

Summer visitors to the beach vanished with the cold weather. A few swimmers continued to come down each morning at first light to take their dips. They had some trick, some slight of hip, by which they changed from nightclothes into swimming suits while covered by a dressing gown—the act took place on the end of the wooden wharf—then off with the robe, into the water, ten strokes out, ten strokes back, and the dressing scenario run in reverse. These swimmers came every day, in mist or rain or snow, all through the winter. According to some theory in Helsinki, such sport was supposed to cure all sorts of maladies, including arthritis and middle age—but close observation revealed to me that these were all formidable females and I lost interest in the spectacle, believing it couldn't be very healthy.

Worse than the weather itself was the fact that there was nothing, apart from school, for the children to do. School was school, when the classes finished the doors closed. The boy or girl who wanted sports could join an athletic club and train for track or gymnastic events as weather and indoor facilities permitted, but sports seemed to play but a minor part in the lives of Finns, at least of middle-class Finns. As for dramatics, choral work, dances, and so on, none of these were to be found, either in school or out, for young people to engage in.

University students—the elite in Finland—could find diversion and entertainment through the activities of their "Student Nations," and in the wide variety of cultural opportunities of the capital. Adults could forget days of drizzle in nights of drama; *My Fair Lady* was playing at the Swedish theater to its second year of full houses; *Mark Twain*, in the person of Hal Holbrook, was a spectacular success; the Royal Norwegian Theater group was bringing *Hedda Gabler;* Helen Hayes and her troupe were coming with three American plays. More than a dozen theater groups, amateur and professional, had their repertory programs, and at the apex of entertainment stood the Finnish National Theater, under the direction of the poet Kivimaa. This great institution ran two theaters, one classic, one experimental, where one might find selections as old as Aeschylus or as new as Anouilh. In a real sense the Finnish National Theater was the cultural symbol of a race whose daily inhibitions found a natural outlet in drama. As the art was enthusiastically supported by the state, the best talents could be recruited for acting and directing, and tickets could be sold at a price that everyone could afford.

However, such lively night life was not for young people. Even the movies, for the most part, were restricted to people of sixteen and over, or eighteen and over, on account of brutality, sexiness, or both. Young people were expected to stay home—a good theory, but one hard to practice in the cramped quarters of modern apartment living. Young girls, slim and shy would come down to the beach and collect under street lamps to gossip and makes noises at the boys. And the boys, too shy and embarrassed to stop, would hurry by to go and kick balls or drive their tinny motorbikes round and round in the sand. Both groups seemed fatalistically bored. Sometimes the boys wrestled or fought—there was a good deal of pushing and fighting among young Finns—but after a while the contestants would get up, shake off the sand, and amble off through the dripping trees. If there was fun in life, little of it seemed to filter down to the young people.

So in a way school work became the only diversion during the months of darkness. We could see this in Kim, who was working very hard. Her six-day schedule was a grinding routine, and to make matters worse, her class, contrary to the norm in Finland, was noisy and obstreperous. She seemed to be getting very little lift from her school work. I think she often wished she were back in Norway, but it was not her way to complain. True to Scandinavian traditions she was taking a large number of courses which would continue year after year in a linear fashion to the end of her high school years: European History, Scandinavian History, Religious History, Psychology, Singing, Biology, Chemistry, Physics, Geometry, Algebra, Swedish Literature, Finnish, German, French, Gymnastics, and something called *skrivning* which was neither penmanship nor essay writing but something of both. The hours varied from one to four per week in each subject.

Kim said very little about school. Sometimes I tried to help her, though often the problems were beyond her Swedish and my mathematics. It surprised me to find that instructors felt they could teach higher mathematics to students who were not allowed to ask questions; it surprised me even more to find physics taught entirely out of a book, without the help of laboratory exercises and demonstrations. Little by little I was disenchanted with Finnish secondary education. The students worked hard, it is true, but much of the work seemed a mere accumulation of facts and all of the teaching didactic.

One morning in early November Kim came downstairs to breakfast with her face set tight.

"Daddy, you said ice sinks . . . in the spring. . . . Does it?"

Long experience had taught me to be wary: this was not the real question. Kim had a way of stalking her problems like an Indian, moving from cover to cover but never letting herself be seen. Her class had apparently been hearing about Archimedes' Law, but understanding very little. No floating blocks of wood of various densities had been used, nor heavier objects suspended from a spring balance, to illustrate this elementary proposition. Yet without Archimedes the special properties of melting ice would be incomprehensible. It was getting late; I was still trying to recapitulate the Greek's discovery in a cup of coffee when the girl rose to get her coat.

"Why don't you ask the teacher about it, Kim?" I said.

"I did. Never again, though."

"Why?"

"He began hollering at me: 'Ohho. So in Norway they teach that ice sinks? And in America, I suppose, ice flies through the air?' "

"Then the man's a damn fool."

"Daddy . . . I know all that. But I can't do anything about it, can I?"

So now, at last, the real difficulty was out: it was Kim's school, about which she had had misgivings from the first day. Half of the boys were repeaters from the previous year; sometimes they made so much noise that no one could hear anything. Kim had told us this but, preoccupied with Ben, we had not thought about it.

"I know you think I exaggerate," Kim went on. "But I don't."

"I'll see what I can do," I said. Kim picked up her books and went running for her bus.

Elisabeth was steaming her face over a plate of oatmeal: "If we have any more trouble over schools, I don't think I can stand it."

Then Wendy came tripping downstairs and helped herself to oatmeal. I could tell from the accusing look she gave us that she had been listening to the whole discussion while fixing her hair upstairs on the landing. Wendy loves nothing so much as to be in the thick of a disaster.

"We just can't pick up and move the family home," I said.

"Why not?" Wendy said. "I think that would be great."

"You don't have to face it every day the way I do," Elisabeth went on. "Every day almost Ben runs away from school; the kids are laughing at him he says, or his eye aches, or some such foolishness."

"Well, throw him in bed. If he's sick then into bed and the hell with it."

"He's not sick," Elisabeth spouted, "and we tried all that."

Then Wendy broke in. "I don't know what you think, but you'd better do something about Kim. She's really in with the goons."

Later that morning I called Professor Reuter to ask his advice on what to do. True to form, Ole said it was "quite

68

impossible" to do anything at this late date, all schools being terribly overcrowded. Yet he would see. And true to form he called back that night to say that a place had been made for Kim at the Zilliacus school, one of the progressive co-educational schools in town where he himself taught a class in Latin. At the end of the week Kim shifted. It was amazing to watch the change in the girl after a few weeks at the Zilliacus school. She liked her studies and her teachers and she soon began to talk about this or that girl who was a "friend." For one of the children anyway, things were beginning to work well.

As for Wendy, it was impossible to guess whether the girl was learning anything other than good grooming at that Neue Svenska Flika Skola. But one morning I screwed up my courage and basted up my Swedish for an interview with the school's head mistress. This big lady, a plump comfortable woman of about fifty, beyond academic alarums of any kind, said that Wendy was "always an excitement" in her classes.

"Does she speak any Swedish?"

"No. Not at all."

"Does she try to learn Swedish?"

"No. I think not."

"Should we do something? Make her work more at home?"

"No," the good woman said. "Just wait. One has only to wait."

I gave up wondering about Wendy. She had never wanted for words in the past: she would pick up Swedish by osmosis, or, more likely, she would soon have the whole school talking English. Either way would be all right, so long as it meant peace at home.

In some ways, I think, the Finns suffered from the oppressive darkness more than we did. We at least had an escape route open. There was even a kind of excitement about seeing how bad the weather could get, for you knew that after December 21 all the days would be better and spring would be sweeping back over Europe like a tidal wave of Mediterranean light. But to my Finnish friends this was a four-month period of despair; one-third of their lives were lost in it.

Up at the Business School the teachers became progressively morose. At first they tried to promise that the rain would not last. But it did. Then they said that when the sea froze over, the sky would clear and the beautiful cold blue weather would come. But the sea did not freeze, the windy drizzle kept on, and my colleagues took to avoiding me, as though they themselves were somehow guilty of the weather.

They must have thought I had lived among oranges and begonias. (The Finn, I saw, is a humble creature: he loves his country, will fight for it, die for it if need be; but he cannot imagine any foreigner honestly liking the place.)

One of my students, who had followed her courses at the University in spite of children, a drunken husband, and at last a divorce, wrote me in November that she was leaving school and taking a job in the west of Finland. She had no clear idea why, only that she felt compelled to go:

Last summer I saw jolly old England. I don't know whether I learned any English, but I was getting culture. I traveled around to all the places one is supposed to go. I "had fun"— but it wasn't very funny. It all seemed so aimless and expensive. Now I am back in my slough of despond and nothing will get me up out of it . . .

So fall slogged toward December and the light faded from the swamp that was our sky.

One could easily see why Finnish writers are so profoundly naturalistic, oppressed by physical boredom, lassitude, melancholia. The mist seeps through the cracks in the wall, mud crawls in on every pair of boots, clothes never dry, the trees struggle with the wind and the sea hounds its waves to the farthest marshy reaches of the bays. Lights lost in the south —over Estonia—are not lit up by TV programs in Russian rebroadcast from Tallinn; lights overhead, the old lights of the north skies, are not lit up by the news of a new contraption successfully jettisoned into space.

The world is the old world still, and only the old sun can cure its ailments.

Sometime toward the middle of November, however, we crossed an invisible line; though the dark period remained, for perhaps another two months, we ceased to think about it or to feel it. The magic word Christmas changed the outward scene. There was open talk of *Joulupukki*, who he was, what he looked like in Finland; and there was much hush-hush discussion of things being made in school. The kitchen at home became a carpentry and ceramics shop where every afternoon after school the youngsters came to make wooden decorations for a tree and to cement collections of Italian mosaics into tiles and hot plates. Steve, home in pitch-dark from his afternoon with the Park Auntie, had his own work to do, his piles of nails, tools, and tiles with which he decorated the floors; Elisabeth crunched around trying to get supper among the heaps of glued and cemented boards; one might get a piece of colored glass or tile instead of peas in the soup—but we were happy. We had come to Finland, hoping to escape for a while from the centrifugal forces that pull American families apart. Dark weather and the reticence of our neighbors had isolated us and forced us to depend upon each other. Friends five thousand miles away across the ocean were never closer than now.

Sometimes in the evenings, after the young ones were abed, Elisabeth, Kim, and I would go out for a walk in the streets. This was almost the only exercise we could get. Up on the main road a few blocks away was a small café called a *Baari* where we could stop for a cup of coffee or a bottle of Finnish-made coke. The Baari stayed open until ten o'clock and was the only public place in the neighborhood where a young man and a young girl could share a table and a moment of quiet together. They seemed so repressed, these young people, eating together with lowered eyes, always so well-mannered. Often they passed an entire meal without uttering a whisper of conversation. Perhaps these very repressions account for the strange and sometimes admirable traits of Finns—their reputed drunkenness, yes, but also their genius in defensive war; their gloomy natures, but also their spectacular outbursts in art, architecture, design, and drama. Finns were Finns. Sigrid Undset, the Norwegian writer, once called them "the most talented race on earth." She was, however, glad to live in Norway.

At the end of November we received our first shower of wet snow to add to the illusion that the dark time was passing.

(It was only an illusion. The next snowfall occurred at Easter.) On a wind blowing heavily from the sea the thick flakes crowded out of a grey sky. All day the snow came until by evening the ground was clean and white. During a lull in the storm, Elisabeth and I skied through the streets to the park on the western end of the island. The police and veterans' summer houses were all dark, but the woods were bright enough to ski through.

We went down the trackless lanes to the final sheet of rock where once we had seen an Amazon washing rugs in the surf. Now the slope of rock was white and the sea black. We could hear the waves coming ashore but could see nothing of them. And out on the rim of the darkness the islands stood covered with phosphorescent light, more striking than anything we had seen of them in summer.

Then the cold wind turned us around and headed us for home. Home was this place that luck had brought us to. The Nordgrens' lights were out. The Spooks' lights were out, but the Spooks were home as we could tell from their open bedroom window. It always seemed to be looking askance at us at night, when we came to our doorstep. Home was a place where Christmas tiles littered the floor; where rubber boots were thrown against the door, and mittens, socks, coats, hats, scarfs, book bags were heaped on the nearest convenient bench or stairstep; where baseball mitts and Swedish comics sprawled with open books and naked dolls on the dining table. Here at least was a corner of this foreign land that was forever America. Forever for two years.

It was beginning to snow again. Outside our living room window was a single street light around which the flakes swarmed like moths. That was the only visible light, and it was hard to believe that it did not stand on the very breaking edge of the world.

Tytti

Elisabeth needed help around the apartment, and even more she needed adult companionship, so we placed an ad in English in the *Helsingen Sanomat* and the result was a call from the Palace Hotel. To a background of hissing steam and banging pots a girl's voice said, "Please, you should not give that job to anyone until I can come." After we had seen Tytti Kaija, we had no thought of taking anyone else.

Tytti went through our hermetically sealed apartment not like a fresh breeze but like a whole gale off the Baltic: off came her coat and spiked Italian shoes, on went a striped Marimekko smock and slippers; then, flinging all the doors and windows open, Tytti stripped the bedding off the mattresses, hung it over the balcony, and went to work with the only swatter we had, Ben's baseball bat. Next came the rag carpets and a stiff Jugoslav rug; these she took to a fence outside and beat them until the last puff of dust and lint had blown away into the yard next door. After that, with flour on her hands, a fish supper in the skillet, and a pail of diapers for the machine shop downstairs, Tytti disappeared, leaving everything wide open in our apartment.

"I'm getting out of here," Elisabeth said, taking her market bag. "I'm frozen."

Tytti: she had the face of Danny Kaye and twice the animation. She was, in fact, the queen of swat in the Helsinki baseball league. Long-legged, strong-willed, ruddy of complexion, there was laughter or fury, gentleness or murder, constantly alight in her blue eyes. Without more formalities this Karelian daughter of the *Kalevala* adopted us and brought us up to be Finns. If the apartment needed dusting she threw everything outside and went to work with pail and mop and Lutheran fury. If supper needed cooking, it came on the table in strange but delicious disguises, and always accompanied by a mountain of boiled potatoes. Tytti protected us from the neighbors. One day when she was swatting things outside, an old harridan appeared on the balcony of an apartment nearby and began screaming across the street that Tytti ought to know it was "after hours" for beating. Tytti merely brandished her club the fiercer and yelled back some insult learned on the baseball field. That was the end of the interruption.

Steve alone opposed Tytti's iron will. One morning Tytti announced that she was going to "train" Steve.

"Steve's only a baby," Elisabeth reminded her.

"He's old enough," Tytti replied firmly.

"But he's only eleven months old."

"Then he's late. Already at six months are Finnish children all trained. You will see."

Elisabeth went shopping again. She couldn't stand the wailing when her smallest son was suspended over the raging whirlpool that is a modern Finnish toilet. Tytti's interest in toilet training was not because of the numbers of diapers she had to do, but rather because this was the way of things in Finland, a matter of national pride. I had my doubts about the procedure. It seemed unlikely that a child would learn anything from the experience except terror of water and a certainty that the big people are a wild dangerous race. I wondered, too, whether children helpless and exposed naked to all the perils of Lodore might not be expected to become in later years the very repressed and stonily silent creatures we saw all around us. However the problem was only theoretical: Steve refused to be civilized. Months later Tytti gave the project up, calling the young man "just a horrible stubborn American," and this we considered high praise from a Finn.

Tytti came once a week in the morning and once in the late afternoon. Most of the time she worked in the kitchen of the Palace Hotel—a forty-eight-hour work week for her, with

74

several nights on late duty, and two Sundays of the month committed. She worked hard and lived frugally. There was never time to eat at the hotel, she said, though sometimes she got a little of the brandy or wine "if it comes back and if the chef doesn't see it."

So far as we could tell Tytti made all her own clothes. She wore either a brown tweed skirt or a dark blue one; on special occasions, a party or a birthday, she might wear a single-piece dress of her own model. The only luxury she allowed herself were nylons; they cost 70¢ a pair and were of poor quality, but still, she was twenty-two-years old and unmarried and a girl had to think about her future.

Once I asked her how much she was making at the Palace Hotel.

"Twenty-two thousand Finnmarks," she told me.

"A week?" I said.

"A week?" she shouted. "No, a month."

That was about $70 a month, less than nine hundred a year. All this she turned over to her mother, for Tytti was the breadwinner for the family. They lived in a subsidized apartment over in the poorer part of town, in eastern Helsinki, which was commonly referred to as the Communist section; there was a younger sister who was working for the state tax bureau and taking night courses in order to prepare for her university examinations; and there was a tall slim young man of sixteen, the youngest of the family, who sometimes got odd jobs to help fill the family coffers. All in all the family probably did not have more than $2,000 of income annually. Tytti carried the main burden. Mrs. Kaija had decided that the younger sister was the one most likely to succeed at the University (though both girls were remarkable linguists, able to speak English, German, Swedish, and some French), and Tytti accepted this decision without complaint.

Two older brothers were sometimes mentioned. One was married and had several children, so that he could contribute little or nothing to the support of the family; the other was down with tuberculosis but refusing to take care of himself or to follow doctors' orders. He would soon be dead, Tytti said, but that was his business.

75

The family had once lived prosperously in Viborg, the ancient fortified seaport of eastern Finland. Forced to leave after the war they had settled temporarily in a number of western districts before coming to Helsinki. Tytti's father had never been able to re-establish himself. He had tried his hand at several jobs, finally running a kind of delicatessen on the outskirts of the capital; he lost money and lost heart. After his death Mrs. Kaija took over managing the family, and Tytti had to give up schooling.

One member of Tytti's family drew her ire; she never mentioned him without a burst of brimstone: her Communist Uncle. There were many kinds of Communists in the country; the distinction was important and had always to be reckoned with in any assessment of the surprising strength of the Communist party in Finland: First were the Finnish agents of the Kremlin, small in number, probably, but well-trained functionaries in inner party circles and ready traitors to any Socialist-Capitalist government. A second much larger group were the idealistic Communists, minor functionaries in the party (The People's Democratic League), who carried on its extensive social work and recruited so effectively in the poor mining areas and northern forests of the country. These people believed in nineteenth-century purely Finnish Communism. Half a century of world history had swept over them but left them undampened with facts.

A third group were those whose fathers and grandfathers had voted red or fought with the Red Guards during the 1918 civil war. That was a sufficient platform for them.

A fourth segment of the Communist votes came from those who were not Communist at all and would not have wanted communism in Finland. But they thought the Social Democrats weak and therefore voted with the Reds because they believed that only steady pressure from the Communists brought them the social programs they wanted.

A fifth group—and Tytti's uncle may well have been one of these—voted Communist, or talked Communist slogans, because they disliked all government and enjoyed keeping things stirred up. The bovine good order of Norway and Sweden was not for them. If they could not fight an invading outsider, then they would fall with a will to fighting Finns.

Tytti could not say which of all these kinds of "Communists" her uncle was. The distinctions were too academic for her:

"They are fools. All of them. What are they thinking, we should be Communists, after all the Russians have done to Finns!"

Tytti probably never paused to think how much she actually owed people like her uncle. To her the matter was very simple: "I would rather be dead, than live like Russians." Yet Tytti and her family lived in a good apartment built by the city; half the rent was subsidized. Her education was entirely free. Had she gone on to university, her major cost would have been only in time lost from work. If she was sick, she could have the best of Finland's excellent medical attention, including hospitalization and surgery, for little more than a dollar a day. If she married and had children, she would be entitled to children's allowances, maternity allowances, and other family benefits; out of work, she could claim unemployment insurance. Accident insurance, old-age pensions, and disability allowances would also be available to her. In all these ways Tytti's meager income of $900.00 per year was augmented by an invisible but very real amount. She paid nearly 15 per cent of her income in taxes, but the benefits available to herself and her family in any emergency must have been worth the equivalent of all they collectively earned in a year plus the added intangible value of security. In a way both Tytti and her uncle owed each other something: he helped to give her a high scale of living in spite of a small working-class income; she, with her simple direct way of looking at the world, helped to guarantee Finland's continued independence.

Tytti, of course, had no idea how much we came to know her country through watching her. Late daughter of Karelia, dispossessed of her childhood home and her chances for a good education, she came in youth and energy simply to make war on the sand and squalor of one American encampment. But she turned out to be our firmest tie with Finland. She taught Bronwen Finnish, Ben baseball, Elisabeth cooking. She even grudgingly consented to talk Swedish to Kim and Wendy. She took Steve to her arms like a child of her own. If there was a moment of spare time around the apartment, she liked nothing so much as to take Steve off into the woods to collect whatever was in season—pine cones, sticks, flowers—and bring it home for decorations. In return we got Tytti her first raise in salary in two years by the simple expedient of telling the chef we were going to take her to America. We weren't, of course, but the lie was good for 3,000 more marks per month.

Others of her race might hide themselves in silence or in ceremony, but not this home-run queen. Tytti showed everything on her animated face. One day she would come gushing tears over some altercation with her mother, the next day shouting with laughter because the chef had almost electrocuted himself fixing the cold-storage machine. One moment she would swear she was going to run away on a ship to America, then the next she would remember how lonely she had been as a maid one summer in a wealthy Copenhagen family. Here at least were trees, lakes, islands, and they still belonged to Finns. We could see in her a passionate physical love for her country which steadied her and kept her spirits free, whatever the monotony of her personal life.

As far as we could make out Tytti entertained no thoughts of marriage, though boy friends, she admitted a little scornfully, were never very hard to find. Her duty was apparent: her tall young brother must finish his education, and her sister must have her chance to go to the University. As for her own prospects, she hoped someday to be taken off the "hot stove" and put on "salads and desserts." It was not a big future.

It was Tytti's practice to take a bus from Lauttasaari to the railroad station and then to walk the remaining mile and a half home rather than pay the three and a half cents a transfer ticket would have cost. For all her stinginess with herself she had no real idea of where the money went. Mrs. Kaija ran the family finances with the secrecy of the Bank of Finland. At twenty-two years of age Tytti must have looked forward to a life of eternal hard work; she resented her mother's autocratic ways, but she did not consider running out on the family.

One day in December she came to the apartment in a sulphurous rage. Her young brother was missing. He had done a stint of work at a mail-order house during the Christmas rush and now he had disappeared.

78

"Disappeared?" Elisabeth cried, thinking of bodies floating in Helsinki harbor.

"Yes. For four days he is gone."

"But have you done anything about it?"

"What is there to do?"

"Report it to the police."

"The police?" Tytti shouted, wide-eyed. "What business is it of theirs?"

"To try to find out where he is, of course."

"I know where he is!" Tears of mortification were spouting from her eyes. "I know exactly. I could walk there now. Up in that woman's apartment. An older woman has got him, and she has got all his money too. Oh, I should go there and . . . scratch her eyes out."

And then suddenly Tytti subsided, with half a smile and a wicked gleam in her eyes: "Mother, she would like to know where . . . Imagine, for four days with a woman, and he's only sixteen! *Voi, voi*—my little brother."

Language

"Boy, this Finnish really murders you," said Ben, tutored one
week and shining with enlightenment. "You say *Uni* it means
Dream. But you say *Uuni*, and what is it? . . . A blinking *fireplace!* . . . Er—no, wait, wait—maybe I got it backwards.
. . . Well, it's something like that anyway."

But the light of hope soon faded from his eyes. *Fireplace*
was not a word you needed much around a school, and *Dream*
got you nowhere. Ben had a practical boy's mind. If language
didn't deal directly with balls, ins, outs, offside, and "the heck
you did," it probably didn't deal with much of anything.

Certain rules which he learned at the very beginning made
Finnish seem deceptively easy:

Words are pronounced exactly as they are written, all double
consonants and double vowels being voiced.

The accent is always on the first syllable.

All grammar follows the rules, there being almost no exceptions.

So far so good, but having learned this much, or at least
heard and believed this much, Ben could see no way to apply it
to the jumble of noises that surrounded him. True, by apply-
ing himself for an hour he had learned how to count to a
million, but even this was of no use, for the small kids in first

80

grade were only learning their ABC's; they didn't have plusses and take-aways yet.

So Ben, after the first few weeks, quietly retired into picture books (the land of *Uni*) and tried no more. His tutor became discouraged: "He works. But nothing will go in. It is as though he should shut his ears." And his teacher at school confirmed this impression: "He lives somewhere else—in America, perhaps."

Ben talked a good deal of going home: Was it a long distance? How many days would a ship take to get there? Would hockey and skiing have started there yet? All this discussed in a matter-of-fact way: many people had gone from Finland to America, it couldn't be very difficult.

I tried to persuade him to be patient. Eventually something would get through that made sense and then he'd be on his way. But one of Ben's troubles was that he understood himself too well: he would fall behind the gang at home; he might lose a year and then what would he have to show for it? A language he'd never use again.

So we moved on from week to week with Ben, tempting him with talk of what we would do when the snow came, bribing him with the promise of a bicycle in the spring. But probably we would never have succeeded in keeping him in school had not Laurel and Hardy come on the movie circuit in Helsinki. Helsinki was going through a revival of all the old comedies. Here was a tangible immediate reward for not making a complete break with the Finns; every week Ben and Bron and I went to see those irreplaceable comics whom they called Lordy and Hardy.

Bronwen fortunately suffered none of Ben's devastating realism. Learning Finnish was to her like putting together a marvelous picture puzzle. No one had ever told her that language had to have form and a purpose, sound alone was enough. Neither had she ever heard of the purgatory of grammar. Bronnie simply opened her ears to everything around her and came home echoing with the sounds of that language:

"Oh, Mummy, you know what? Listen, isn't it pretty what the teacher taught us today?

81

> *"Mitä itket, tyttö raukka,*
> *Tyttö raukka, neito nuori?"*

"It is. But what does it mean?"

"Oh, I don't know that! But it sounds so beautiful."

(She was singing a song from the *Kalevala*, wherein a young maiden finds that she would rather drown herself than marry and leave home—a song for Ben, in fact, but he wasn't able to hear it.)

Bronwen, of course, was beginning at the beginning in a class that was just learning to read and write. Moreover Finland had not yet mechanized its teaching. The bardic tradition, so strong in that country, still prevailed in the schools. Children grew up hearing, chanting, singing, memorizing, dramatizing the old, old songs that are both innocence and tradition for a country, the deepest unconscious bonds that hold a people together.

For all his violent reaction to Finnish, Ben had my sympathy. Finnish is a hard language. There are few loan-words from German, English, or Swedish on which a beginner can find a footing. The whole structure of the language, and hence the way of thinking, is foreign to Western minds.

Finnish has no articles, definite or indefinite. It has no gender, not even he and she for pronouns. Finnish has no future tense of verbs. It has almost no prepositions; instead it plays scrabble with the endings of nouns and adjectives. Compared to this language Latin is simple-minded. Finnish nouns require fifteen ordinary endings, then there are more changes for plurals, negatives, questions, emphasis, for polite or familiar usages, et cetera, et cetera. In short, Finnish is a language so difficult that only children can master it.

The laws of grammar may be followed with mathematical exactness, but learning how to apply those laws seems like learning arithmetic beginning with calculus. What profiteth it a man to find that there are no exceptions to the rules when instead he must memorize ten thousand rules?

There are other difficulties in learning the language. For example, a glance at a line of Finnish would convince one that it had been written with a machine-gun loaded with K, T, P, V, and R. These consonants bristle everywhere. (As a matter of fact words beginning in K, T, P, V, and R make up nearly half of the words in the dictionary.) When jaded memory slips the least bit, confusion takes over. Often, in the indoor market or local food store, I stood at a loss to remember what the word was I had to have. *Potato* might come out *egg* or *apple* or *good morning*. Faced with an embarrassed salesgirl I might reach into Pandora's Box and try for the simple word *Ruoka* (Food). But anything in R might slip out. Was it *Rauha* I had asked for (Peace)? or *Raha* (Money)? or *Raskas* (Heavy)?

No wonder that look of panic on the face of the salesgirl—an instant of horrified catatonia before she fled.

Perhaps I had actually approached her with *Rakas* (Beloved), or asked for *Rakkaus* (Love).

"One moment," the girl would gasp. "I'm sorry, but I do not speak English. . . ." Then out the back door, across the street—God knows where. She would never come back.

Yet, for all these difficulties, Finnish is a fascinating language. One senses, working at it, that one is on the corner of a continent of migratory peoples whose unwritten history can be dimly glimpsed only from the trails of language which run back into their distant past.

Finnish looks and sounds like written and spoken Japanese; indeed there are some interesting similarities between the two languages. Finnish also looks and sounds like that mysterious language of the Pyrenees: Basque; and at the same time it appears to have remote affinities with Eskimo. Finnish is a close relative of Estonian, a distant cousin to Hungarian, and Finns will sometimes grudgingly admit a kinship between their language and Turkish, Lapp, and certain minor languages of north central Russia.

When Zacharius Topelius spoke of his people as being "two wild-grown Asiatic shoots [the western Finns and the Karelians] of a many-branched decaying stem" he was speaking of what little can be surmised about their racial origins, for they probably came from somewhere east of the Volga and west of the Urals in the northern part of Russia. Perhaps no one will ever know exactly. Their own literature gives no hint of their homeland or of the migrations that brought them to the west.

83

They brought only a religion or a mythology: heroes, trailing clouds of glory and works of magic to be sure, but heroes who were singers, blacksmiths, fishermen, warriors, wives, mothers, maidens, and who settled in a land that is recognizably a mythological Land of Swamps. Of the travels of ancient Finns nothing remains in the *Kalevala* comparable to the cartographic descriptions in the *Odyssey* or even to those impressionistic sketches of Leif's wanderings told in the Icelandic Runes. The Finns came with their bards, and the bards sang of the greatness of the heroes, around winter fires or in great singing competitions, but the stories they recounted were imaginative, religious, and democratic rather than epic, aristocratic, and based on fact.

Another curious thing about Finnish is that until very recently it was only a spoken language. Swedes thought the tongue too barbaric to bother with. They conquered the country, civilized it with war, priests, and merchants, and ran it as a frontier duchy for more than six hundred years without feeling the need of a written Finnish language. The first Finnish book was the *ABC Book* (1542) by Michael Agricola, a native disciple of Martin Luther, who had virtually to create the written language. The third book was Agricola's translation of the New Testament.

But not until the early nineteenth century did anyone speak of Finnish literature, and not until the 1860's did anyone seriously believe that Finnish children should be taught to read and write their language. When Elias Lönnrot toured the countryside collecting songs, stories, folklore from ancient singers and old farm crones it was as though the good country doctor had stepped back fifteen centuries to sit at the feet of those who had once listened to Homer. Lönnrot's *Kalevala*, first published in 1835, is often called the Finnish Epic, though it is not an epic in the Western sense. Rather it is a broad but meandering stream from many sources of legends and stories brought together and unified by Lönnrot's editorial genius. Nothing like the *Kalevala* exists in Western literature or mythology. It is a strange, mystical, sometimes deeply human song, like a fairy tale in spirit but written with an adult sense of loneliness and passion. The depth and variety of the Finnish folk literature was probably not suspected by Finns themselves until Lönnrot's time. Since then the Finnish Literary Society has compiled and published further researches in folklore, herbal medicine, folk tales, superstitions, enchantments, sayings, puzzles, etc. The work now runs to thirty-three volumes, surely the largest collection of its kind in any country.

These were the songs and stories Bronwen was hearing and learning in her class with Mrs. Laitinen. It was luck for Bron. All too soon she would be in the hands of the literary scientists who would take a poem to the dissection table, as they would a chloroformed butterfly, and with efficient pin and scalpel reveal all its parts.

I envied Bronwen. Finnish is a beautiful and expressive language, a language of imagery. Intimations of this I could get from my students' names, or from studying the dictionary, or from listening to the pungent syllables in the market place or in the National Theater.

Where in English we turn to adjectives and qualifying phrases to describe a particular kind of "hill," the Finn has ready two dozen different nouns that identify the size, contour, location, or structure of the mound in question, and how it was iced or aged into shape. We speak of a "bear," but the Finn cannot. It is not sufficiently exact. He has several words, that range from the Teddy Bear (*Nalle*) to the shaggy misanthrope (*Kontio*) who prowls his range red-eyed and expects to be left alone.

Exactness has its limitations. Finnish does not serve easily for abstractions. (There are many poets but few philosophers in that country.) An abstract idea or a generality must be hemmed in with a forest of hardwood words in the hope that the skittery notion will have been trapped therein.

Months of walking in the wilderness of Finnish words brought me to few clearings and still fewer lookouts. But I could begin to hear the whispering sounds around me and catch some of the flashing lights through the forest—some glimmer remaining from the First Day, and a suspicion of magic:

> *Siitä vanha Väinämöinen,*
> *tietäjä iänikuinen*
> *teki tiellä venetta*

85

laati purtta laulamalla.
Lauloi virren: pohjan puutti,
lauloi toisen: liitilaian,
lauloi kohta kolmannenki.

Unfortunately the practical Ben never caught this drift of light from the wilderness. He learned to ask for butter, bread, milk, meat, and chocolate. Soccer players and frustrated small fishermen soon taught him the expletives, but beyond learning such useful Finnish words Ben closed his ears and dreamed of happier places. I knew we were licked one evening in December when Mr. Nordgren hailed him at the back door:

"Hello, Ben. How does it go?"

"Oh . . . not so good."

"That Finnish, you call that pretty tough stuff?"

"I guess so."

"What do you know, then?"

"Well, I know *Uuni*. You know what that is, Mr. Nordgren? *Uuni* and *Uni*. That really murders me."

The land was ours before we were the land's.
She was our land more than a hundred years
Before we were her people. . . .
Something we were withholding made us weak
Until we found that it was ourselves
We were withholding . . .

—Robert Frost

𝕴ndependence Day—December 6

A great storm had been brewing all week in the Baltic. Now it overflowed its basin; the tide, which was no tide but wind-driven water from as far as the Skaggerak, climbed three feet during the morning, four, then five. Spume reeled across the gull-nest islands at the mouth of the bay; the beach went under; the summer wharf began to come apart as the waves surged under the planks. Then wet snow came spitting down from a racing sky.

In the morning the children had been dancing like curlews before the teeth of the surf, fetching ashore the oars, seats, rudders, fishing gear, driftwood which struggled in over the piecrust fresh ice. The summer boats, hauled up and tied in the sheltering trees, began to stir uneasily. By noon, several swamped skiffs farthest out had come away, lumbering down with the stacked flats and bathhouses into the marsh at the end of the cove where older boys could get ropes on them and moor them to the trees.

Beaufort 8 (a gale), the weather man said laconically over the radio, while the big wind was withering the Baltic. White and blue flags crackled from the apartment poles, the foot-thick walls of our building hummed in the gusts and the metal roof boomed out its weird discomforts.

At 3:00 P.M. the day was already getting dark. We went to fetch the children on the road. It was time to be getting dressed for the independence parade. Ben and Bron, dripping like otters, took us to see the latest excitement—a fish shack that had come floundering down from one of the islands up-wind, and blundered onto the wharf to hang up and pull its nails. There was nothing anyone could do to save either the wharf or the shack. We changed into dry clothes, then, booted and coated against the snow, took the No. 23 bus into town. We had been told to get off near the National Cemetery and then follow the students carrying torches.

I had expected a large crowd, but there were only scattered pairs of older people moving down the snow-dusted sidewalks. The rest were students, boys and girls, wearing their white caps and running down the tree-lined avenue in high heels or oxfords to join in dark masses of people collected in a field. They were ranked according to their "Student Nations," their provincial districts. Each group had its flags and we could hear the laughter and cheers which greeted late arrivals.

After a while we came to the main gate of the cemetery where, under triple stone archways, a special squad of students were lighting torches made from wicks and cans of fuel oil nailed to the ends of long sticks. The flames blew horizontally among the stooped intent faces. From the arches we made our way along a gravel road which ran up an aisle of bare trees. On either side were the geometric gardens of graves. On the top of a low hill we joined a small crowd of people, all motionless in their heavy black coats and Homburgs, waiting. They stood around three sides of an open rectangle. Braziers of oil on stone posts poured a hectic flare and black smoke down over the area. At the far end of the rectangle a huge stone cross, as plain as a carpenter's square, rose dimly from a pedestal of steps, and nearer us was a massive block of polished granite beside which two soldiers stood stiffly on guard. Even in the darkness Ben and Bronwen recognized, from postcards they had seen, that this was Mannerheim's grave.

Nothing happened. For a long time only the snapping of flags overhead and the occasional roar of down-blowing flames broke the silence around that plot and grave. At last Bronwen whispered, "Is Mannerheim dead?"

"Shhhhhhhh!" said Elisabeth.

Some of our neighbors stirred, looking down to see who the speaker was.

"But is he?"

"Of course," Ben answered. "Whatcha think with a rock like that on him."

Is Mannerheim dead?

He was fifty-one years old when he came back permanently to Helsinki. He had gone to Russia before the bitter years of oppression in Finland. After thirty years of a brilliant career as an officer in the Czar's cavalry, an explorer and diplomat in Mongolia, and as a Russian general in the First World War, he was leaving Russia. At that time, in late 1917, the Czar and his family were under arrest; Kerensky, in a flurry of social theories and political incompetence, had come and gone; Lenin and Trotsky were mopping up in St. Petersburg and moving on to Moscow.

General Mannerheim did not "escape" from revolutionary Russia. He traveled from the Crimea to Moscow, from Moscow to Petersburg by train and carriage, wearing his uniform and getting revolutionary soldiers to help with his luggage. He stayed a week in Petersburg—long enough to see that apathy among the old rulers had turned the future of Russia over to the Bolshevists. Bluff, a Finnish citizenship, and his extraordinary "command presence" got Mannerheim the rest of the way home.

A week earlier, on December 6, 1917, Finland had declared her independence. She had, like the American colonies in 1776, only a self-appointed government, no foreign policy and no army. Moreover Finland was both overrun with confused Russian troops and on the edge of Red revolution herself. Independence would still have to be believed, fought for, and won. Within a month Mannerheim was called upon to begin a new military and diplomatic career. His work for his homeland would span another thirty years. The country would face a civil war, Communist uprisings, a great depression, a near-Fascist *coup d'état*, three more wars, and the perils of the postwar settlements, before his career would be done.

Is Washington dead—whose military skill and statesmanship made a nation? Is Lincoln, who saved it? Is Churchill gone—who for a while embodied the truculent genius of freedom? Carl Gustav Mannerheim was all of these men to his country.

The graves look down a long slope to the sea. So many graves! Acres of them, among trees and hedges, the mounds softening with snow. It was cold on that hilltop. Nobody in the crowd moved. Finns stood there with endless patience, barely shuffling their cold feet. We could see beyond the arches where the fields were blooming with torches but as yet no columns marched in.

"I'm cold." Bronwen glared.

"You'll have to wait. We'll have cocoa after."

"But I'm freezing."

"How long do you think Finland has been a country?" Elisabeth asked.

"A thousand years," the girl answered.

"A hundred," Ben said, more leery of numbers.

"Forty-three years," Elisabeth said.

"Heck, Daddy's older than that!" Bronwen said, disgusted that so much fuss should be made over so ordinary a thing. "Why don't they get going?"

It's an awful job, I thought, getting Finns lined up and pointed in one direction.

It had been cold and snowy that day in late December, 1917, when Senator Svinhufvud, head of the Finnish provisional government, had come to General Mannerheim and asked him to be the supreme commander of the defense forces. The name was about all that Mannerheim had at first, but in the northwest (in Southern Ostrobothnia) free peasants had already banded together and begun to train in expectation of independence. These could be turned into a nucleus of a liberation army—the "White Guards." Mannerheim also learned for the first time that 1,800 young Finns had been spirited away, while Russia was fighting Germany, and sent to the enemy for training as a Jaeger battalion: these could serve as the beginnings of an officer corps.

General Mannerheim's first decision was to move his headquarters out of southern Finland. In the northwest he would be out of the reach of Russian troops and near to Swedish supplies.

Although Russia's new masters, early in January, gave official recognition to Finland's declared independence, it had been on the assumption that Finland herself would become revolutionized and would then join with the rest of the Soviet Socialist Republics in one great marching force of the working class. To cut Finland away from this plan would certainly mean war with the Russians, as well as civil war with revolutionary Finns. In the south, Finland's civil state was in almost as complete disorder as Russia's, although there was no apathy here. Radical socialists and the self-appointed "Red Guards" held the initiative: they were 30,000 strong, well organized, and would soon grow to more than 100,000. Russian land and sea units would reinforce them with another 40,000. Arms were already available in the many Russian garrisons in the country.

For all the difficulties that would face his Liberation Army, Mannerheim, in accepting his command, stipulated that there must be no intervention either by Swedish or German armies; Finns would have to win their independence:

> I insisted [he writes in his *Memoirs*] that a people's freedom, to be lasting, must be paid for with its own sufferings. . . .
> Senator Svinhufvud was sceptical: "You have no army, no soldiers, no arms—how then can you break the enemy's resistance?"
> I replied I was sure it could be done.

Mannerheim went at once to Vaasa. It was a close escape for him, for Helsinki was soon taken over by a Red *coup*. There Mannerheim set up his headquarters, chose his staff, trained his men, and filled the ranks with such notable peasant leaders as Matti Laurila. When he was ready, he took up the Independence War which was at the same time to be a Civil War.

"We were about to take a leap in the dark, but there was no lack of resolution." The White army in a surprise move disarmed Russian coastal garrisons and secured the railroad to Sweden. Then they started south and east, preventing where possible any conjunction of Russian reinforcements with the local Red Guards. Mannerheim was a professional; he made no mistakes. Against him was a large ungoverned mass of disaffected peasants and opportunists: their vision of the war was rarely more than local, their primary impulses not so much to establish a Soviet Socialist Republic in Finland as to wrest land from the wealthy gentry.

It was a brilliant winter campaign for the White army, its strength augmented by Swedish volunteers. Decisive battles came in March and early April in the lake land around the industrial city of Tampere. Soon after, Helsinki itself was freed with the help of the German Baltic Division recently landed on Hanko, the southern tip of Finland. After that the Whites ("the Butchers" as they were always called by the Reds) moved on inexorably to Karelia, the port of Viborg, and the rich Kymi valley towns. On May 15, Finland was free.

The scars from that war were cut deep, the memories still burn. Civil wars are fought with guilty consciences and therefore utmost fury. Atrocities were rife on both sides. Thousands of innocent people, and many more thousands who had only the vaguest notion of what the fighting was about, were murdered by brothers and neighbors; 80,000 Red Guards were rounded up and incarcerated for years in prison camps where, during the first year, 10 per cent died of starvation, cold, or sickness.

This is a people, as Topelius wrote, who have "perseverance allied to a certain obstinacy . . . an unwillingness to become angry, but a tendency, when roused, to indulge in unmeasured wrath." The bitterness of the civil war still shows, unabated, in every parliamentary election or domestic issue.

Mannerheim must have been a prickly hero. Scion of a baronial Swedish family, his education and years abroad had given him a breadth of understanding rare in itself and entirely wanting in the new rulers of Finland. To make matters worse, Mannerheim had a blunt self-confidence, a formidable command of facts, and an unbearable way of being almost always right. Like Churchill he was too big a man for the bumbling ways of peace, though irreplaceable in time of crisis.

Thus a mere two weeks after the end of the Liberation War Mannerheim was informed by the acting leaders of the government, Senator Svinhufvud and Dr. Paasikivi, that the army and defense forces were to be "under German direction." Protesting this unwise and unnecessary invitation to German domination of Finland, Mannerheim resigned and went abroad. "The members of the Government had not a word to say to me when I left the chamber, no one rose to offer me his hand."

Worse was to follow. Svinhufvud, the son of a sea captain, was a small-town judge who had been exiled during the Russian oppression for refusing to suspend the laws of Finland in favor of Russian laws. He was a stout-hearted patriot, but one of limited vision. (His name means The Pigheaded.) He and his government were apparently persuaded, as late as autumn, 1918, that Germany was going to win World War I. On October 9, just a month before the end of the war, the Finnish Diet duly elected Prince Karl of Hesse, brother-in-law of the Kaiser, to be King of Finland.

This fantastic hallucination passed with the collapse of Germany, and then Senator Svinhufvud resigned. Mannerheim was called back to be Regent until new elections could be held and a new constitution drawn up. Under the direction of the country's ablest jurist, Professor K. J. Stålberg, a republican form of government was adopted rather than that of a constitutional monarchy. (Perhaps it was unfortunate, in the light of subsequent events, that Finland was not tied more closely to Sweden, but at the time this was an absolute impossibility.) In any case, Finland's government is fully democratic and its constitution has served the country well since its adoption.

I looked at the stolid men around me, standing so mute and patient in the snowy red darkness at Mannerheim's graveside. Many, middle-aged now, had probably fought under him in the two recent wars with Russia: 1939-40 and 1941-44. Their fathers and uncles would have fought in the Civil War. Whatever their thoughts or emotions, nothing showed in their faces.

There is a tendency now among Finnish writers and journalists to belittle Mannerheim with trivialities, as though to make him more "human." But history is too full of him. There was nothing inhuman about him. Courtly, reserved, he was an aristocrat with a sense of responsibility equal to his many talents. While he was given the skill and the opportunity to save his country from destruction—not once, but three times!—

93

nevertheless it is in the Finnish nature to grumble and grimace over that fact, to deny it and make jokes—and to be secretly proud that it was a Finn who did it.

We waited and we waited, our feet smarting with the cold—and at last we saw the students coming through the archway and up the aisle of trees in a long river of torches burling and blowing under a hectic banging of flags. Not a word or sound, no music, no commands. The first ranks crossed the open area and climbed the stone steps under the cross, the flagbearers filed in behind the grave; then in an almost endless stream the Student Nations poured out onto the lawn before the quadrangle and ranked themselves in silence on the broad slope.

Soft and thin in the darkness the voices rose in chorus under the cross, singing *Vårt Land* (Our Land), Runeberg's national anthem. We could not see the leader of the chorus, but felt the movements of his arms translated into chords, hard minor chords that swelled out of the immense darkness and were blown away by the wind. After that, someone spoke from among the raucous flags, telling the listeners not to forget the students who in the past had fought to save the land, and had to fight again: the voice spoke in Finnish, a language which is both the glory and the prison of these people. The speaker followed his lecture with only a brief paraphrase in Swedish, thereby himself forgetting the hundred years in which a national consciousness and sense of independence had been the masterwork of Swedish-speaking Finns.

Like a wedding, the ceremony at Mannerheim's graveside was soon over. The shadowy lines moved out through the arches again to begin the long march into the center of town. Two kilometers of students. We could see the first Nations limbering their length across the tracks to Acadia Street; from there they would pass down Mannerheim's Avenue to the Esplanade, down to the sea and the government buildings, then back by way of Alexander's Street to the great square in front of the Lutheran Cathedral. We took a straighter route into town where, by the Esplanade, we could watch the marchers from a restaurant.

"How many cakes?" asked Bronwen, glued to the front of a glass cabinet that was piled with delicacies.

"Two," Ben said promptly. "Right? On Independence Day —two cakes."

I wondered about the Swedes. Why this mute distaste for anything Swedish that stays like a birthmark on the older Finns? The battle for Finnish equality has long since been won and the Swedish-Finns, now numbering only 6 per cent of the population, are a vanishing minority. Little things are usually given as the reason: the singsong language, though surely Swedish is a beautiful and expressive tongue; the stiff formalities of Swedes, though upper-class Finns secretly admire and adopt these same formalities.

Part of the rancor stems from the past World Wars, which Sweden was lucky enough to stay out of, thereby becoming rich and guilt-ridden. Though Finland in its worst days received sympathy, volunteers, and cash, Swedish help never went beyond that. In numerous crises demanding political action—a firm defense pact, a northern alliance, or even the much-discussed union of the two countries—Finland was always left to find her own way; the bluster of the Kremlin was enough to warn Sweden off.

The grudge goes back much further, too. Swedish people ruled here a long time. They came as fishermen and traders, stayed to make their homes along the coasts, built seaports and cities, forts, factories, and universities, carried the ledgers of business and the flags of empire. The Finns were farmers and woods people. By feudal standards the Swedes were enlightened rulers over a poor uncouth populace whose very language was unwritten and nearly incomprehensible. In 1556, Gustav Vasa deeded the whole of this area as a Grand Duchy to his son—thereby establishing early a sense of unity in Finland.

Swedes brought trade, Christianity, government, education, and Western concepts of law. They also brought the endless wars of empire. For five hundred years the land of swamps was afire in the struggle between Sweden and Russia. Strange to say, the slow-witted stubborn Finnish peasants remained loyal to the Kings of Stockholm to the end. When, in 1808, Czar Alexander I finally extinguished Swedish ambitions and annexed the Grand Duchy of Finland, "most people then living in Finland," according to Topelius, "thought all was over.

. . . But they were mistaken. Only now was it possible to build up a future."

Alexander must have liked Finland. He returned to her the Karelian lands in the east, taken in 1721; he promised to abide by Finnish laws and the Constitution; Finns were to have their own local and national governments, their courts, schools, churches, customs, currency, army, et cetera; they were to rule in all matters save foreign policy. Alexander II extended those liberal measures of independence. For eighty years, under Russian suzerainty, Finland was virtually free. True, it was the wealthy (primarily the Swedish-Finns) who benefited most. The peasants suffered as before from bad weather and crop failures, though work on the railroads, the naval fortifications, and jobs in the developing industries brought some relief and betterment.

All that was good in the Grand Duchy was buried, however, by subsequent events. Those Alexanders had been worldly men. The Nicholases fitted better the Czaristic manner: some sinister blackness and suspicion pervaded their minds. When the cries of their people became too loud, they knew only how to apply new terrors. After 1895, under the orders of Nicholas II, Russification began in earnest. Nicholas dissolved the Finnish parliament, suspended the constitution and local courts, conscripted Finns into the Russian army, and declared Russian to be the official language of the country. General Nicholai Bobrikov was the talented instrument of this policy until 1904 when he was assassinated by a young university student.

The torches of liberation, touched off by Eugene Schauman, smoldered during the few short years of moderation that followed Russia's defeat by Japan, then flared anew in the windy terror that led to the Revolution.

Yet for Finns the years under the Alexanders were years of essential transformation. Out of the long peace came brilliant men and women to celebrate this land, this people: Henrik Porthan, professor of Finnish History; Elias Lönnrot, country doctor, who collected the songs and folklore of Karelian singers and constructed out of them the Finnish epic poem, *Kalevala;* Johan Snellman, country teacher, journalist, statesman, who championed the Finnish language and Finnish schools; J. L. Runeberg, national poet, whose poems of *Ensign Stål* fired the people with an unruly pride over their fortitude and loyalty in war; the scientists Castrén and Cajander; the statesmen Svinhufvud and Stålberg; the painters Edelfelt, Järnefelt, Schjerfbeck, and Gallen; the musicians Sibelius and Palmgren—all of these, to mention only a few, constituted the first waves of freedom. Self-discovery moved on to pride, and pride to a sense of destiny.

All Swedish names, Swedish-Finns.

There were other waves following, purely of Finnish origin, and they have not abated yet, but the first wave was Swedish-Finn. The greatest gift of Sweden to Finland was made after this country became a Russian Duchy. The tidal flood, both Finnish and Swedish, came to be a national movement long before it turned revolutionary. Only the stupidity and paranoia of despots succeeded in turning it into an independence movement.

Mannerheim came as a late crest of that first wave. Returning from Bolshevik Russia, he saw clearly that Finland must stand alone or be extinguished in the chaos of revolution. The Independence War must be won. Only after that could the problems of social justice, health, employment, land be corrected.

Torches moving in the wind, students marching. When the last of the long column had bobbed past our restaurant windows, we hurried out to watch the torches flooding into Alexander's Square. Christmas was in all the shop windows, in colored lights and tinsel. (I wondered what Russians would think if they could see Helsinki now.)

As we rounded the corner of the University, we found a large crowd of people already jamming the sidewalks. We were conspicuously out in mid-traffic and face to face with a tall policeman. It was like blundering into the center of a football field at the moment of kickoff. The crowd watched the policeman, and the policeman watched us. Although we were blocking traffic, he did not whistle or shout orders—he knew we were foreigners; no Finn would ever get himself so far out of place—instead he regarded us with suppressed amusement as though curious to see what goofy move we would try next.

And then from Bronwen, who had never spoken a word of Finnish in our presence before, came a flood of whispered school phrases: "*Voi kauhet . . . mihin voidaan mennä? Ei o'mitään paikkaa. . . .*"

The tall policeman smiled and bowed over her, saying in words that only she could understand: "Little girl, please, take yourself around the corner and around the block. There you will find places."

Alexander's Square, like Mannerheim's grave, was lit by braziers of oil on pillars festooned with spruce branches. Under the statue of the Czar the Student Nations were crowding in to take their formations. Down the long avenue more students were coming, marching in route step, their torches flaring on their faces as the lines of fire flowed into the square. The only sound was the howling flames from the braziers and the snow-muffled footsteps.

When the square was full, the University Chorus broke into song again on the dark steps under the Cathedral. Some senator spoke—unbelievably for less than four minutes—then the whole echoing area gave voice to that music which more than any other tells the imagery which holds Finns together: Sibelius' "Finlandia Anthem." After that the independence celebration was over, the fires quenched, and the silent crowd melted away.

We went home to Lauttasaari, put Sibelius on the record player and turned the volume full on to let our East German neighbors know that they hadn't buried us yet.

Out in the dark were the bare islands and snow-blind skerries. The storm was pounding the bank of our shore road. Ben and Bronwen, forgetting the cold, ran out to join the salvage operations of their friends. The summer pier was humped and broken, the fish shack had disappeared. Men, home from work, had come down to wade around in the black muck of the surf and haul their swamped boats higher into the trees. Under dim lamplight each man worked by himself.

98

> History is written by the victors.
> —VÄINÖ LINNA

That Other War

There was another war at this time so different from the Liberation War that it seems to belong to another time and another people. It is a war only hinted at in the usual histories, but it is the general subject of some of the best books in Finnish. One begins:

> The effect of the death sentences on the slack population, which had not foreseen such an eventuality, was on the whole mildly stupefying . . . But in Jussi Toivola's last moments there was one minor incident that irresistibly provoked laughter because it was somehow so typical of him. The rebels were shot in a shallow grave dug ready for them in the graveyard, and Jussi chanced to be the last. Whereupon instead of remaining standing he lay down in the pile of corpses—to save trouble, like. Wasn't that Jussi all over? Only he was not shot lying down, but ordered to get to his feet.

Among the many dim-lit faceless people who never celebrated December 6, there was one whom F. E. Sillanpää* chose to illuminate that other independence war. His name was Johan Abraham Benjamin's-son in the parish registry, Jussi when he was a boy, or Janne among pals, Johan during his short period of relative prosperity, and Juha when he was old and dirty.

* *Meek Heritage.*

99

His face was covered with a mongrel growth of tangled hair; only the sharp nose was clearly visible. This was because hair grew round his eyes as well, and as the peak of his cap cast a shadow, one saw in that region of his face only two sunken harsh points of light into which no decent person cared to look.

The good farmers in the neighborhood were happy enough to be rid of him. They regarded him as a "cunning rogue and skillful agitator"—though he was nothing of the kind—because there was something in his eyes "suggesting awareness of what one would not at any price admit existed in oneself." When it was learned that Juha Toivola had been involved in a murder during the rebellion, "judgment was pronounced upon him without further ado."

Sillanpää begins his story of one minor Red Guardsman at the very end: the rest is merely explanation. Yet Jussi may be regarded as one of a large class, and the circumstances of his life, during the latter half of the last century, were common enough to be almost universal. He was the accidental son of Old Benjamin, a small freeholder who was sometimes drunk, often improvident and lazy, and whose happiest moments were spent with a neighbor's slovenly wife or in the petty cruelties he could practice on his family:

> The boy . . . recognizes the familiar smell of liquor and tobacco and sees Benjamin's hairy face from an unusual angle, level with his own. A rather dreadful being, father. . . . The incalculable being is still smiling and doing things. It takes the plug of tobacco out of its cheek and in slow deliberate fun pokes it into Jussi's mouth. The boy is afraid to resist, to hit out; the mouth twists into a peevish howl. To sodden old Benjamin it brings a tiny sickening pleasure. Maja's boy . . . he cannot quite remember whether he has ever given Maja a proper beating.
>
> Maja comes into the living room just as Benjamin is forceably pushing his tobacco-smelling finger into the boy's mouth.
>
> "What are you up to now again—Drunk?" she asks.

"Easy, old hag," Benjamin roars in his hollow old-man's voice, rage patently feigned, as he pushes Maja away.

"Swiller, what do you think you're going to live in next year? Will you put the boy down?"

"Hell's cow, are you going to hold your jaw?" snarls Benjamin, turning fiercely to Maja. Jussi takes advantage of the diversion to jump down from the fireplace ledge, his heels jarring the floor; rubbing his lips he darts out into the yard.

Maja, plump and vague, unwanted even in her youth, has by dumb acquiescence become Old Benjamin's third wife. Benjamin dies during the famine years of the eighteen-sixties, but not before he has traded away the deeds to his land for a last Christmas jug from one of the neighbors. Turned out by the sheriff, Maja and Jussi load their belongings on a sled and go to seek Maja's prosperous brother, Kalle. They spend a night at a village "clinic," among other dispossessed wanderers and beggars; a woman dies and her clothes are snatched away before her jaws have stopped moving. At Kalle's farm Jussi is left to find his way with a grudging uncle. Maja humbly disappears, to return only when she is ready to die.

At Kalle's place the farm hands live together in a separate room, Jussi sleeps in the bakery, and the master and mistress have a room to themselves. Jussi is slow-witted like his mother; it takes him years to understand his privileged position as a poor relation. Nor does he quite grasp the life that goes on around him, the play of the young boys and girls up on Pig Hill.

Kalle and his wife prosper. They aspire to better society. Kalle changes his name to Karl and hopes ultimately to be accepted by even the Swedish-speaking families in the parish, "those with tongue-twisting names and offended countenances who never have been seen at any farmers' celebrations." But a boyish prank of Jussi's spoils Karl's play for favor among the gentry (he screwed the nuts off the carriage wheels of some of the better people visiting the farm one day), and that night Jussi is on the road again.

He hires out at a nearby farm, he finds work with lumbermen, he rides rafts of peeled logs downstream to market. Protected by a surly pride, he finds his way in Old Benjamin's footsteps. As he was sired, so he marries, by mischance, then watches his starvlings arrive. He works his grubby tenant acres, grows old. Nothing that ever happens later is as real as the smells and sights of his first days; these are his closest possessions; he trails them after him like a cloud of black flies from the many unblooming Edens he has to leave.

Sillanpää, writing soon after the Civil War, can see consequences still secret in the times:

It would be hard to think of a more purely artificial subject for study than the exact nature of Juha Toivola's attitude toward that time of national distress known as the period of Russian Oppression. . . . People of Juha's type could not with the best will in the world have said what had all of a sudden made the situation of the Finnish "people" so exceedingly difficult. As the farmers were obviously growing fatter and there were no signs of impoverishment or leanness in the gentlemen living in the parishes, the lowly people were utterly at a loss to know what the distress and confusion in those quarters was about. "Their jobs must be in some kind of danger," they thought.

Sillanpää puts his finger on the pulse of Civil War when he portrays the uneasiness of the Master of Paitula, one of the local gentry. The Master is a Finn, not one of the lofty Swedish-Finns. He has probably never thought of attaining so high a social state. But frugality, hard work and a certain native craftiness have made him land-rich and therefore vulnerable:

The present unrest . . . is grave enough to awaken anxiety, yet fraught with something before which the deepest, loneliest soul of man is helpless and secretly inclined to submission. At odd moments the Master has felt the desire to surrender . . . but when his eye falls on the tangled beard and stupid pricking eyes of a disgusting old fellow like Jussi, his stomach turns and he knows hate, the hate that springs from a conflict *of one's own making*.

Franz Emil Sillanpää (Nobel Laureate) was the son of a tenant farmer; he knew the harsh determinism of land and weather; he also knew the benediction of summer's long white nights, those mystic moments of suspension and delight by which subtle Nature rewards her toiling people and ensures the perpetuation of the race. Studies in biology at the University confirmed this fatalistic-romantic outlook in Sillanpää, and an instinct for psychology led him to understand the confused gropings of poor people for a meager dignity and a half-full belly.

History speaks for the few, the effective ones: Mannerheim, the senators, the industrialists who knew what they wanted of a free Finland and where they had to go in Civil War to make it a reality. But Sillanpää speaks for a much wider majority, the landless peasantry. His soft voice is joined by those of Minna Canth, playwright and crusader for women's rights, and of Toivo Pekkanen who writes with love and agony for people who like himself grew up *In the Shadow of a Factory*, Finns of the industrial camps, twice dispossessed of their soil.

The causes of the Civil War are hard to see in modern Finland. To the great credit of the victors, in due time they conceded to the vanquished. Land reform was hastened in the twenties, under the *Lex Kallio*, and was concluded during the settlement of refugees after the last war. Most farmers now own their own land and government subsidies for agriculture are large enough to be a national problem. The factory worker and his children enjoy the many benefits of the enlightened socialism practiced in Scandinavia. Equality of women and the right to decent medical care were written into the Constitution—Finland being the earliest of any country in Europe to do so.

Never in the years 1915 to 1918 were such things foreseeable to the dim minds of the Jussi Toivolas:

Youth roamed the streets and highways, danced and made merry, and some mysteriously vanished in circumstances strongly tinged with a flavor of forbidden high politics. (They had, in fact, gone to Germany, to learn soldiering with a view to the coming separation from Russia.) On the whole, life was a day-to-day affair.

Until the crash came in Russia. . . . What was to come next, now that good business and abundant employment on the fortification works were suddenly at an end?

Jussi—Juha—joins the Red Guards, calls himself a "temocrat," relishes using the epithet "the Butchers" on those whom he does not know. Newspapers from the cities excite him with the vague news of a "general strike." One of his sons is a successful taxi driver in Tampere and a Socialist. Hilda, his favorite daughter (fulfilling an ancient curse from the *Kalevala*) is boarded out in the city and drowns herself. Jussi's old horse grows spare and dies.

And the Revolution goes on, swelling with a sense of its own importance. . . . At Toivola both want and misery now reign. . . . For days at a time the family goes hungry, with potatoes and the brine-water from pickled sprats as sole diet.

But Juha is now an errand man at the local headquarters. He enjoys the smiles he gets and the reputation for being a hustler. He likes to ride out to the red-necked prosperous farmers, levying requisitions on them for hay or rugs or furniture in the name of "Socialism and Temocracy." Yet even when the Butchers arrive at the local defense line on Kuuskoski ridge, the war seems unreal to him, little more than the kind of play Old Benjamin delighted in—shoving a quid of tobacco down someone's throat. The firing on Kuuskoski becomes commonplace, even comforting.

When the front is at last breached, in the spring of 1918, and refugees are streaming away over the ice to escape and hide, Juha doesn't even understand defeat. He has gone to fetch wood from the shed as the firing thins out and becomes spasmodic:

What is all this? He stops and stares into the darkness: "This is Revolution and I am a Revolutionary!" It had been pleasant to mutter that to oneself when it all began, but now it seems to hold meanings too deep for Jussi to penetrate.

"If we could all go back to the old order now. . . . I have saved well over five hundred marks, and that is something to the good."

But there is no going back. The Master of Paitula is found dead and Jussi Toivola is rounded up. His innocence is of no interest to anyone. Eight others, men and women, are locked in jail with him. On a fair spring night the nine are taken out and marched to a grave already dug for them in the graveyard. One by one they are ordered to strip off their clothes and are shot. Jussi can't remember the shoes Hilda was wearing the day she went away, much less the slogans which he, still half-disbelieving, is dying for. But there is the matter of his clothes: he hesitates to undress "for his drawers are very ragged."

Christmas Spirits

When the lights go up like an arcade of Christmas trees over Alexander's Street, the children from all over the suburbs come towing their parents into the city to see what the good *Joulupukki* has brought to Finland this year. Fathers and mothers are no less ecstatic: Finns are givers and spenders, not savers and worriers. Money itself means little. Their attitude is "Buy it. Who knows what there will be in the shops next year?" Christmas is for children and all people are children at Christmas. Crowds pour in, traffic is tied up, the Alko shops (State Liquor stores) treble their business, the tall policemen look like jugglers working in their white gloves, balloons tumble in the wind, and out of the night sky drifts the gleaming snow.

Christmas is a month-long celebration. It begins with Little Christmas on the first Sunday in December, a tree ceremony for children. After this in quick succession come Independence Day, primarily a Finnish rite, and the Swedish *Lucia*, this year's bride of light, crowned with candles on the steps of the Cathedral. Then innumerable all night parties for the adults, the nativity of the Christ child, a night watch of candles placed on the graves in all the cemeteries, *Joulupukki's* boisterous visit to the homes, and finally, in an extravaganza of fireworks, the birth of the New Year. Thus for the critical last month of the year the long gloom of fall is chased away and the sun, still hesitating far in the south, made welcome anew.

Many details were strange to us: the candles burning in all

the windows, the sheaves of wheat hanging outside the doors for the winter birds, the doormats of pleated spruce boughs, the dish of warm rice, cinnamon, sugar (and one almond in the pot for the one who would next be married), the pouring of molten tin into cold water so that in the splashed shape of the metal some outline of future good fortune might be told.

On the last days of school Christmas pageants are given by each class: it is then that songs and plays rehearsed for weeks go on stage under blue lights and the whispered agonies of the prompters. The tableaux run to rabbits and fairies as often as to mangers and wisemen. Recitations from the *Kalevala*, folk songs and folk dances, are played out with an intense sense of the dramatic: the young boy of nine who, as a rule, wouldn't say more than three words a week to grownups suddenly appears alone in the spotlight and makes an oration or recites with perfect aplomb his fifty lines of poetry.

Even more impressive is the "handwork" done in school by the younger boys and girls. In the first year they begin knitting, sewing, embroidery (later wood work for both sexes) often while the teacher reads aloud from the classics or stories from Finnish mythology. Proud, indeed, is the small Magi who has worked six secretive weeks to embroider a table mat and who now can inscribe in a tall careful hand the first message he has learned to write: *Äidille*—For Mother.

Sometimes there is snow, more often drizzle and mists. Beside the Baltic, after four months of darkness and wet weather, Christmas needs all its candle power.

Philip Binham, friend and fellow sufferer among the unshakables at the KKK, invited us to his home to celebrate Little Christmas. The family lived north of the city in one of those well-planned new suburbs where all classes of people live and where it is only a short walk from home to shopping areas, schools, and to open forests and fields. Philip, by virtue of being a teacher, qualified for subsidized housing and therefore his family could live decently if not lavishly on his small income. As to essentials, his two children were as well off as those of the shipping magnate down the street.

Philip's Finnish wife was one of those people in whom you sense at once, behind her repressed moods, the melancholy, passionate, stubborn qualities of the race. Marja hated two things (Swedes and Russians), and loved two (food and music). She prepared for us a feast of open sandwiches, hot dishes, wine, cake, cookies, brandy, coffee, at which she herself would only nibble and sip.

"Why? Why can't I eat?" she exclaimed. "Food is good. It is good when people can eat all that they want." But Western ideas had begun to permeate Finland and Marja had to suffer the torments of beauty.

Marja's father, Väinö Sola, had come to join the festivities and see his grandchildren. A stocky barrel-chested man of about eighty, bright-eyed and still steady on his feet, he ate with gusto and went ahead telling us stories in Finnish even when he learned we couldn't understand a word. He seemed to believe that if he talked long enough and fast enough something would get through.

After supper Philip got out some family costumes and directed a production of *Prinsessa Ruusunen* (Sleeping Beauty of the Roses), a Christmas favorite. Then carol singing with Marja at the piano, and the rest of us holding hands as we walked around the tree. We had had little idea of who Väinö Sola was until this moment: but when a great tenor voice reverberated from that stocky body, and when he roared with the laughter of Rigoletto at the antics of the little ones playing elves, we knew we were with the Caruso of Finland.

We learned later that this man had sung his way across sixty years of his country's best and most difficult history. His ambition had been very simple: to bring the great operatic music of the world home to Finland. Not just some of it, all of it. He had played the lead in more than a hundred different operas, had translated fifty into Finnish himself and contracted out many more to other musicians. With Marja as his accompanist he had traveled twice to the Finnish settlements of America. Though honored and revered in Helsinki, Väinö Sola said that his greatest pleasure had been to take an opera troop to all the small villages in the country where no musical events had ever been given before—to do that and to watch the faces of the people when he got into the great arias.

Marja was like her father, talented both in piano and singing,

108

and always reaching out for the music and art of other countries to enrich the lives of her children. Philip, of course, could give the family an urbane and witty surface polish, but Marja was its life force.

Philip took his wife's moods—even her distaste for Swedes —with bland common sense. Those days were past. The divisions and hatreds of earlier times had been primarily economic, though always given a social and racial coloring. Now Finns were in the ascendancy, Swedish-Finns a dwindling but cultured and valuable minority. Philip once went so far as to say, "I've civilized you just a little, Marja, don't you agree?"

She agreed, with glittering eyes.

I could see that Philip's influence was about like the cool shade a good pine might cast on the slopes of Vesuvius.

On the way home from the Binhams' we had to transfer from one bus to another. We were standing in the lee of a corner near the Tech School buildings with other Lauttasaari-bound people, when two young men came singing around the opposite corner and stopped to light a cigarette. Snow had been falling all evening; now it lay three or four inches deep on the sidewalks. More snow was sifting down. As the two boys huddled their heads around the sudden flare of a match, laughing and expostulating by turns, they seemed slowly to flow down the wall and out on the pavement until they lay full length in the snow. Snow whitened their jackets and the wind frustrated their matches. One could tell from their high-water trousers and pork-pie hats that these were two Tech students celebrating the end of another round of examinations.

No one said anything, no one in the crowd even glanced at the boys. A lady came along lugging a heavy bag, and walked right over the feebly waving legs without a break in her stride. No cops came flogging up. When our bus arrived at last, one of the boys was asleep and the other was singing some mournful military song. For all I know the two spent the night bivouacked there, though they were not on the corner the next morning.

Irma Rantavaara, who never tired of finding things for us to see and do, gave us one party in her apartment and, I suspect, arranged for several other invitations. One was at the home of

Professor Kivimaa (Stone Land), the head of the Finnish National Theater. This gentle man, a poet as well as a dramatist, and his black-eyed beautiful wife, could not have been more hospitable had we been Alfred Lunt and Lynn Fontanne. Irma, herself a director and devotee of the National Theater, was there, and an English dramatist who had just come to Finland to help in the production of *The School for Scandal*.

These were the highest people in their professions in their countries. Elisabeth and I were no match for them, but it is Finnish hospitality to give the word "welcome" without reservation or distinction. We were Irma's friends, that was enough: our business at the Kivimaa's was to eat and drink, toast and be toasted, talk, enjoy, and feel at home. The professor could relate his wife's odyssey in finding a cook as lightly as he could describe the backstage calamities at the theater or the latest plays of Beckett or Aristophanes. There was an air of culture without pretense in the Kivimaa home, a rich deep sensitivity to art of all kinds which was like an assumption that needed no proving. The simple hospitality of these people set off their accomplishments as the French wines set off the many excellent dishes Mrs. Kivimaa had prepared.

Later, as we were leaving, shaking hands in the living room, Professor Kivimaa asked if the children would not like to see the special performance of *Prinsessa Ruusunen* at the National Theater. I replied that I had tried to get tickets but all were sold out. He smiled and said, "But of course you may take our box. Whenever you wish, you have only to telephone."

So we saw the ballet-play of *Sleeping Beauty* and Bronnie was a star-showered princess for months afterward. Even Ben wanted to attend this play. He wore a coat grown too small for him, and his hair, wet at the drinking fountain in the hall, was slicked down like a November thatched roof. The professor's box was second only to that reserved for the President of the Republic. As I looked out on the sea of faces, all hushed for the rising of the curtain, I couldn't help thinking: Where but in Finland would such kindness be shown to the family of an ordinary English teacher?

Finally, after many parties, and a trip to the country to cut a Christmas tree, we found ourselves almost ready for the entrance of the main actor: *Joulupukki*. On Christmas Eve, Tytti asked if we would go to the graveyard with her to light candles; she was meeting her family at the entrance to the national cemetery where we had recently watched the processions at Mannerheim's grave. It was a drizzly evening. As we walked down the dark avenue beside the graveyard we could see small clusters of wavering lights, like a thin field of poppies under the trees. At the stone arches we found Tytti's mother, her young sister and lanky brother. We shook hands and then Mrs. Kaija led the way along the gravel paths: she was one of those quiet, solid mothers who always lead the way. The hedged rectangular plots were so similar that soon even Mrs. Kaija was lost. The only illumination was from lamps set at the head of the graves. After much discussion and exploration the stone on the grave of Mrs. Kaija's husband was found. Tytti's brother had a metal base and a candle. He lit the candle and set a cylindrical piece of glass over it. Then Mrs. Kaija put an evergreen wreath on the grave. Tytti said it was too bad the snow had all gone, for in snow the graves look very beautiful under the trees in the candlelight. There were no prayers or tears. The four Kaijas stood but a moment looking around, glad that this grave looked as well as its neighbors; then we moved on to find and decorate the graves of an uncle, a brother, and two boys killed in the war who had been the Kaijas' next-door neighbors in Karelia.

We came at last to the top of the hill, near Mannerheim's tomb. There were dark shadows moving all around us; low voices talking and constant shuffling of feet on gravel paths. In the dark, with the myriad candles flickering in the woods as far as one could see, one suddenly grasped the enormous number of the dead. The place seemed like an encampment of soldiers waiting by their fires for the time when the old General should rise up and say they were needed again.

Ben and Bronwen had suffered cold and delay enough on this hillside; they were anxious to go home. As we walked back along the avenue to the bus stop, their spirits revived at the sight of two *Joulupukkis* racing past on bicycles, their red robes flying behind them. Ben and Bron had adapted themselves to the new mythology without difficulty. The fact that

Joulupukki's name meant Christmas Goat did not bother them any more than that he rode a bicycle. A reindeer and a sled, after all, were of little value in a city, especially when there was no snow. The important thing was that he existed, beyond all doubts and rumors.

Joulupukki did make his rounds that night to Ducks' Slope No. 2. He entered dramatically (twenty-five minutes late) just as we had turned off the lights and were holding hands singing carols around the candle-flaming tree. Bump, bump, a shadowy figure in the doorway, lugging a sack—crash, the door opening —"Hallo. Hallo."

"*Terve!*" shouted Ben.

"*Terrrrrveh*, boy," replied *Joulupukki*.

Soon the big red elf was emptying his sack (which looked very like a pillow case) upon the table, reading out the labels on the boxes with some difficulty: *Keeem, Vendyy, Brrron-ven.* . . . When the presents were distributed and placed under the tree, *Joulupukki* was given some cocoa and marshmallows, which he had never had before and which he managed somehow to ingest through his white beard and mustache. Then he joined hands with us, and in a good Tech School baritone sang a few last carols.

Between songs Bronwen voiced what must long have been a source of pain and doubt: "Did you know we lived here?"

"Yes. I did," *Joulupukki* assured her.

"Not still in America?"

"I heard."

"But you were pretty late," Ben said. "I thought you would never come."

"Oh, I come." *Joulupukki* grinned through his cocoa-stained beard. "But, you know . . . my car . . . it all broke down."

"I was afraid you would miss us," Bron said.

"No, no. I never miss children."

"Good old *Joulupukki*." Ben laughed, and put his arm around the red-clad figure.

Ben's Winter War

After Christmas, Ben was advanced in school from Mrs.
Vornamo's first grade to Miss Tanner's second. We took the
change to be glad tidings of something, though Ben remained
noncommittal. He eyed everything that happened in school
with suspicion and though he was happy to be with an older
group of boys, he could also see clearly that in arithmetic he
was steadily dropping behind his friends at home. He had
already had second-grade mathematics. Still, the promise of a
bicycle in the spring held him in school—a sort of grail image,
indistinct but worthy of his suffering and nobility.

Bronwen we no longer had any doubts about. She came
home singing from school: "Oh, Mummie, we had the yummi-
est food today."

"Good, Bronnie. What was it?"

"Oatmeal."

Bron was beginning to make friends. One of them came
every morning at breakfast time to walk to school with her.
This was Maila, an impassive youngster with bobbed hair. All
of a sudden she would appear out of the dark—a calm ghostly
face at the window—and survey the strange things we were
eating. Some sign language would pass between the girls, and
Maila would withdraw to our entryway and wait. Nothing
could induce her to enter the house. She stood stoically outside, in bitter wind or Siberian drizzle, until Bronwen was
ready. Then both girls would go running down the gravel
drive swinging their book bags and jabbering in Finnish.

Kim and Wendy, too, seemed pretty well settled in their Swedish schools, though in fact we really didn't know very much about either. Kim would have thought it somehow her fault if the Devil himself came to teach in her classes, and Wendy would have enjoyed every moment of it if he'd gone to hers.

Even Steve was happy attending his classes in trench digging and winter warfare under the dripping trees at the Park Auntie's nursery school. It was surprising to us that these small plastic-covered gnomes could survive such constant bad weather. Rain, sleet, slush, snow, back to rain again—all were the same to them; the important thing was to get on with the ditches. Even the Park Auntie in her knitted bucket-hat or sou'wester seemed to enjoy bad weather. Only once was school not held—on a day when the cold went to 5° F. and a strong wind was blowing.

In a way, this period was more melancholy than late fall. From January to June is a long stretch. Winter was in the north, according to the newspapers, but Helsinki lived in a swamp of weather. After January we gave up any thought of snow, put away our skis and steadied ourselves on a course for Easter, when we would go to Lapland.

One Saturday afternoon Elisabeth and I returned from the city to find Ben slicked up in his best clothes coming down the stairs holding a small black suitcase.

"I'm going home," Ben declared. "To America."

"America!" Elisabeth cried. "But I haven't fixed supper yet." She went in a fluster to put her packages in the kitchen. There was nothing of trouble on Ben's open face, not even worry. He had spoken with friendliness and conciliation—with a gentle condescension which suits a boy who expects to have to explain difficult things to his parents.

"How are you going to go?" I asked.

"I'll take a boat."

"Trouble in school, Ben?"

"I'm sick of that school."

"What was it this time?" Almost every week Ben had come home early because of some altercation.

"I don't know. They're always jabbering about something, making faces. They laugh at me."

"So it was a fight, eh?"

"Not much," Ben said with a shrug. "Some old woman, that's all. She got mad. I couldn't figure out what she was hollering about."

Elisabeth came back from the kitchen. I could see she expected me to do something swift and diplomatic. But I had suddenly the feeling that I was looking at this boy for the first time—not as my son, with all the notions that attach themselves to that relationship—but as a boy, with blue eyes and half-combed hair, who had made a sensible decision and was preparing to carry it out. Ben did not even seem to think that we were primarily concerned in his business, and there was that air about him which made me feel he was probably right.

"How about your ticket?"

"You can give me the one you have and I'll use it now. Okay?"

"But where will you live?" Elisabeth cried.

"Well, I'll get a room. I'll go to school, too. Somebody will give me a room, I know."

"What will you eat?"

"I'll get a job selling papers, or selling something anyways, like at Tanzi's store, you know. They always say 'Here comes Ben, the boy with the smile on his face, looking for a candy bar.' They'll give me a job, I bet."

All this spoken with calm good sense and attention to detail. I breathed a long sigh, exhaling all the arguments I might have used as a parent under such circumstances—they seemed no more than exercises of pressure.

"What really happened in school, Ben?"

The boy shook his head. "I don't know. At recess we were wrestling and some old woman got mad . . ."

"Miss Tanner?"

"No, just some old woman, another teacher, she started twisting my arm . . ."

"What did you do?"

"Ran away, naturally. I can't fight everybody, can I?"

"Well," I said, coming to some sort of a decision. "You don't have to go to America to get away from old women."

"But I gotta go," Ben said. "I'm behind all the other kids. Can't you see that? . . . You think I want to be a dumbhead all my life?"

Suddenly Ben's mother, unable to speak, stooped over and kissed the boy, and for the first time tears welled up and glistened in his eyes.

"Don't worry, Mother. I'll be okay till you guys get home."

"Oh, Ben, don't you—don't you know—I need you around here?"

"What for? To take care of Steven?"

"Yes, other things too. . . . Oh, we'll never learn that blasted language! We've got to stick together . . ."

So it was settled, without logic but by an exchange of tears. Elisabeth picked up the suitcase and started up the stairs; the boy shrugged and followed. Pretty soon I heard them laughing in the boy's bedroom:

"Why, Ben, you goose, you haven't even packed your pajamas."

"Yeah? Not my toothbrush either. Oh, well . . ."

We worked out a plan for Ben to study arithmetic at home in the mornings. We sent to America for a third-grade math book. Home study would require supervision and persuasion, of course, but there was really no need for him to attend a Finnish school. Math and English alone would determine whether Ben kept up with his class or not.

Fortunately at this juncture the first real cold spell of the winter blew down from Lapland and almost overnight the brackish sea around Helsinki froze to a sheet of ice along the coast. At once, even when the ice was thin and flexible, hordes of Lauttasaari skaters came out to skim the bay and try their chances of getting out to the islands.

No snow came, but the skating was excellent and gave our young scholar something to look forward to after his multiplications were done. Sometimes Ben and Elisabeth and I took Steve on a sled and bored our way upwind two or three miles to the islands. Then, turning, we could come skimming home over the black ice in long rattling strokes that covered the

116

distance in a matter of minutes. We couldn't skate very far toward Helsinki because of the ship lanes cut by the icebreakers, but one day we circumnavigated our island of Lauttasaari, learning how large it was, how well planned as a suburb, and aware always of that stunning mushroom water tower looking down on us from the hill.

Winter stayed only ten days; after that the rains came, and then a big storm which devoured in white gulps the outer margin of ice. On the last day of skating Ben and I went out toward the islands to watch some fishermen squatting by their holes. The surf was clearly visible, destroying the ice not more than a quarter of a mile away from the fishermen. As we approached we could see the men rising and falling a foot or more as the swells moved in under the rubbery surface. The fishermen did not seem to worry. They stooped over their holes, holding their bare hands together, catching nothing. By the next morning the broken ice was piled up on the shore and the sea was roaring its ancient threats again.

The dreary time returned . . . and yet there was one compensation. Ben had been slow to learn reading; indeed, he scarcely read at all. Now, bloody but unyielding in Babylon, he sat down to hear the waters of his native language and discovered that invisible country—home: *Young Mr. Jefferson*, the *Rover Boys*, *Huckleberry Finn*, *Ethan Allen*, *Lou Gehrig—Pride of the Yankees*, *Chief Joseph*. Suddenly these, and many others, became men for him, not things you have to learn about in school, but good men who had also suffered and endured.

As though by a miracle Ben taught himself to read English. If we sent him upstairs to take a bath, an hour later we would find him perched on the rim of the tub, his knees up to his ears and his nose in a book, the limpid waters of Babylon cold and untouched before him.

Yet, as we soon learned, all was not settled at the school. Whispers of some colossal ruckus began to come back to us. Bron heard that the principal was going to call the inspector to see about Ben—she thought this was a policeman. Then one afternoon, some two weeks after Ben's departure from school, Mrs. Pastinen, Bron's tutor, called on the telephone. She was very embarrassed to intrude, but even more upset over what had happened: could she come over and talk to us?

Mrs. Pastinen came and had coffee. This small intelligent woman, wife of a diplomat, said that she had called only because her friends, Mrs. Vornamo and Miss Tanner, were themselves too shy to call: something terrible was happening in school, the older teacher said she had been assaulted by Ben and insisted that the principal call in the chief inspector and have the boy expelled, not only from Lauttasaari schools but from all schools in the city.

"It is so," Mrs. Pastinen said, trying to soften the indictment, "that the teacher is old; perhaps she is tired from too much work to do, she doesn't understand. . . . But it could be serious, you know . . . if Ben should want to go back to school."

The principal, it appeared, being uncertain what to do had done nothing, which only made the older teacher more enraged. Meanwhile Miss Tanner, Mrs. Vornamo, and Mrs. Laitinen had all been fighting a rearguard action for the boy—and our keeping him out of school had made his guilt appear more certain.

"But what did he do?" Elisabeth cried, red with shame that we had caused so much trouble.

"The teacher says . . . he's a sex maniac! A dangerous American sex maniac."

"A what? Ben is only eight years old."

"I know. I do not believe all what she says . . ."

"I don't believe anything," I shouted. "What exactly did he do?"

"He . . . he ripped her dress off!" Mrs. Pastinen suddenly could not suppress a smile, "In the playground, in front of all people."

Finally the story came out, and I could see the kind of misunderstanding it was: Ben had been scrapping with his classmates, the teacher in charge of the playground had told him to stop, he had not heard or understood, she had taken hold of him and he, thinking he was being ambushed from behind, had wrenched himself free and escaped. But lack of any communication had built the thing up into a tempest.

118

Certainly there was no sign of guilt in Ben's face, when we told him, after Mrs. Pastinen had gone, what she had said.

"Me? Rip her dress off? No. Ha-haaa. That's a good one. But maybe a few buttons popped."

That was the end of the matter as far as Ben was concerned. But it was a messy way to leave school: three teachers had fought for him, another was after his scalp, and the principal had acted with uncommon restraint. I persuaded Ben to go back and make amends, and I suggested a peace offering of flowers for the older teacher.

"Flowers? To that old biddy? Why?"

"Because . . . well, because she was wrong."

He thought it over for a while, then said he would go.

Ben was never one for fancy clothes. Indeed his only known concession to sartorial splendor was, if pressed hard enough, not to wear jeans to bed. But for the day of his return to school his mother insisted on clean, pressed jeans and a clean shirt. He submitted to these demands with silent disapproval. Having agreed to take flowers, he couldn't worry about trivial matters. After breakfast Ben and I walked up to the *Kukkia-Blummor* shop where day and night the fresh flowers looked out on our dreary world with exotic splendor. Three flowers are the ceremonial number in Finland. Ben chose carnations, two white and one red. These were laid in sprigs of maidenhair and wrapped in green tissue, then tied up like a cornucopia: no disguising the contents of that package.

Ben, suddenly faced with the fact of his mission, eyed the flimsy bundle with distaste: "All right, I'll take it . . . but if anybody laughs at me, somebody's going to get a good pop in the snoot!"

Then he started up through the woods and over Windmill Hill in order to avoid the paths used by his schoolmates. The betting wasn't high that he'd ever get to school. Windmill Hill had a number of caves on it. I half expected we'd find him that night holed up in one, cooking squirrel over a fire. But, Ben came home in the afternoon full of pride; his classmates had cheered and welcomed him back, even called him "the famous Ben."

"What about the flowers?"

"She got them all right. Miss Tanner went with me."

"What did she say?"

"Who, Miss Tanner?"

"No, the tough old woman."

"Oh . . . she began to cry and said I was a good boy and all that sort of junk. Man, was I sweating to get out of there! Finnish women . . . you can have them . . . one minute they want to tear your arm off, next they're blubbering all over you. . . . What's for supper, Ma?"

And a verse of a Lapland song
Is haunting my memory still:
"A boy's will is the wind's will,
And the thoughts of youth are long, long thoughts."
—LONGFELLOW

A Torch of Birches

Easter was in the capital with armloads of flowers; the ice had long since gone from the marshes of the Baltic, and the young sun halfway north in its new year was already stealing the edges of midnight. In the full light of day you saw people suddenly stop in mid-traffic and turn their faces to the sun, with closed eyes, transported by that pagan worship that has a Christian name.

The trip from Helsinki to Lapland is over a thousand kilometers long and a journey back over more than ten thousand years, beyond the happy stone age Lapps, to the grey river beds and bare-shouldered mountains where lately the glaciers left and lichen crawl upward under the six month snows.

"I won't be here next week," I told my first class at the KKK. "Something important has come up."

"We know," replied one of the girls, the class grinning.

"What do you know?"

"It is said . . . to be very beautiful . . . in Lapland."

Philip Binham was going with us. He had helped book a place at an unknown lodge, in an unknown village; reservations had had to be made in October, for all the beds and bunks are soon sold out for the week-long excursions at Easter. On the appointed Friday evening we carried our incongruous bundles of skis and packs through the well-dressed crowds and the glass temples of modern Helsinki down to the railway station. Philip had already found our compartments on the wooden carriages which had once served the officers of the Czar. Bronwen and Ben had never seen a sleeping car before, much less one whose tiny rooms were three bunks high; with a shout they both claimed the upper bunks.

The train of Easter skiers was enormous, seeming to stretch halfway to Lapland, but it started on the minute and soon we were moving at a leisurely pace past the fertile farms of southern Finland. Through the open windows poured a stream of chilly air, but there was spring in it. In the stretches of woods spruce candles were lit pale green. The birches, too, were turning at the tips, as though their sap were blood. At first we saw snow only in blue patches on the north slopes of the hills, but later the snow was everywhere over the fields.

This was the rich part of Finland, a country of hut-builders; houses, barns, sheds, and hayracks dotted the fields. At Hämeenlinna a stubby castle was spotlighted on a hill (now a reformatory for women); at Tampere, where the decisive battle of the Independence War was fought, the engine picked up new cars from the west and headed north again. Finland looked well groomed and well painted in the spring twilight. We sat on bunks whose sheets had already been turned down by some thoughtful maid, had a snack of sandwiches and hot tea, and considered our good fortune.

"In the good old days . . ." I said.

Bronwen instantly rebuked me: "The good old days. The good old days. What are you always talking about them for? Don't you know—*these* are the Good Old Days!"

Indeed she was right on two counts, and the first one was enough: it was hard for a passer-by on a train to imagine there had ever been anything but prosperity here. We were passing through Häme country. Not so long ago, and for all time before that, this was poor, hard farmland. In the nineteenth century nearly everyone lived by farming. Rye was the staple; potatoes were poor nubbly things shrunken with disease; a cow and a horse were tokens of prosperity. The people were not worse off than their neighbors in the east—they were not serfs—but their lives were a constant struggle in short seasons against bad weather and the overwhelming forests. During the winter men logged the forests, rafting the logs downriver in spring to put a few coins in their pockets. Farther north the people spent the winter boiling pitch from mounds of pine logs, draining the tar into barrels. In summer they rowed their barrels downstream in narrow river boats to the seaports of Ostrobothnia—then back, perhaps a three-week haul, for another cargo.

Häme country—in a way the source of Finnish strength and the wellspring of Finnish literature. From Kivi's Juhani to Linna's Koskela, the Hämäläinens have enraged and delighted the Finns. They are supposed to be the slow, stoop-shouldered, silent people; the dry-witted people who stayed; the Vermonters of Finland. As virtuous as mules, the Hämäläinens have peopled the pages of literature. But no less have they written the history of Finland, out of poverty and endurance.

Bronwen couldn't know this. She saw peaceful red houses, trimmed with white, and flowers in the windows. In the shadows were seven hundred years of rain, ice, starvation, tuberculosis, and war.

Once from the windows of the train we saw a stream in flood, dammed by ice. The grey fields round about were under water and children in flimsy coats and rubber boots were standing on a bridge launching sticks of wood and bits of bark on a trip to the sea. The children stopped as our cars rocked by, turning their eyes upon us in a solemn moment suspended. A man pushing a black bicycle through ankle-deep water did not even look up. The picture reminded me of something I'd seen, a painting by Järnefelt: a burning field where stumps and brush are being cleared, a family stooped in clouds of smoke through which dimly in patches the endless distant forests flatten. In the center of the picture is a skinny girl (Bronwen's age) dressed in a smudge of rags who is dragging a torch of birches to the fire. She looks out on the world from a strangely old face with eyes like dead white coals. More truth is spoken in that girl's eyes than are told in volumes of history.

Just a century ago came those bitter times known as the Famine Years, not new to Finland, but cut into the heart of a story by F. E. Sillanpää:*

* *Meek Heritage.*

In the midst of well-timbered forests these people—the term Finnish Nation meant nothing to them—struggled on from week to week and month to month. . . . There came a June when a Harjakangas farmer going out into his yard at three o'clock in the morning would see in the soft reflected light of the clouds snow on the slopes of Pig Hill, gleaming white ice on the lake, and tangled yellow sprouts in the rye fields.

Then at Christmas:

Maja was still in the bath house; she had gone there after the others, having lingered behind to bring in secretly the customary layer of straw for the living-room floor. A poor decoration that straw made; it was part of a batch pulled that morning for cattle-feed from the thatched roof of a barn.

Coarse chaff cake, watery sour milk, mutton, turnip stew. The solitary dip casts a yellowish light on the lean faces around the table. . . . "It is hard to think that it'll be spring before pine-bark will be fit to eat."

The lofty heavens with their stars look down on this phase in the history of a lowly people . . . the heavens see immense forests where gold in millions slumbers beside a dying beggar and a flame-eyed lynx.

Such conditions were universal in Finland. With 94 per cent of the people living off the land, poverty, tuberculosis, and seasonal starvation were the common lot. The good land was generally held by the large landowners, each with his crofters and hired hands whose tenure there was upon the whim of the master. Sociologists, in their dry lingo, report that this last group—the farm hands—made up as much as 40 per cent of the work force. These wandering, homeless, familyless males lived here or there, drifting wherever jobs offered a little food and a barn or perhaps a kitchen to sleep in; their possessions filled a limp knapsack the way turnip stew filled their stomachs; overcome with "the fate of Sunday evenings" they might breed and move on unknowing, or settle down in a corner croft with their bewildering offspring and their debts.

It is the common claim of people who write books about Finland that "feudalism never took hold here," as though the perverse and democratic people somehow kept out the pretty notions and pretensions of Swedish nobility. (The claim is best made on a full belly.) A simpler explanation is more reasonable: Rule, in this land of swamps and bog-hoppers? Who would want to?

Finns had feudalism without the banners, the serfdom of poverty and ignorance; they were bound to the master's land by hunger and children. Failing, the family could take to the roads, it is true, and sleep under hayricks, wrapped in all their freedoms.

Above all Finns had the feudalism of endless wars for absent lords. For five hundred years they were, in the words of Zacharius Topelius, "the bloody shield of Sweden," when the empires of the Stockholm knights clashed with that of the Czars. Topelius adds:

From 1714 to 1722, when the greater part of the country was ravaged down to the very ground, impoverished depopulated and abandoned into the hands of the enemy, the hope, though not the loyalty, of the Finn began to falter.

It was hard to read this cruel history now in the evening shadows over a spring land, but it was there: in the distaste for anything Swedish; in the suspicion of anything Russian; in the Communist vote and the frenzy of splintered political parties; in sardonic laughter, mystic poetry, and the troubled melancholy of Finnish music; in the raw love of land and liberty.

Late at night, thinking of Järnefelt's girl and the others of her tribe, I lay in my bunk rocked by the easy motion of the railway carriage. There was no hurry in the train, just a certainty we'd get where we were going on time. Sometime during the night Ben fell off his third-story perch, but he landed unhurt on a pile of packs and Philip and I stuffed him back into the blankets. We were deep in forests: I could tell by the engine hooting like an owl down a canyon of spruce.

In the morning: Oulu, Kemi, Tornio, towns that had given America many Finnish immigrants. Then six hours due north on a bus, following the broad valley of the Torni River, back out of cities to scattered farms; back out of spring shelling the roads, into frosty snow where herds of reindeer loped through the woods.

Our destination was a solid single-story cabin built and maintained by the *Suomen Latu* (Finnish Trails) for Easter skiers and summer campers. The cabin nestled on the side of a small mountain about a mile from the village of Äkäslompolo. Decamping from the bus into deep snow, we lugged our gear up a steep path to the cabin. The sauna was hot. After that, supper of meat soup and potatoes and a gluey pink cornstarch pudding flavored with lingonberry and alum, then bed in the crowding cold of late March.

We were a mixed crew in the *Latu* cabin: four lanky Finnish boys in search of kilometers, six shy girls in search of Finnish boys, one Britisher, six Americans, and fifteen young Germans who had come to ski in Lapland under the guidance of three older men, veterans of the war. In addition to the cabin and a temporary cook, *Suomen Latu* provided us with the trip leaders, Paavo and Jussi, two bright-eyed wiry young men who looked small on foot, but who were equal to any bulging pack and tireless on running skis. All of us had been recently at war with each other; it could have been a difficult fellowship, but the handsome young Germans seemed not to know there had been a war, and the rest of us skirted the subject.

The day began at seven o'clock with the clatter of firewood going into the stoves and the clump of ski boots through the big room. Then breakfast: boiled potatoes, pickled fish, cheese, pickled beets, hard bread. (From these ingredients we also made sandwiches for a noonday snack.) After that a steaming bowl of oatmeal. Jussi had built a birch fire outside, over which we could heat the bottoms of our skis and rub them down with wax. In an hour everyone was gone, down across the valley toward the sprawling white hulk of a *tunturi* (a bare-topped mountain). Kim wanted to go with Paavo and the Germans on a fifteen-kilometer jaunt. Wendy had taken up with a young *Mädchen* who had hurt her foot; they decided to ski down into the village of Äkäslompolo where, it was reported, they might arrange to go for a reindeer ride. The rest of us planned to slide along easy, climb the mountain behind the cabin and get our bearings in Lapland.

This was country like none we had ever seen; the forests were open and parklike, rising in knolls and terraces to the edge of timber. And there, in a short space, the spruce and pine ran out, while the dwarfed birch straggled a little higher. Above treeline the mountain piled up its glistening fields into flat domes and shoulders. There was no end to the routes we could follow. The snow was cold and powdery in the forest, and up on the fjell-side it was raked by the wind or baked into glaze.

From the top of the mountain we could see five other *tunturis* nearby, and except for the bulk of Ylläs, for fifty miles in any direction. Swamps and shallow lakes spread patterns of white over the great valleys. Far to the north beyond an immense black forest rose the cream-white cumulus of the Pallas mountains, piled up like clouds under a cloudless sky.

After we had explored our little *tunturi*, we slid off the back side into the forest to build a picnic fire and eat lunch. Then home, through frosty snow and blue shadows. After supper Philip, Elisabeth and I climbed once more to the top of the *tunturi* to watch the sun slanting into clouds in the northwest. Its course was flattening down to horizontal. (In summer it would be aloft for a six-week day.) The arctic sunset flamed into crimson. Down below us the lamps of Äkäslompolo burned dimly around a blue-white lake; on Ylläs across the way the light changed from peach to cherry to rose, the features of the mountain seemed to soften in repose, and then the colors drained from lavender to grey to some midnight phosphorescence of the snow itself.

Back at the cabin we found the older Germans waxing sentimental under the influence of a bottle of good cognac and a captive audience. One was standing in the open floor beyond the tables, giving an enthusiastic lecture to a mute audience in his native tongue. "Good friends and comrades," he kept saying. The young Germans, visibly unmoved, sat and waited for the cognac. The Finns sat respectfully attentive, though always embarrassed by speeches, especially speeches of praise in an unknown language. When the first German was done, the second started in, then the third, the largest and most inspired of the leaders. The smoky hall must have reminded him of winter barracks in Lapland, for a sonorous epic of *Kammeradschaft* rolled out of him. When he was done, Paavo rose in one corner, thanked the speakers, and said (in Finnish) that tomorrow would be another long day; we had better get to bed.

Later, in the dark Bronwen leaned out of her upper bunk and whispered, "What was that big guy talking about?"

"Nothing much. About how good it was to be back in Lapland again."

"But why was he so mad?"

"He wasn't mad. Just giving a speech."

"Well, he was hollering all the time."

"I know. He said he'd been in Lapland all during the war, the people were wonderful to him, always his good friends. Then he said skiers should always be friends because they know the good things of life."

"Oh." Then after a moment: "Why didn't the other Germans listen to him?"

"I guess they'd heard that speech many times before."

Six days and nights would probably be all we would ever know of Lapland winter. They passed quickly. One evening Paavo and Jussi took the young people down to the village for an all-night dancing party. On another evening a farmer we had chanced to meet invited us to come and have a sauna with him. His was an old-fashioned smoke sauna, the best and gentlest of them all, in a bathhouse as black as polished ebony and as fragrant as a cured ham.

Afterward, around cups of coffee in a clean lamplit kitchen, the farmer told us, casually and with many jokes, how he had taken his family on skis and a reindeer sled over the mountains to Sweden during the German retreat through Lapland. It was not a hard trip, he said, but one he would not wish to make again. Then he said there was talk now that reindeer meat would not be fit to eat because of something the atom bombs were doing to the North. But how could that be? How could bombs in Russia affect the meat of Lapland, especially when the animals all looked all right? He studied his hands under the lamplight as though in their deep lines he might somehow read an answer to this mystery. But perhaps it was only talk, he said; there was always too much talk in Helsinki. Life was better in Lapland.

One day, when the tops of the mountains were in a surf of clouds and snow was already spitting down, we decided to go on a Makkara Tour, as Bronnie called it, a trip whose real objective was the cooking of chunks of sauna sausage over an open fire. In the woods there was wind and falling snow, but the weather was far from bitter. We climbed the valley that leads to the open fields of Ylläs and after a couple of hours discovered a sheltering bluff behind which to build a fire. Then the sausage: red and dripping grease, turning black and curling around its shrinking skin. Wet boots, wet mittens, falling snow, ruddy faces—I wondered whether any but the Scandinavians knew that such skiing existed.

After the feast Bron announced that she wanted to go " 'sploring where no one else ever went." The rest wanted to climb *Ylläs* to the summit. So I took the girl on a trip to a valley and lake which lay in a deep cleft between *Yllästunturi* and the next mountain to the north. Our route led over a shoulder of *Ylläs* out of the scrub birches over a shoulder of rocks, like a wintry graveyard, where we had to pick our way head down against the horizontal snowflakes, then to a great snowfield that curled down and down into the valley. Finally we came into a woods of massive pines, a forest primeval, where the wind let up and we moved along without effort between the great reddish trunks. We were in a kind of rift valley between the two mountains. I reckoned we had nearly three miles to go before we would reach Äkäslompolo again.

The girl went ahead. She wanted to break trail. New snow over hard crust made the going easy. I watched her lithe light body move, leaning forward in a half-running glide with just a springy hitch at the hips which all children learn unconsciously in Scandinavia. How natural it was, that mile-eating stride, when the snow was good and the wax right. Skiing was not important: Bron would not remember much of Lapland or Finland, but something would remain of snowy hills and forests, in the back of her consciousness among her definitions of peace.

Down at the edge of an alder swamp we found the beginnings of the lake. The wind was waiting for us and we stopped to tighten our parkas before starting on. I got out the compass and took a reading, as there were no tracks marking the even white surface ahead. Soon we were moving in a cloud of snow.

After a while Bronwen said, "Why did they burn Lapland?"

"Who?"

"Whoever it was."

"The Germans?"

"One of the girls said so."

"What did she say?"

"Well, that big guy the other night, you know, telling everyone what good friends he had in Lapland and all that—was he a German?—and one of the girls was sitting there . . ."

"A Finnish girl?"

"Yes, and she said sort of in a whisper, 'Yeah, pals. What did he burn it all down for?'"

"That was in the last war," I said.

"But did he do it himself?"

"There were a lot of Germans up here fighting Russians. And the Finns, who had to make peace with the Russians, had to get the Germans out. The Germans wouldn't go, so the Finns had to push them out."

"But why burn everything?"

"The Germans were pretty mad."

"But somebody might want to live there! That's stupid."

We went on a little way and then I took another reading on the compass. The snow was coming thick, in that opaque white space the wind kept driving us aside. I decided we would have to face the wind and hold to a straighter direction.

"I'm cold, Daddy," Bronwen said, bent over and shivering.

"It isn't very far now, Bron," I said.

"But I'm freezing."

"Then take my hand. No wonder, your mittens are sopping." I gave her one of my gloves and took her other hand inside my own. After a while I could feel the warmth returning to the slender fingers.

"Do you like coming to the mountains, Bronnie?"

"Sure. But are there wolves?"

"Not here."

"We read about them in school."

"That was in the old days."

What was it Frost had written? "Snow falling and night falling fast, oh, fast . . ." the stubble of a farm going under and himself "too absent-spirited to count"? Coming to Finland was in part because of that: to hold back the universal loneliness. One travels but a short distance with a small girl's hand to warm one's own. This was one of the few stands we, as a family, could make against time and change. Something of the unspeakable loneliness of Frost's wintry words—hard to imagine words more plain—took hold of me like a shiver.

"Pretty soon we'll see the forest just ahead," I told her.

"I thought Finns were against Russians," she said, puzzled.

"They were."

"But you said Germans."

"It was all mixed up. First the Russians fought the Finns. Then Finland and Germany fought Russia. . . ."

"Why did the Russians want to fight the Finns?"

"They didn't really."

"They didn't?" she asked, incredulously.

"Russians were afraid that Germany would go after them by going through Finland."

"Did they?"

"No. Not that time."

"What side were we on?"

"We were five thousand miles away on the other side of the ocean."

"But anyways we were for Finland." That much she felt sure of.

"We were, but we couldn't be."

"What? I don't get it."

"We were fighting against Germany, so we had to be against Finland."

"That's crazy!" she cried, and gave me a long long look.

Fortunately I didn't have to go further into the strange arrangements of World War II, for from somewhere off to the right came the barking of a dog, high and nervous and quite unwolf-like. Then in a moment the loom of the forest was in front of us and we found a well-cut trail leading home through the village.

Light and a Shadow

After returning from the snows of Lapland, we found spring in possession of the south country. Rapidly as the fall had shut us in behind its curtains of mist, even more rapidly did the high sky come to open the windows on another summer. The University term was almost over; classes were entering their last month; after that only the final examinations remained. By June 1 the schools would close and our friends would all be hurrying off to their refuges in the country.

In March we had become Americans again and bought a car—a red Volkswagen bus. Elisabeth's parents, Judge and Mrs. McLane, had decided to visit us in late April, and they wanted her to drive to Leningrad with them for a four-day tour behind the Iron Curtain. Accordingly, Elisabeth arranged with the Finnish Travel Bureau for the visas and bought the coupons which would entitle them to guides, meals, accommodations, taxis, and entertainment in Czar Peter's famous city.

After a couple of weeks of waiting, Elisabeth was summoned unexpectedly to the Soviet Embassy for an interview. This, it was said, was only a spot check which the authorities made of all people going to the USSR, purely a routine matter, but in Russia even the word "routine" has come to have a Lubianka ring.

Elisabeth presented herself before the enormous cold grey buildings which stand on a drab hill surrounded by iron in the diplomatic section of Helsinki. Entering timidly at the gates, she was questioned by the guards and grunted by. Then she walked up the hill to a side entrance where the visa office was located. (Even in Helsinki one feels the otherness of that world behind the iron gates.) But to her surprise she found the officer in charge an affable middle-aged man, not at all the xenophobic bureaucrat she had expected. He rose and shook her hand, offered her a chair, then sat back in his own, fingering a pencil and feigning not to understand her definition of herself: "Housewife? In Russia there are no housewives. Is she different from other wives? What does she do, for example, for the good of the country? In Russia wives work. It is a good thing for everyone, especially for the men."

The officer was plainly enjoying himself and the questions he asked were of no particular consequence. Elisabeth concluded that he merely wanted to see what she looked like. Eventually, with the amused and half-weary air of one accustomed to American notions about Russia, he stamped her visa and scrawled in his name.

"You are a very brave woman," he said solemnly, passing back her passport.

"Brave?" Elisabeth repeated, getting jittery at the thought.

"Americans always come to the Soviet Union in herds. Never alone. It is as though they are afraid to come alone. But . . . have a pleasant journey. Please come back afterward, if you care to, and tell me what you found in my country."

This worldly man had made permission to enter Russia both pleasant and easy. Elisabeth had almost hoped it would be a trying process, for it was a well-known fact around Helsinki that no country was so difficult to get into as the United States. We ourselves had known students to be embroiled for two or three months in meaningless red tape before obtaining permission to attend a college in America.

Elisabeth and her parents spent their first night in Hamina; next morning early they passed the Finnish frontier guards, crossed the mile of no man's land, and stopped at the barricade and paintless building which blocks further passage into Russia. In a large room they submitted their documents and passports to a single official standing behind a circular desk. Only two other people were in the room, a man and woman sitting at a table in one corner whose whole purpose seemed to be to scrutinize anyone in the room including the official behind the desk. None of the worldliness of the visa officer in Helsinki filtered down to this slow-witted border policeman. He spoke only monosyllabic English and seemed to be angry and suspicious over everything. All money had to be declared: every last dollar, kopec, or finnmark, together with jewelry, rings, and other personal effects. Inspection of the VW bus and its queer little engine took nearly an hour. In a front compartment of the car the official discovered a walking map of a small section of wooded country west of Helsinki. This he took and studied minutely, impervious to explanations. Either he could not understand that much English or he was not interested. Finally he took the map into another room where it was presumably studied by a higher official and photographed.

But the item which really aroused the dark forebodings of the man was a blue box of Tampax: here at last was the evidence, small diabolically powerful sticks of dynamite fused and ready to go. . . . These innocent-looking Americans! As any explanation would have been both difficult and embarrassing, Elisabeth held her peace and waited while the official took out the sticks one by one, shaking them, hefting them, studying them narrowly. He laid them all out on the counter and wondered what to do next. The couple in the far corner stepped over to have a look. Finally, Elisabeth tore one of the tubes open with her nails and unraveled the contents on the counter. A match proved that the packing was only cotton, and, after another consultation behind the door of the inner office, the customs guard brushed the torn Tampax into a basket, passed the remainder back for her to pack, stamped the passports, and with a surly grunt waved the expedition on.

Now the three adventurers were on an excellent and completely empty road running along the northeastern end of the Gulf of Finland. They had been told in Helsinki not to detour from the main road, not even to stop, and these warnings were further emphasized by other check points which they encountered along the way. The officers had clearly been notified to

135

expect a strange red bus bearing German plates and an American family, for they repeated the previous inspections as though knowing exactly what to look for.

"Damn!" growled Judge McLane after a couple of hours of such halting progress. "Stop at the next wood."

"But we are not allowed to stop, Judge."

"Let them shoot then, but I'm going to the bathroom."

In a bleak way the countryside was fascinating. This had once been Finnish Karelia. Seventeen years had elapsed since the Russians had come, and in that time the farms, never very rich, had gone to weeds and the buildings weathered down to sway-backed frames. Even the ancient Hanseatic port of Viborg, once Finland's second city, looked grey with decay.

Farther along the road, near to Leningrad, the trio passed a number of seaside resort homes where workers go for their annual holidays: large Victorian wooden buildings, decorated with gingerbread, and stained a faded blue and pink. These were buildings erected to illustrate a fairy tale—a fairy tale that is still being recited, although the children have long since grown up to grey hair and the world of Father Stalin.

Leningrad, of course, was different, that beautiful Parisian city of low cream buildings and wide boulevards beside the bridges and canals of the Neva. The visitors saw the Hermitage, which was crowded with people avidly seeking a glimpse of Russia's great past and enthusiastically looking for evidence of its greater future. Then on to the Czar's palace, Peterhof, still under repair because of its recent tenants, the Germans. The travelers visited a modern housing development, they stopped to see the beautiful stations of the Underground Metro, and in the evening saw the incomparable Kirov ballet. Their Intourist guides were intelligent and charming university graduates who were imbued with the excitement of modern Russia. It was, the guides felt, a good world they were building, one where everyone would have enough room, food, clothing, vacations, education, medicine. They talked openly and frankly about Russia; housing was the worst problem; whole families still had to live in one or two rooms. But that would change. Russia had survived invasion by the Germans, undergone a nuclear revolution, and come to lead the world in space machinery. Now, perhaps, there would be time to build up the social foundations of the country.

These young guides were far from the robot propagandists that the three visitors had expected. If they showed a somewhat childlike pride in their country, it was energized by their enthusiasm at being able to help in the building of what they believed was to be the perfect socialist state. There was, after all, something in life for a woman beyond promoting her husband's career. If these young people did not seem to see the pathos of modern housing in Leningrad and the long queues of people waiting to buy a bit of meat, if they had little knowledge of the changing world outside Russia, they were at least enthusiastic and constructive citizens of their own country. One could only wish them success in their hopes, marriage, children, and a chance to travel.

Yet there was another side to the Soviet Union which the visitors saw, the hard, cynical, militaristic side of official Russia. Indeed, there was no way to avoid seeing it. Huge posters were hanging from the buildings in Leningrad, each one proclaiming the present national heros, members of the Politbureau, Premier Khrushchev, Lenin—and the smiling handsome Yuri Gagarin, who this year would be the main attraction at the May Day celebrations. (Stalin was noticeably absent.) I think Elisabeth was a little shaken by May Day in Russia, not so much because of the military power grinding down the highways, but by the fanatic exultation of the crowds. These were not people fed on bread and circuses, but on fear and bombs, and there is no more dangerous diet.

I had to miss seeing Russia. In a way I was glad, for I didn't trust what I would see in a four-day visit and I was pretty sure that I could study the big neighbor better through the eyes of Finns than as a tourist. Finland, too, was having its spring festival, though of a very different kind. May Day, and especially the night before, Walpurgis Eve, are set aside in Scandinavia for students. Walpurgis is a strange rite. Named for an English nun who lived in Germany, it must certainly be of much more distant origin, a kind of Hallowe'en when witches are supposed to be abroad. And if not witches, then students. For this is the night when those who have successfully passed the "matriculation examinations" at the end of their general schooling may don their white student caps and paint the town with gin and rioting. Many of the students would never go on to university, but at least they had proved their right to admission, and in Finland there is no social distinction made so much of as that of being a Student.

All afternoon on the thirtieth of April, trucks and buses full of new students paraded down Mannerheim Street to South Esplanade, then down to the seaside market place, up North Esplanade and across the city. Traffic stammered to a halt, the sidewalks filled with shouting people, and the caterwauling from the trucks was deafening. To climax the evening's witchery, just at midnight a tuxedoed young man, chosen by vote of the governing powers of the Student Nations, would slosh through the fountains at the base of the statue of *Havis Amanda*, climb the pedestal, and then, propelled by gin and a sense of destiny, clamber up her lovely dark and slippery frame to crown her with his own white student cap.

I spent the evening in the raucous city, then at two in the morning walked home to Lauttasaari. Dawn had not yet come, but in the north and east a band of red was broadening under the pure sea green of the sky. The street lamps were burning dim. Over the islands at the harbor mouth a cloud of tinseled gulls flickered in the air, screaming their claims to a mate and nesting place.

Steve was soon awake. With the light coming fast at 3 A.M., he knew it was time to begin the day's work. This was the third night in a row that Steve had roused himself soon after midnight and the strain of it, coming on top of a heady Finnish Walpurgis, was too much for me. But threats, songs, milk, bread had no effect on this young man—he knew it was time to get up and get at the excavations. I wished Elisabeth would come home and tend to her housewifery. Finally, limp with fatigue at four in the morning, I gave Steve a bottle of milk liberally diluted with Finnish gin. That did the trick. When the sun rose bleeding over the dewy trees Steve was at last asleep—straight was the path of gin for him and the need of a world of men for me.

In due time the travelers from the east returned with the VW bus to Helsinki. They were discouraged by the noisy militarism of Russia, but even more by the difficulty of attending to even trivial human concerns. They had found, as many have before them, that the individual is suspected of being guilty by virtue of his mere existence. In this case they were guilty of burning gasoline. Near Leningrad they had tried to refill the tank, only to learn that rubles were of no use, gasoline coupons were necessary. They had not been issued coupons and no one had spoken about them before. At a series of stations they had received only a hard-faced "Nyet" and a wave on to some other station. It began to look as though the expedition would spend the night stalled on the forbidden side of the Leningrad highway, after which, to make matters really interesting, visas would have expired. Finally a woman attendant, who understood their quandary and telephoned to the transportation authorities in Leningrad, received permission to sell them enough gas to get the car over the border.

At the final check point, Judge McLane found he had miscounted his Finnish money by approximately $2.40. Since he could not otherwise account for the disparity of his incoming and outgoing funds, and since it was strictly forbidden for anyone to take any rubles out of Russia, this complication consumed another two hours. He was not stripped and searched in the border post, as some people have been, but he was subjected to an interminable quizzing by an official who spoke practically no English.

Humiliating as it was for an American lawyer and banker, the Judge had finally to admit to the official that he had "made a mistake" in counting his money.

"A mistake?" sneered the official, obviously relishing the situation. "A mistake!"

"Take the money then and do what you like with it," the Judge suggested.

"Great American businessmen!" The official reluctantly pushed the money away.

Afterward, when the three were finally released, they crossed no man's land again to the Finnish border station where two blonde smiling University graduates welcomed them back and served them with coffee and delicious coffee cake. The Judge, who had scarcely sung a note in his life, went outside the station and burst into a great hymn:

"Hallelujah, hallelujah, hal-le-lu-jah!"

I took the Judge to my last seminar in American Literature at the University. We were studying the New England poems of Robert Frost and Philip Booth. Since he knew both of these men personally, I knew he would enjoy the class. Back from the company of wall builders, the Judge could relish the mischief of spring and the certainty again that earth was the right place for love. My students, however, had other ideas about this class. They had brought two bottles of wine and a dozen beautiful plum-shaped glasses. Such aids to study were not mentioned in the syllabus of the English Department, and wine drinking was probably against University regulations, but I could not read the regulations, and besides, wine and a book of verses, with or without the bread, is in the best Maytime teaching tradition. We opened the bottles and the girls asked the Judge to tell what it was like in Russia. At first he was reluctant to say much: a man's first reactions in coming to a new land are apt to be unbalanced by what he expected to see, and small things get to mean too much. Yet, people were generally better off than he had expected, and he was glad for that. It was a good thing that the Intourist Guide had showed off the new suburban housing with such pleasure, and yet pathetic that she had, in fact, been talking about plain boxes of masonry, designed with T squares and unadorned by any color or architectural grace.

Russia was now, he said, rather like America just after the Civil War, full of ignorant boasting and prideful chauvinism, a kind of I-don't-know-anything-about-the-rest-of-the-world-and-brother-I-don't-want-to-know-anything attitude. Perhaps they would get over it, as Americans were getting over it.

One of the girls asked, "What did you first notice when you came back to Finland?"

The old man laughed and turned up the palms of his hands: "Everything . . . everything. . . . Even the air is different. I wish I could tell you."

Fulfilling her promise, Elisabeth went back to the Russian Embassy to make her report to the gentleman who had called her a very brave woman. She was full of impressions and fuller still of questions; there were many things she wanted to ask this pleasant Russian officer. But he was gone. No one seemed to know where nor whether he would come back.

Part Two

The best in Finland emerges not in adversity or danger but only when utter, irremediable and final disaster threatens.

—PATRICK O'DONOVAN

The Russian success is temporary. Communism will ultimately collapse because of its inherent impossibility. Thus final peace terms will be dictated by Finland. . . .

As soon as the soldiers of the victorious Red Army return to their homes, revolution will break out. And the government will be powerless because, you see, the Germans will have stolen all the barbed wire.

—LINNA's Honkajoki

Had a farmhouse but they burned it to the ground.
Don't know even where the spot could now be found.
In the County roll 'tis safe inscribed and sealed—
But no matter, more was lost at Mohać's Field.

—*Hungarian song*

𝕭order Seas

The boat from Kotka to the islands was to load at 11 A.M. but
by ten o'clock she was already down to the sheer strake,
jammed with boys and girls, packs and tents, guitars, handbags,
and food for the two-day celebration. The *Lokki*, scarcely
more than an outsized double-ended fishing boat, had a decked-
over cabin and wheelhouse forward and a large open cockpit
aft. Designed to carry fifteen or twenty passengers, she now
had sixty-five—and a hundred more waiting at the stone wharf
for a chance on the second trip.

Two young birch trees had been cut and tied fore and aft
on the *Lokki's* flag poles, their heart-shaped leaves fluttering in
the wind. This was Midsummer, the Scandinavian fiesta. The
cities would be emptied and the shores of lakes and seas would,
in the evening, be alight with thousands of driftwood fires. But
the sea was bitter cold still, and clouds were moving in from
the western islands thick with the promise of rain.

June 23. One lives with the weather in Finland.

Captain Arvo Korppas tramped down to the stone pier with a
packet of island mail and said he guessed there was no need to
wait for more passengers; he'd be back from Kaunissaari in
about three hours. He obviously did not worry about the
cargo his *Lokki* was carrying. Festive shouting filled the chilly
air, a song was starting up around a guitar player sitting on the
roof of the wheelhouse; people were still jumping on and off
the *Lokki*, changing their minds in mid-air. Captain Korppas, a
stump of a man, stepped heavily aboard and motioned to his

son to slack the lines. Then he backed the *Lokki* away and headed for the channel. The boat seemed to settle down comfortably behind its bow wave. Out beyond the first island, spray began to burst from the bow and sweep the deck. We could see the guitar player and his companions scrambling down from the wheelhouse into the mass of people in the cockpit.

We waited all day in Kotka for the *Lokki* to thin out the crowd on the wharf. Everything was at a standstill in the city, the streets empty, the lumber ships along the waterfront decorated with birch trees and then abandoned. Not even a restaurant was open, for no one, it seemed, was willing to sacrifice a moment of this bedrizzled holiday for the sake of a few extra finnmarks. Up the Kymi River a few miles we found the handsome hand-built "Fish Shack" that the Finnish people had given to Czar Alexander III and his pretty Danish wife, Dagmar. Unlike his father, young Czar Alexander had done nothing for the Grand Duchy of Finland; but he had loved to sail on the lakes and watch the salmon-trapping; he had done no harm; and after him the harsh days of Nicholas II and General Bobrikoff had come. These were reasons enough for celebrating the memory of the high-domed slow-witted Czar.

It was eight thirty in the evening when Captain Korppas brought his vessel down the channel for the last time. The wind was blowing hard outside and the trip had taken him twice the normal time. Along with the remaining passengers on the pier we loaded our gear aboard, put on raincoats, and huddled together in the lee of the *Lokki*'s windward rail. When the boat cleared the harbor islands, she was already porpoising.

Ben and Bron were with us, Steve was farmed out to Tytti's family for the month, and Kim and Wendy were off visiting classmates at their summer cottages. We had no clear idea where we were going except that it was to stay with a man named Kantola on an island called Kaunissaari. We had no paper to show, no deposit had been required of me when, two months earlier, I had made arrangements to come here through the Finnish Tourist Association in Helsinki.

146

"I want a rock in the eastern Baltic," I had specified to the lady at the desk. "Preferably with sea gulls and fishermen on it."

She, giggling, had come up with Kaunissaari, twenty kilometers southwest from Kotka and not far from Russian waters. The lady had telephoned the owner of the one phone on the island and left a message for the man with whom we would be staying. "Kantola," she had said. "Aarne Kantola. Good, all then is arranged. He speaks no English, neither speak the sea gulls any."

Aarne Kantola had not written to confirm the reservation, and the lady at the Tourist Association office had not expected a reply. I wondered whether our host would have forgotten us, or whether, owing to our long delay in coming to the island, he would have given our beds to others equally anxious to avoid the rain.

The June night could not darken, but it was murky with clouds. Now and then the *Lokki* at half speed plowed an olive sea wide open and sent showers of spindrift hissing to leeward. But after an hour of open water the boat ran in under the lee of a low island. A steep sand beach, a rarity in any part of the Baltic, stretched along most of this sheltered eastern shore, and just above the beach many tents, like yellow and orange mushrooms, sprouted under the pines. Now and then a whiff of campfire smoke blew down to us—a poor night for cooking out, but a fine one to be tenting with one's girl.

This was Kaunissaari. At the far end of the island the sand gave way to boulders and the boulders sank into a crooked shoal, emerging shortly to form a treeless grassy island. Into the mess of rocks and breakers Korppas swung his *Lokki*. Though no buoys showed to guide him, the old man seemed to know the channel by the shape of the waves. Somewhere in the ragged moment of crossing I caught sight of a great red bonfire spiraling up on a beach. Then we were across the shoal, curving down toward two small jetties and running into the smallest basin that was ever called a harbor. One dim light shone down from a post on the *Lokki's* wharf where a score of people had come down to lend a hand and welcome the new arrivals. Around the basin were a dozen grey fishhouses and small docks, beyond them in the pines the few lights of the village.

We were stiff and cold from sitting in our raincoats, but we managed to creak ashore with the others and stood there wondering what to do. Then from the crowd a short man detached himself, pushing a homemade wooden wheelbarrow. He wore a black beret and the sleeves of his work shirt were rolled up over strong brown arms.

"*Amerikkalaisia?*" he asked, in a soft voice.

"Kantola?"

"Welcome," he said, holding out his hand. In a moment he had piled our packs and suitcases on the barrow and lifted Bronwen to sit on top. We started off over the dock to a lane which, between pole fences, led toward the cluster of small houses halfway up a gentle hill. The wooden wheel of the barrow creaked from side to side, bumping up over the stones. Aarne Kantola grinned and told Bron not to fear; he had made the wheelbarrow himself and it had lasted twenty years. Rain dripped from the pine needles overhead and glistened dully on the stones.

"Bad weather," I said.

"Bad," Aarne agreed. "Tempest comes. (That excellent word *Myrsky*.) But—there is coffee, and the sauna is still hot."

Kantola's house stood beside the lane a short hundred yards from the water. It was a well-constructed board-and-batten house of two stories, painted a mustard yellow. Behind it were a lawn, garden, hayfield, then the sheltering spruce and the booming western shore. He had given us the main living room to stay in and set up cots for sleeping, although the room was already overloaded with furniture and bric-a-brac. Two candles and an oil lamp gave us light. Between the windows stood a polished mahogany harmonium; near it was a large glassed-in bookcase; and on the walls several stern ancestors looked down from dark oval oak frames.

Mrs. Kantola came in at once, a big handsome woman of middle age, and with greying hair, bringing towels for the bath and bread and milk for the children. After we had settled ourselves she led the way outdoors and across the lawn to a log cabin where, inside the door, the warm heavy air in the dressing room began to thaw our bones. Assuring herself that there was enough cold water, and that everything was neat and clean, Mrs. Kantola left us, saying that coffee would be ready when we had finished our baths.

Aarne's sauna was the best we ever bathed in; compared to it the efficient electrically heated flash boxes of modern city apartments are saunas in name only. This one was large enough to be worthy of a *Kalevala* hero. The fireplace, built of white-washed rock and topped with cement held half a cubic yard of smoke-blackened stones. As is true of all country steam houses, the sauna serves as a laundry and borning place for babies, so there was a second firebox in which stood a large caldron brimming with hot water. Both fires were now out; no seeping of bitter smoke could come to burn our eyes, but the log walls and the benches, black with years of use, exuded a fragrance of smoke. The pile of rocks warmed the room, but did not stifle the air. Each dipperful of water, turning to steam with a rich smothering sound, filled the room with a downward flooding heat that tingled from the roots of our hair to the tips of our toes.

Kantola had cut and bound fresh bundles of birch branches, dense with scented leaves. Seated on the tiers of benches we steamed and beat each other into a running sweat. Then it was time to step down, fill the pans with water, and soap and scrub ourselves. After a rinse we stood awhile outside the sauna to cool off, watching the vapor billow upwards from our bodies into the grey sky. Then back to the benches for more dippers of water, more steam. After three such changes of hot and cold our skins glowed pink and seemed to soften, though this was but a surface sign of the softening and sense of well-being which flowed all through our bodies.

I found myself trying to remember the scent of steam and birch boughs so well described in a passage in the *Kalevala;* even there, however, the poet had missed the real fragrance of a sauna, which is smoke. We smelled like perfect country bacon when we left the bathhouse and went to join the Kantolas in the kitchen.

(One writes of steam baths with a sense of broken trust, for there is no subject that brings a grimace quicker to the faces of Finns. More than a hundred years have passed during which Western visitors have been discovering Finland; in all that time saunas have remained the special wonder for the traveler. How long, Finns ask, how long before people will accept the fact that Finns take baths? Is there nothing else to write about? A sauna is not a religious rite, not a mystical experience for stone age masochists, but a bath—a pleasant and sociable way to get clean.)

After helping us to coffee and delicious coffee cake, Aarne Kantola showed us the lane to take to find the Midsummer bonfire. The sky around midnight was only a stormy twilight; we could see well enough to follow the cart tracks across two fields and through a neck of the woods to where, on a shingle beach, the fire was shouting sparks into the drizzle. Perhaps twenty couples stood around the fire in an ever-shifting audience. A Finn on an outing is a well-dressed Finn: the boys wore dark suits and oxfords, the girls wobbled around the beach on high heels. Oblivious of the rain, they stood there steaming in front and soaking up the drizzle behind.

Nearby in the woods stood a small dilapidated dance pavilion. Two couples were dancing to the thin music of a phonograph, but the rest of the group seemed to be waiting. At one end of the pavilion the girls clustered, whispering together and looking pathetically hopeful; at the other end the boys hung together, equally shy, but making a big ceremony over passing a bottle.

Midsummer night—the annual fertility rite, older by ages than the Grail legends of the poets, and familiar still to Chinese, American Indians, and Scandinavians.

Who were these young sons and daughters camping here? There was an unshowy frankness about them which gave authenticity to their performance. One could not help admiring a civilization which treats sexual matters with such directness. These people were not carrying out the standardized practice of trial marriage, but their time had come, and parents probably knew, while awkward Finn boys and shy Finn girls spent a cold midsummer dawn together.

After two days the campers vanished, leaving their bottles

and cans by the spent fires. We followed their footprints on the long eastern beaches, explored the bouldery west shore and the northern tip of the island where the lumber vessels from Kotka came pounding by. All that week the *Myrsky* blew. Aarne scythed his field, piled up the hay on sharp-pointed poles to dry, tended to his half-acre of summer potatoes. He did not fish; the fish were all out in deep water he said and would not school inshore until September. No one else around the harbor, not even the sea gulls, went fishing. The men were repairing their boats or building new ones of pine planks cut from their own lots on the island; nets hung over frames outside the fish shacks, blowing like lace curtains, ready for the moment when the sea would come alive.

In the autumn, after he had made his catch and salted them down in barrels, Aarne would cruise to Helsinki for the October market festival, sell his "Baltic Sprats" and kegs of spicy small herring, "Silakka," and load up with a winter supply of potatoes. After that there would be logging to do on the island, while the small children went to the one-room elementary school and the older ones lived on the mainland to attend higher schools. Life on Kaunissaari seemed very much the same as that of the islanders in Maine.

Kaunissaari was a peaceful bucolic place. Cows roamed the lanes munching flowers, Kantola's wooden wheelbarrow was the only vehicle, there were no electric lights, and one telephone in the kitchen of a Korppas served the entire village. Boys learned fishing, boatmaking, net tying. Girls played dolls and kept house in the pretty little playhouses which are as much a part of a Finnish farm as the sauna. We learned the Finnish way of picnicking—taking a small pot with us and making coffee over a fire of pine cones and birch bark.

For all the peace of the island, though, there was no getting away from war. One came suddenly upon grassy trenches and machine-gun nests and rifle pits, on the tumbled-down log roofs of bunkers, on mines rusted and half buried in the sand. Kantola had spent a part of the war here. Kaunissaari had not been attacked, but he could remember the day when, near the end of the Winter War, Russian troops massed behind tanks had attacked over the ice toward Kotka, attempting to flank the Karelian defenses. With both horror and pleasure he spoke of seeing Finnish artillery bursting red against the limitless white of the frozen sea, of dark figures running, tanks floundering into pools of broken ice, men drowning. The attack had failed, but the war had brushed by that close to his home.

One morning when the wind was down and the sky summer pale, Aarne stopped us to point out an island to the southeast we had not seen before, a high grey cathedral shape over the easy sea.

"*Russland, Russland!*" he said, using the Swedish name to be sure we understood. His normally soft musical voice was harsh, like the cry of a perigrine hawk wounded in some way it could not comprehend. "Suursaari. All lost, all lost."

Suursaari (Great Island) had been his wife's home before the war. Her father and grandfather had lived there fishing and farming. It was the finest island in all the Finnish archipelago, having a deep harbor on the south side, thick forests, and from the cliffs a view in all directions over the eastern sea. In the old days people from Russia, Estonia, Sweden, and many other countries had come to summer there. Now it was a Russian base. Suursaari and its neighboring islands, together with much of Karelia and the seaport of Viborg, had been taken over by the Soviets after the war. Compared to it Kaunissaari was but a rocky slip of land. The Finnish Government had come in to blast and dredge the tiny bight on the southern tip which people use for a harbor. "It is not so much," Kantola admitted, "but it suits. We live."

Aarne Kantola had a simple man's understanding of war. Why should anyone want to attack Finland? Finns had never in a thousand years waged an aggressive war. They asked nothing of their neighbors but to be left alone in this land of swamps. Why then the unprovoked attack in the winter of 1939–1940?

Aarne probably did not know it—for the secret had been kept even from the Parliament until war broke out—but Suursaari was lost to Finland long before the Winter War. It was lost the moment Stalin decided that the Soviet Union and Nazi Germany must sometime come into head-on collision. The

Anschluss of the Nazis in Austria probably convinced Stalin that the time was not far off, for immediately afterward, in April, 1938, he initiated secret negotiations with the Finnish President and Foreign Minister concerning the defenses of Leningrad. (This was six months before the Munich crisis, eighteen months before the outbreak of World War II, and three years before the German attack upon Russia.)

Stalin was a logical and farsighted man. Even in 1938 he could see that Finland, willing or not, must surely become involved in an attack by Germany upon Russia. Russia's second city, Leningrad, and its great naval base at Kronstad would be two immediate objectives for the Nazis. The attack would be of the usual pincers kind, one claw reaching to surround Leningrad from the southwest, across Latvia and Estonia, the other coming down through Finland and Karelia. Geography made that inevitable.

Indeed there were other good reasons for the Germans to strike early into Finland: to the east lay Russia's arctic railway, running south from the ice-free port of Murmansk; to the west lay Sweden, whose rich supply of iron ore and wealth of manufacturing would thus be assured of remaining neutral in favor of Germany.

Many factors had combined to create a power vacuum in Scandinavia. All the countries were small, the population of Finland, for example, was scarcely more than that of Leningrad. All were neutral in their own way, and only Sweden had a modern defense force. But what was worse, there was no compelling sense of unity among the peoples of the north. They disliked each other. Swedes thought Finns a violent and unpredictable race, Norwegians uncultured sea rovers and ski sports. Both Finns and Norwegians had developed to a high degree the domestic habit of despising Swedes. The habit persisted, even when all were in jeopardy together.

So Sweden, which was rich compared to its sister nations, was willing to talk about a "Scandinavian Neutral Bloc," or a "Northern Alliance," but it was not interested in working out the details.

Finland's defensive position was even more exposed than that of Norway and Sweden. The entire Åland archipelago in the west had been demilitarized by international treaty, the so-called Mannerheim Line on the Karelian Isthmus was largely a romantic notion of newspaper writers, and military prepared-ness in any modern sense was almost nonexistent in the coun-try. General Mannerheim in his *Memoirs* entitles a long chap-ter of this frustrating prewar period "Eight Years Racing the Storm." He lays the blame for Finland's defenselessness (and therefore her inability to negotiate) on a succession of socialist governments who always put its social and economic aims ahead of even a minimal defense appropriation.

Mannerheim probably understood better than any statesman in Scandinavia what was happening in those years of drifting into war. He had spent thirty years as an officer in the Czar's armies: he knew the dark workings of the Russian mind and the overriding necessities of Russia's defense. Nevertheless, as the years before the storm narrowed down into months and weeks, he could not persuade his government of Finland's peril. The Ministers had no better understanding than did a simple man like Aarne Kantola: Finland was not going to at-tack anyone, why should anyone attack her? Such a thing was immoral and unthinkable.

When, in the spring of 1938, secret negotiations got under way between Russia and Finland, the Kremlin's demands were still vague: If Germany should attack Russia through Finland what would Finland do? Would it accept Russian military and economic aid? The Finnish Foreign Minister, unable to imag-ine such an eventuality, gave no immediate answer. Four months later he replied that his country would repel *any* great power seeking to gain a foothold in Finland. Then he asked for Russian approval of a project for the Åland Islands to be forti-fied jointly by Sweden and Finland.

This proposal hastened more concrete Russian demands. Stalin was wary of Finland's historic friendship with Ger-many; such fortifications might be turned against Russia, bot-tling up its fleet in the Gulf. Therefore Russia declared it would be willing to allow the Ålands to be fortified only if Russians were permitted to take part in the work and to con-trol the use of the forts. Meanwhile Russia asked permission to place both an air base and naval base on Suursaari.

Finland refused, stating that both proposals were contrary to Finnish sovereignty and neutrality.

After the Munich crisis in the autumn of 1938, Sweden, too, became alarmed over the defenselessness of the Åland Islands. Germany might take them over; that would be bad enough, but what was to prevent Russia from occupying them first? Another attempt by Sweden and Finland to negotiate the joint militarization of the islands got as far as a name—the Stockholm Plan—but a loud rattle of sabers from Moscow brought these proceedings to a halt.

Sweden's abrupt withdrawal from its own Stockholm Plan was clue enough for Stalin: Finland was indeed alone. Russia's next demand, in March, 1939, was specific: to *lease*, for thirty years, Suursaari and several neighboring islands in the eastern Gulf of Finland whose fortification would protect the passage to Leningrad. Finland refused to discuss the proposal.

Mannerheim, as Commander in Chief of the army and Head of the Defense Council, was privy to these discussions. He strongly opposed his government's actions. "I was of the definite opinion," he writes, "that we were bound to meet the Russians in some way." He even went further, suggesting that Finland should offer to withdraw the frontier in southern Karelia farther to the west; Leningrad was within shelling distance of Finnish soil and this could only be a provocation to Russia. As for Suursaari and the other islands in question, these, he said, were of no military value to Finland; in any crisis they could not be defended, and would have to be evacuated.

"Russia will not hesitate to obtain its aims by force of arms," Mannerheim warned. Moreover he felt certain that the Finnish people would understand and accept the proposal once it was explained to them. He offered to "risk his popularity" by being the one to take the matter to the people. "But," he says, "I met with no understanding."

This proved to be the last chance to negotiate a settlement with Russia. One month later Litvinov stepped down from his post as Commissar for Foreign Affairs. In his place stood the man of iron, Mr. Molotov.

There were other ways to skin a Finnish lion. Molotov

turned to the business of making a Nonaggression Pact with Germany. Germany wanted time for its coming work in the west; Russia wanted time to develop its defenses—the same delay that England and France had bought a year earlier at Munich. This time the sacrificial country was not Czechoslovakia, but Finland. Molotov asked and received, as the price of peace on the Eastern front, "a free hand in Finland."

A week later, on September 1, 1939, World War II began. With Germany occupied with Britain and France on the Western front, Molotov moved. One by one, beginning on September 22, he summoned the Foreign Ministers of Estonia, Latvia, and Lithuania, to "discuss a pact of Mutual Assistance." One by one, a week apart, the Ministers of these little nations journeyed to Moscow and signed their countries out of existence.

On October 5 it was Finland's turn to be called. When the Finnish delegation, under the leadership of the statesman and jurist, J. K. Paasikivi, refused to discuss that sort of mutual assistance, Molotov presented alternative demands: Russia would lease for a naval and coast artillery base the peninsula of Hanko, lying midway between Helsinki and the Åland Islands; the great Lappvik anchorage would be available to Russian ships; the islands in the eastern Gulf of Finland would be ceded to Russia outright, together with part of the Karelian Isthmus in the south and the Fisher Peninsula in the Arctic; fortifications on both sides of the frontier on the Isthmus would be "demolished."

The significance of these first steps was not difficult to see. "The Soviet Government," said Mannerheim, "will soon, as has been the case with Estonia, produce new demands. They wish to establish good conditions for aggression."

Stalin may have had a soft spot in his heart for Finland—after all, Lenin had been sheltered there—but sentiment never affected his mind. When Mr. Paasikivi stated Finland's plain case, that it wished only to remain outside all conflicts, Stalin replied, driving a pudgy finger into a map at the Åland-Hanko invasion area: "I understand this, but I assure you that it is impossible. The great powers will not permit it."

Meanwhile Molotov's plans were going forward. For more

than two months now the troop trains had been rumbling north over the Murmansk railroad; new concentrations of soldiers were seen in Karelia, both north and south of Lake Ladoga; a division newly returned from the Polish front was identified massing near the southern Finnish frontier; and all along that eight-hundred-mile border Russian aircraft were flying daily reconnaissance missions. When all was ready it was time, in Molotov's words, "for the soldiers to negotiate."

One small diplomatic nicety remained to be arranged: a border incident which could be used as provocation for war. General Mannerheim had anticipated some such expedient and pulled his artillery back out of range of the border. He had done all he could. He had mobilized the army and the reserves under the guise of practicing war games. Still the government procrastinated. On November 27, 1939, Mannerheim wrote in a long communication to the government:

> While everything has pointed to a gigantic conflict approaching, the indispensable demands of our defense have been treated with parsimony. . . . Even now, questions regarding the most urgent necessities of the armed forces are treated in as leisurely a manner as if we lived in normal times. . . .

But time had run out. One day earlier a Russian battery on the Isthmus had opened fire on a Russian outpost near the village of Mainila, killing four men and wounding nine. "We don't wish to exaggerate the importance . . ." said Mr. Molotov in his protest to the Finnish Ambassador in Moscow (one can almost hear his chuckle) and then the wires to Finland were cut and the tanks began to roll.

Thus the long talks which began with a request to lease Suursaari ended in a war which both sides did not want and which was never formally declared or justified by any of the common euphemisms. One cannot but believe that throughout this period the Finnish Government set a new standard for pigheaded diplomacy, but whether any other course would have spared the country cannot be said. Stalin was right about the German attack. He was right that the great powers would not permit this ancient Finnish bridge to go unclaimed. But he was wrong about the determination of Finns to battle an invader.

At the end of November, 1939, the Winter War began—a minor tactical incident in the snows of the far north to those who were watching the gigantic conflict just getting started in Central Europe. That Molotov expected "the Finnish question" to be cleared up in a few weeks there can be no doubt. On the first day of operations he installed the well-known Finnish traitor, Otto Kuusinen, in the tiny border hamlet of Terijoki and declared that Kuusinen's *Democratic People's Government of the Finnish Republic* was the only official government of Finland. Russian soldiers, as they set forth against the "capitalist butcher warmongers" of Finland, were given slips of paper warning them to be careful not to molest the Swedish frontier on the other side.

Yet perhaps even pigheaded diplomacy may have played a positive role. One wonders whether the very perverseness of Finns, their utter inability even to find the words to discuss independence, may not have been, on the last thin edge of decision, the fact that saved them. Estonia, Latvia, Lithuania—all more reasonable countries—were swallowed up the following spring. Finland fought, and gained its only possible objective, a temporary settlement.

. . . Or so I thought, looking across the water from Kaunissaari to the high blue cathedral of Suursaari. Aarne Kantola, scarcely more than a boy, had fought in that war. He didn't look much like a hero, just a strong simple man. His wife's island was gone now. It was only twenty miles away to the southeast, twenty years away in time. But the distance was incalculable for one who seeks but a strip of shore for his home, fish for the bellies of his children, and freedom to be a Finn.

It was the best war to date for both sides had won. The Finns, though, had won slightly less than the Russians.

—VÄINÖ LINNA

Borderlands

If the prewar map of Finland once looked, as I have said, like the picture of a man standing on a misshapen world, his two arms flung up as though in a shout of exultation to the Western world, during the Winter War the map suddenly altered: the man stood on his shaky world, but his arms were flung up in desperation and his cry to the neighbors was "Hurry." In 1939, however, none of the Western democracies could hurry or give help.

I had long wanted to see something of these eastern borderlands, to examine for myself the terrain in which the Winter War was fought and study the changes that are not mentioned in articles on modern Finland. So, after a week on windy Kaunissaari we returned with Captain Korppas to Kotka and loaded up the VW bus for a camping trip to the north. It is not far from the Gulf of Finland to the first fjells of Lapland; no more than six hundred miles. The roads were dirt but wide and well kept. We were in no hurry, a hundred and fifty miles a day was enough. Most of the larger towns had set aside excellent camp sites, so there was never any need to press on; we could stop and chat, picnic, or look for an out-of-the-way rapids mentioned as a *koski* on the map.

After leaving the rich valley of the Kymi River and crossing a low watershed, we came into the great Saimaa drainage basin. Farms dwindled down to small family holdings and forests of pine and spruce took over half the land. The other half was water. Although the Kymi River, running down to the Baltic

159

at Kotka, drains a wealthy forest area, compared to it the Saimaa basin is an inland sea and forest empire. One third of the country's wood-producing land pours its annual cuttings downstream into an archipelago of lakes which all drain south into Lake Saimaa.

One whole day we spent winding through the channels of the Saimaa on the steamer that runs from Lappeenranta to Savonlinna; three more days passed before we worked our way out of the maze of lakes to the north that are the Saimaa's tributaries. Wood, timber, saw logs, peeled orange logs of Norway pine, white-birch logs, pulpwood, fence poles, logs for plywood knives and furniture, lumber and pulp and paper —one has to see such quantities of wood and the steaming sulphite mills to grasp the meaning of statistics.

Kotka itself seemed but a small island in a sea of lumber. Timber rode in on flatcars; lumber was stacked up all over town in buildings as high as three-story apartments; the river was thatched into whirling pods of pine and birch, waiting for the saw. While brawny women were heaving cordwood into coasting schooners, men stacked the freighters with lumber to the booms and chained it down for great circle voyages. A year's cutting would take almost a year shipping.

In Lappeenranta: more logs boomed together into huge islands, waiting in the bays. On the lake: more logs peeled and chained together like enormous faggots, rafted for two kilometers out behind the stately tugs. At Savonlinna and Joensuu: more logs swimming down the boomed channels to the lakes below. Never an end to the logs, day or dusk in summer, moving to the sea.

Before the war the natural outlet for this harvest of timber was south through the lakes, then through the short Saimaa Canal to the port of Viborg. Such enormous supplies of wood, so easily and cheaply transported, brought prosperity to Finland in the twenties and late thirties. But the war had changed all that. Viborg was gone and the canal cut by the new frontier. New methods of overland transport had to be devised, and new ports dredged and built: Kotka, Hamina, Loviisa. The work was urgent just after the war, for the sale of wood products abroad meant not only a daily livelihood for Finnish laborers but investment capital for other industries, and thus the possibility of meeting the demands of the Russian War Debt.

Strange to say, in spite of the extent of lumbering in this southeast region, we rarely saw any sign of cutting, and never any of the slashed and brutalized hillsides so familiar in America. Finnish forests lend themselves to selective cutting. Finnish forests are drained and limbed and kept as clean as parks. Moreover, as the very future of the country depends upon not overcutting, for decades Finns have practiced the most advanced conservation measures.

Our roads wound between the lakes and swamps, over sandy knolls of pine and blueberry, down again into spruce and birch. We could rarely see any distance ahead, the trees buried us. Now and then a farm, with red or yellow buildings, held back the forest. And now and then there was a white village lazing in the sun. From Koli's ice-white quartzite cone we looked down on a lake sixty miles long where nothing moved but the shadows of clouds. Except for a few high hills this was a flat country of trees and shining water.

Directly across the lake from Koli, in what seemed unbroken forest, ran a single-track railroad from Sortavala in Russian-held Karelia straight northwest to Oulu on the Gulf of Bothnia. To capture this track had been a major objective of Russians in the Winter War. With it in their possession they would have been able to cut the country in half and shut off all supplies coming from Sweden. But they failed. Out there in the low hills, invisible to us, but not very far away, were the little villages of Suojärvi, Tolvajärvi, Ilomantsi, Kuhmo where one by one the attacks in the winter of 1939–40 were blunted, stopped, and turned into unexpected victories.

All this seemed very long ago. Driving through this border country, we rarely saw any of the scars of that war. Spruce closed over the torn hills, blueberries covered the tank tracks. Villages had been built back better than before. Burned farms became new farms where the momentary task of stopping Russians had been forgotten in the eternal work of holding back the wilderness.

North from Nurmes and Kuhmo, except for a scattering of

towns, we were on Finland's perpetual frontier. The soil was sandy and poor. Some mining was going on in the area, but it was a meager resource. The region was reputed to contain a large number of Finnish Communists; all we saw were the farms hacked by enormous labor from the hard-scrabble hills. Poverty showed itself mainly in a lack of paint. Houses and barns weathered to shades of grey. Yet, for all that, we saw not a single tarpaper shack. The homes were small but strongly built log cabins, the yards bloomed with flowers and the fields with fireweed. Bright lines of laundry, like a ship's flags on holiday, declared the independence of each family.

One could not help but wonder how this lonely country was ever defended against a determined invader. Who would be there to man strategic defenses at the critical times? How could sufficient men be collected, housed, moved, supplied in the forests, in the snow and darkness of winter? The answer can only be found in the tactical genius of General Manner-heim and in the resourcefulness of Finnish soldiers.

The Winter War, of course, in any strictly military sense was hopeless from the start. Russia was forty times larger than Finland. It had been preparing its attack for at least three months, while Finnish diplomats said "No" in Moscow and didn't believe war possible. Russia had 26 divisions, 2,000 tanks, armored brigades, a fair air force, and unlimited artillery to throw in at chosen points along an 800-mile border. Mannerheim had 9 divisions including reservists, a few tanks and antitank guns, some ancient airplanes, and supplies of ammunition good for one or two months.

Of all the peculiar exploits which have earned for Finns the Russian soubriquet of The Unusual People, surely the Winter War is the most astounding. The story need not be elaborated in detail here, for it will always be remembered and can never be adequately explained. (One might as well expect to see the people of Massachusetts take up arms against the United States, and for 105 days prevent the U. S. Army from pene-trating beyond thirty miles into the Berkshires.)

The Kremlin's plan for conquest was simple and logical: attack with maximum strength and simultaneously at six widely separated points along that long border. The strongest force, 12 to 14 divisions and a thousand tanks, would be concentrated on the narrow Karelian Isthmus, to break the "Mannerheim Line" and plunder west along the coast into the industrial heartland of Finland. Another strong force, north of Lake Ladoga, would move west through Sortavala then south into the Saimaa basin to divide the Finnish forces and harry the Karelian defenders from the rear. Three more columns over a two-hundred-mile frontier would drive west to the Gulf of Bothnia, only 150 miles away at the narrow waist of Finland. And a sixth army would move south from the Arctic, dividing and taking Finnish Lapland. Thus it could be expected that in a short time supplies from Sweden coming in over western railroads would be shut off, and the country cut up into untenable segments.

Against such an attack, anticipated by General Mannerheim and his staff, there was only one possible defense: enemy columns must be stopped in the borderlands where the forests had been left uncut, the swamps undrained, the roads and railroads unbuilt; they must, at whatever the cost, be stopped on the wilderness roads where their size would be turned to length, like a snake unable to coil.

Yet almost from the beginning Mannerheim realized that he had made a serious, perhaps fatal, miscalculation: he had underestimated, by two or three times, the numbers of men and machines the enemy could maintain and maneuver in a given area. This was especially true on the tight land bridge of the Isthmus. Even though the terrain was favorable to his small defense forces, they had to face overwhelming numbers at the very outset. Many excellent defense positions had to be abandoned. Worse still, Mannerheim found that he had at once to commit nearly all his reserves. There could be little rest or reinforcement for the defenders. His "covering forces" in the south, which were to hold up the enemy until the main defense lines could be fully manned, numbered 13,000 as against 140,000 Soviet troops and 1,000 tanks. North of Ladoga, from Sortavala to Salla, generally it was a few battalions of hastily equipped ski troops, at most a regiment or two, that had to face the various divisions of that many pronged attack.

"Bad news from all fronts," Mannerheim wrote in his journal, on December 6, Finland's Independence Day, after one week of the war.

But then miracles began to happen: strange names flooded into the papers of a world already turning its back—*Salla, Kollaa, Summa, Sortavala*, names strange even to most Finns, small villages where the waves of enemy first struck rock.

Kuhmo, Aittojoki, Tolvajärvi, Taipale—where whole Russian divisions were cut up and died in the snow. (In Mannerheim's laconic words: "They got piled up to such an extent they could not bring their strength to bear.")

Ilomantsi, Suomussalmi, Pelkosenniemi—watercourses where the floodgates were hammered shut.

In the Western world these unpronounceable names blazed through the night like portents, for the Western world had already given up Finland. It was the time of paralysis and despair, in the south—the Phony War. England was mobilizing; France considered her leaky Maginot line invincible; America was beginning a draft; and Belgium, Holland, Denmark, Norway, Sweden were hoping to stand aside, exempted of everything including their geography.

With the capture by Russian troops in early December of the border village of Suomussalmi, Mannerheim wrote: "The way to the west is open." Yet the way was shut down again. Winter settled in and proved to be one of the coldest in a century. In December and January the temperature hovered around 40° below zero and sometimes went to 50° below. Winter was both an ally and an enemy of the Finns. While it might speed the work of ski troops in the north, sectioning the miles of men and machinery that were bogged down in the wilderness, in the south the rapid freezing of lakes and swamps gave Soviet tanks a new freedom to maneuver.

Nevertheless, December and January were months of Finnish victories. Unfortunately the Western world, unable to send any help, came to believe in miracles. A Swedish Prince wrote poetry—"Righteousness still stands guard in Finland"—while the Swedish Foreign Minister refused again to allow transit to French and British volunteers. Swedish people did send arms, material, food and medical supplies. Eventually some 11,500 volunteers—Swedes, Norwegians, Danes, and Hungarians—got to Finland. They were sent mainly to the northern fronts where they released several dog-weary Finnish battalions for more arduous duties on the Isthmus. The 300-man company of Finnish-American volunteers also saw action, but only on the last day of the war.

It would have taken a vast modern expeditionary force to have materially changed the outcome of this unequal contest. By February the Russian forces, larger than ever and reorganized by Timoshenko and Voroshilov, were ready for the final offensive. Even now, however, Finnish soldiers refused to be routed. For six weeks more their lines held; their capacity to fall back, let through, then counterattack remained as deadly as ever. Summa stood and stood, blocking the path to Viborg. Further north, at Taipale, a few companies endured six weeks of unremitting attack and yet fought on. Linna wrote: "Every night we dragged half our number to the rear and men went mad in the snow." But Taipale held.

Simultaneously, in early February, peace feelers came from Russia, through Sweden's diplomatic offices. This was the break Mannerheim was looking for, the whole object of his strategy. Mannerheim impressed upon his staff and men that now, above all, they must not falter: they must convince the Soviets that a settlement would be less costly than carrying on the war to the intended defeat and occupation of Finland. Finnish negotiators could take courage from the fact that the Kremlin no longer insisted that Kuusinen's Terijoki government—that misplayed passage from a musical comedy—was the legitimate government of Finland.

On March 13 the war ended. Peace came as a shock to most of the people, for even the Finnish Government had little knowledge of how arms and man power had completely run out.

Molotov's terms were considerably more severe than those demands rejected by the Finnish Government four months earlier: Karelia both north and south of Lake Ladoga was to be cut off, the new line to run just east of the Saimaa lake chain; Viborg was gone; the Hanko peninsula to the west of Helsinki was to be leased for thirty years; the gulf islands and sections of the northern frontier around Kuusamo and Salla were to be ceded.

The treaty meant that Finland would give up 10 per cent of

its most valuable land and have to resettle 12 per cent of its population in the west, to say nothing of having to care for the disabled, repair its economy, and prepare at once for whatever new demands the great powers might make upon it.

Why the Soviets on the verge of total victory in the early spring of 1940 decided to give up the conquest of Finland will always be hard to comprehend. General Mannerheim, in his *Memoirs*, reflects upon several possible explanations. The Winter War had created strong pro-Finnish sentiments among the British and French. Perhaps the Soviets, knowing the sham of their nonaggression treaty with Germany, were unwilling to risk a complete break with these two potential allies. Or perhaps they thought it unwise to incite Germany by occupying land so close to Swedish iron ore. Besides, Russia had other urgent business down south, in the Balkans, and its timetable had been set back perhaps six months. According to Mannerheim's calculation, by mid-March Russia's investment in the war against the Finns had run to 45 divisions and 3,000 tanks, "about half of the regular Russian divisions in Europe and western Siberia," nearly 1,000,000 men, of whom 200,000 or more were dead.

In any case, for the time being, this piece of swampy land, more isolated and vulnerable than before, was not considered worth the extra price. The Finnish question could be settled later. More than once Finland's survival seems to have been the result of an accident beyond their own powers—the momentary accident of nonimportance.

One of the unmentioned blessings of the Winter War was the unity that Finnish people suddenly discovered in themselves. For three and a half months, at least, Swedish-Finn and Finnish-Finn became brothers. Red Finn and White Finn forgot the civil war of their fathers. Socialists, Communists, Agrarians, Conservatives gave up their bickering and stony-headed politics and for a moment reminded a frightened world that greatness is not a matter of size but of spirit.

Mannerheim, summing up his memories of that war, writes:

That an army so inferior in numbers and equipment should have inflicted such serious defeats on an overwhelmingly powerful enemy, and, while retreating, have over and over again repelled his attacks, is something for which it is hard to find a parallel in the history of war. But it is equally admirable that the Finnish people, face to face with an apparently hopeless situation, were able to resist a feeling of despair and, instead, to grow in devotion and greatness. Such a nation has earned the right to live.

The Scaly Straits

Late one afternoon in a day of showers, following a road of solitudes, suddenly around a brushy bend we came on a monument, a fierce gaunt splinter of bronze perhaps forty feet long sticking up at a crazy angle in a little clearing. Shaped like exactly nothing at all it became three things: a rifle and bayonet, a shard or shell fragment, and a jab of bronze lightning. On the stone base some names and words about Suomussalmi were cut. Several bunches of fresh flowers wilted on the base, otherwise the monument seemed to have been abandoned to the vaulting brush.

Our road turned off in the wood, joined another coming from the south and presently crossed a bouldery watercourse between two lakes. Suomussalmi was one of those small frontier villages where, as Mannerheim had said, "the incredible happened" in the early days of the Winter War. We followed the road to the open top of a hill where, abruptly, we came into a new town. It consisted of no more than a score or two of buildings, single dwellings and two-story apartments, a school, a general store, a café, a gasoline station all collected around a turn in the road. The buildings looked sturdy and well-painted, set back on either side of the muddy highway. Carnations in balcony boxes were shaking the drops of a recent shower from their white and red heads, and the town's small children were making a game of riding bicycles through the chains of puddles. The girls withdrew to the sides at our approach, but the boys came to convoy us into town, for it seemed to be something of an event when a red VW bus stopped in Suomussalmi.

At the corner where the main street turned west a fine new church of white walls and dark slate corners stood alone in a well-kept garden of stone crosses. We paused a moment to see the church, for modern churches are museum pieces of Finnish architecture, but it was outside that the real story of Finland's religion was to be read: row upon row of crosses set among trees and kept with living flowers. Some of the crosses were for boys of sixteen to eighteen years, some were named only *Tuntomaton* (Unknown). There were 243 crosses in all, a large number for a commune of only a few thousand souls.

We had to hurry and make camp. Out of the west another shower was dragging the hills with rain. A sign "Camping" on a tree directed us to a grassy point beside a shallow bay where we pitched our tent and cut wood for the fire. Returning to the village for provisions we found to our dismay that the general store was locked up; we had forgotten that this was Saturday when all stores close at noon for the weekend. The coffee shop, too, was closed. However, as we stood there in the road wondering what to do in order to provision our camp for the next forty hours, a big hearty woman appeared in the door of her home at the corner of the store:

"Come on. Come on," she called, beckoning us in. We followed her through the door into the kitchen where vats of blueberries were steaming on the stove. Her husband, in his undershirt, was reading a sports journal. He nodded a welcome and stood aside as the proprietress led us through the back way into the store. There she unloaded the refrigerator, got out milk, fresh meat, sausage, cheese, and went out back to fetch loaves of bread. Ben and Bronwen she armed with a week's supply of candy. All this done in a rapid happy chatter of Finnish. There was nothing of the Helsinki formalities about this storekeeper. She went right on with her discourse even when it must have been apparent to her that we knew little of what she was saying.

When I paid our bill and tried to thank her she only laughed and said, "Anyone would know you were foreigners. Of course you should have something to eat."

I asked her whether anyone in town spoke English. She said she did not know unless it might be the garage man who had once been on ships to America. Later in the evening when the youngsters were fed and settled in the tent, Elisabeth and I returned to town to see what might be remembered of the Battle of Suomussalmi. While it was only one battle among many, it was typical, and in a way a turning point in the Winter War.

At the filling station we found the garage man drinking beer with friends and discussing a broken-down tractor. He spoke no English, he said, but perhaps the minister did, just up the road across from the church. The minister's wife, answering our inquiry in good English, said that she spoke none; the minister did, but unfortunately he was away; perhaps the Swedish teacher might know some.

We continued down the road to a new apartment where the Swedish teacher was said to live. It was embarrassing (and very un-Finnish) thus to invade a stranger's privacy and begin asking questions about a war which we in no conceivable sense had shared. But ever since the first dispatches of the Winter War, since the first photographs of that 163rd Russian division frozen in the snow, the name Suomussalmi (Scaly Straits) had stuck like a fishbone in my thoughts. I could only hope the Swedish teacher would be kind enough to overlook our intrusion.

A man answered our knock and after listening to our unusual request, smiled and took us into a simple modern living room from whose wide windows we could look out over the fields to the east. The late sun was slanting under the clouds and brightening the stubble where the hay had been mowed. Rows of haycocks cast long blue shadows, like bars of music, down to the edge of the forest. To the southeast a large lake shimmered. Except for the lakes and a scattering of farms, Suomussalmi seemed entirely alone among forested hills.

Our host, a dark-haired stocky man in his early thirties, called to his wife and introduced her. She shyly welcomed us, but left her husband to do the talking.

"The war? It was not so much, you know. Here it was bad for only a few weeks. . . ." Then he told us of how two columns of Russians had suddenly appeared, almost without warning, one coming down from Juntusranta in the north, the other along a road from the southeast. It was a strong force, numbering about 17,000 men, together with trucks and tanks and other armored vehicles. Against this force the Finns had some 800 regular troops, another battalion of reservists, and the men of the surrounding district who stayed to fight. This was on December 6, in the first week of the war, so that the Finns had had little chance to prepare any defenses. All at once the Russians were there; the town had to be evacuated and set on fire at the same time the first shells were exploding in it.

"I remember only how the street was full of shoutings," our host's wife broke in. She had been only a small girl at the time. "Men and soldiers running everywhere, carrying things, sleighs in the street, horses, people getting in and horses trying to jump away, men holding them." Someone had wrapped her in a warm coat and blanket and tossed her into a sleigh with her mother. Then the sleigh, driven by a boy of nine, had gone off down the hill to the southwest to join others crossing the watercourse and heading into the woods.

"What do you remember of all this?" I asked.

"I remember nothing," she said, "except the fires on the hill."

"Was it cold?"

"I do not remember. We saw for hours the fires."

"Where did you go?"

"To a farm in the west."

Unfortunately, her husband added, the fires did not burn enough. Some buildings could be used by the Russians for living quarters. Others of the invaders lived in their tanks, while the bulk of the soldiers encamped near the town not far from where our tent was pitched. The Finnish soldiers and the local men—a force of about 2,000 in all—crossed the straits and set up a defense position south of the town. Colonel Siilasvuo, an able and experienced soldier, expected a new attack on the following morning, but fortunately the ice on the lake, and that on the watercourse, was not yet strong enough to hold tanks and trucks. Perhaps this and cold weather saved the defenders, for the attacks were never very vigorous. The 163rd Division did not capitalize on its advantage and drive on across Finland.

A few days later Colonel Siilasvuo, reinforced by a fresh

infantry regiment, counterattacked. Leaving only machine gunners to bar the strait, he took his troops on a flanking march to cut the southeast road. Other ski troops were sent to worry the columns stalled on the north road. The counterattacks proved unexpectedly successful. Three miles of the southeast road were rolled up on the first day, and after three more days most of the Russians were either herded into the ruins of the town or surrounded on the snowy point to the west. The rest stuck to their tanks and were burned out or left to freeze.

At this moment of near victory, Colonel Siilasvuo learned that a new Russian division was advancing upon him along the southeastern road where he had left only two companies to guard the rear. But these machine gunners had taken up a strong position at a gap between two lakes. "Molotov Cocktails" broke down a few tanks and bogged down the division—it was the crack 44th Motorized Division from the Moscow district. That evening it found itself strung out for ten miles on a narrow forest track. The crawling machinery stalled and froze; men froze. Men from the wide spaces of Russia feared nothing so much as this endless overhanging dim forest; they stood in terrified herds while Finnish ski troops, who had been fighting almost steadily now for two weeks, harassed them day and night in small patrols, cut the division into sausage links, struck from the woods and vanished again.

"It was a hard fight," our host said. "We poured gasoline on the tanks. We pumped water from the lakes on them at night—anything that would kill Russians—let them freeze to blocks of ice."

At the end, in a desperate three-day convulsion, the remaining men of the two Soviet divisions broke out of Suomussalmi and fled to the northeast under a cover of planes. The three-week battle had finished in a rout.

Our host recounted these things without emotion. The Russians had attacked and they had lost. They were brave men, but not accustomed to going on skis or fighting in forests. He himself had been in on the fighting to recapture the ruined town.

"Just there, by those trees," he said, pointing from the

window, "I remember three men running, like shadows bending over, carrying pieces of a machine gun. And I knew, absolutely, that if they should not get the gun together at once, we should all be killed. I knew that, but I did not think about it. Later when I found myself lying in the snow, at the same time sweating all over, I said, 'That's funny. Minus forty degrees and I am sweating!' We stayed behind those trees in the snow for two days fighting. . . . Then, it was hard to believe that the war was real. Now, it is hard to believe it was so long ago."

Just then his wife, who had been gone for a little while, entered the room with a tray of cakes, cups, and a pot of coffee. "Good," our host said, suddenly smiling. "Please, coffee. Now we shall talk of other things."

> "Ho ho . . . listen everybody," bellows
> Hietanen, stewed on camp homebrew, "I've
> a speech to deliver. I'm a defender of
> the Fatherland. All we Finns wanted was
> to build our houses and saunas here in
> peace. . . . Hahaaaaaa. . . . Blessed are the
> woodenheads, for they shall not sink."

The Unknown Wars

Although the Winter War will always be remembered, few
people recall Finland's next two wars, the Continuation War
against Russia (1941 to 1944), and the following short war with
Germany. The questions that the second conflict with Russia
raised at the time were too difficult to answer then, and the
answers have not become much clearer since. The Winter
War was clean-cut, like the incident at Marathon, but the
second war remains shrouded in confusion and cross-purposes
even in the minds of Finns.

In place of the actual war and the events which are called
history, one is apt to remember best the incidents of fiction
which appeared in Väinö Linna's remarkable book, *The Unknown Soldier*. The people who come most clearly to mind
are, like Hietanen above, imaginary: Koskela (the taciturn
steady one, the western Finn), Lehto (the dark orphan), Lahtinen (the Red), Rokka (the Karelian), Rahikainen (the for-
ager), Lammio (officer and common enemy), Raili Kotilainen
(war maid and common woman).

These people, and many more, one remembers because they
live in a war more true to the real war than anything written
in three and a half years of news reports or official documents.
They are more true of Finnish people, trying somehow to find
a way out of impossible circumstances, than anything written
of Finns in this century. Finns often say they would have gone
mad in the second war had it not been for the funny things
that happened, and the jokes people made under the most des-

174

perate circumstances. Linna does not hide the tragedy of that war, but he makes it bearable:

HAUHIA: "What is it like to shoot a man?"
ROKKA: "I don't know. All I've ever shot were Russkis."

MAATTA: "A temporary sergeant's something even God would think too small a fish to fry."

"What is it?"
"Horse meat."
"Horse meat?"
"Yes. An old horse." Hietanen took the gristle he'd been chewing out of his mouth. "And the signs all point to a gypsy's nag. I can see the whip marks."

Linna knew war and he knew men. The son of a poor farmer, mill hand and factory worker between the wars and afterward, Linna shocked and delighted his countrymen with one of those rare books that is true not of a person or a time or a circumstance but true of a whole nation as far back or ahead as one can look. *The Unknown Soldier* is written with a savage and sardonic realism. It has no heroes, only Finnish men. If such a thing as a hero exists in the book, it is the machine-gun company. Men come, draw their rations and their rifles, take their luck. Some become good soldiers, many do not, but all have to stay and fight. In three years of futile war nearly all the original people are casualties. Only the unit survives, like the nation, to go on fighting.

Sentimentalists have criticized Linna for being too harsh on officers and women, but the reception of the book in Finland testifies to its honesty. Anyone who has seen the story dramatized in Tampere's outdoor theater, there in the woods with the tanks firing and the acrid smoke blowing through the trees, knows he has not seen a play but been flung into the midst of reality.

One reason Linna's book has tended to replace history is that nothing he wrote, nothing he could invent in his most sardonic fancy, could equal the absurdness and improbability of the war itself. Finland joined the Germans in their attack upon Russia, but it was a queer collaboration from the start: the several German divisions fighting in the north were never under Mannerheim's command; nor were the Finns under German command. After more than three years of fighting, when the *Wehrmacht* began to collapse, Finns got out of the war, made a separate peace, and, by the terms of the new treaty, had to go to war with the Germans to drive them out of Lapland.

"Whatever happens, Finland will always be on the wrong side," is a wry political aphorism in that country, but in 1941, after the eighteen months of uneasy armistice which followed the Winter War, most Finns believed they had to join Hitler's march. "One day the world will thank us for it," the idealists said, and practical people thought there was no alternative. Indeed, it is probable that Finland had to join either Germany or Russia. The conditions which led to the Winter War had not changed; the great powers were still going to use that land bridge for any strategic advantage it might offer. Other countries tried unsuccessfully to remain apart from the war: Denmark, Norway, Holland, Belgium, Bulgaria, Rumania, Jugoslavia, Greece, America. . . .

An industrial nation, Finland was far from self-sufficient. It relied heavily upon exports of wood in order to import food, fuel, chemicals, and other essentials. Finns were in no position simply to sit by wood fires and eat potatoes. Such a naïve policy would have brought severe food restrictions, danger of revolt at home, and the country would have been left without arms for its own defense. The whole desperate gamble of the Winter War would thus have been thrown away.

But in 1940 only two possible trade routes were open: with Russia and with Germany. And the stupidity of Russian diplomacy, their arrogant invasions of Finnish neutrality, their cancellation of all trade with Finland, in the end drove Finland into Hitler's arms. If any last straw was needed to tip the balance and make Finland a belligerent in the spring of 1941, it was the knowledge that a year earlier Molotov had said to Hitler: "It is the duty of the Soviet Government once and for all to decide and clear up the Finnish question." Therefore the government of Risto Ryti, under advisement from General Mannerheim, decided the best hope was to league Finland with the seemingly irresistible *Wehrmacht*. President Ryti denied that there was any formal agreement between his government and the Nazis—Finland was a "co-belligerent" not an "ally" of Germany—but the distinction won't stand examination. Effective secret plans had already been made with the Germans: three German divisions were in Finland at the time, allegedly "in transit" to and from northern Norway, but in fact close to the eastern border and ready for the jump off. The German war machine rose up out of Poland on June 22, 1941, and started east; three days later Finland went back to war with Russia.

Finns are still passionately divided about that war. Anglophiles detested Hitler and were willing to face any privations rather than collaborate with him. Others felt that Finland had a historic mission to help destroy Bolshevism, and naïvely thought that a Nazi hegemony over Europe was a promising substitute. Still others wanted merely to get back the lost territories. And some dreamed blearily of something called Greater Finland, uniting the fatherland not only with the Karelian Russians (who spoke Finnish) but with all cousins and distant kin clear to the Urals.

The summer of 1941 was a time of great optimism. Finnish arms, bolstered by German aircraft and tanks and a growing German army in the north, carried the rampant lion on the blue and white flag steadily to the east. Linna wrote thus of the majesty of conquering Finns:

It was an army whose individualism had never been equalled. Other armies may on occasion have resembled it while retreating in headlong flight, but never at any other time. Advancing and retreating, it looked like a scattered horde. In the morning the companies formed in a column, but an hour or two later they had disintegrated into separate little gangs making their way along the road in their own fashion, asking nothing of anyone and listening to no one. One man would stroll along the roadside grass in his bare feet, his boots slung across his shoulder. Another sunbathed as he marched, the upper part of his body bare, his blouse over his arm. . . .

Meanwhile the *Wehrmacht* was racing through the burning villages of the Ukraine toward Moscow, and other German armies, having invaded Estonia and Latvia, were pressing on toward Leningrad.

By late autumn the Finns had recovered all their old territories, the Isthmus, part of Ladoga, northern Karelia, and the pieces lost in the north.

"Hey, it's the old frontier!"

"We're in Russia, lads."

But Lahtinen, limping along sullenly, glowered at the others. "So we are. And we've no right to be here. We're no better than a bunch of bandits."

Hietanen was busily examining their surroundings. "There doesn't seem to be much worth stealing. . . ."

Lahtinen took a swig of water from his canteen: "You know what happens when you go poking a bear in its lair."

Then they pushed on into Russian Karelia, through the infrequent small villages, to Lake Onega and across the River Svir. Day by day the advance into Russia got tougher. Rain, snow, darkness, lack of reinforcements, lack of ammunition, lack of sleep, lack of food:

LAHTINEN: "Hunger has been turned into a tradition in Finland. . . . Our army has gone into battle half dead with hunger for six or seven hundred years, always with a bare ass showing through its rags. . . . If we had bread and decent clothes, where would the heroism be?"

All eyes turned to Lehto. He had taken out his emergency ration and was opening the meat tin with a knife.

"Don't you know that's forbidden?" demanded Hietanen.

A smile hovered on Lehto's lips. "So's killing. The Fifth Commandment, or one of them anyway. Opening a meat can is nothing when skulls are being blown open all around us."

One wonders what General Mannerheim thought, crossing the prewar border. In retrospect it seems to have been a foolish, even a fatal, step. Might the Finns later have received more lenient terms from the Russians had they stopped at the old frontier? It is doubtful. Molotov was no sentimentalist and seemed to have a personal grudge against Finland. Moreover such a move would probably have brought instant occupation of Finland by the Germans.

Yet for Mannerheim, a man with more political sense than most heads of state, the decision at the border must have been one of the most difficult in his career. Mr. Churchill had written Mannerheim weeks before urging him to find a pretext to halt his army at the old boundary . . . but little insidious words of expediency had leaked into the Finnish consciousness: "to continue is necessary if only to render harmless, in a military sense, the areas beyond the boundary." Finland became the invader.

That great and honest Finn was given little time to savor possible victory in his decision. Within a few weeks the Germans were in retreat from Moscow, and those around Leningrad were bogged down for the winter. America had just come into the war. A nagging doubt hovered in Mannerheim's mind and found its way into his journal—a Christmas doubt that became a premonition of the doom which was to be fulfilled fifteen months later at Stalingrad.

At the same time, before the turn of the year when the new war was only six months old, the first "peace feelers" came from Russia. Then the fronts stabilized for two years in a kind of trench warfare. After the summer of 1942 it became clear that Germany might not defeat Russia, and in 1943 eventual German defeat began to look probable, even to plain Finnish soldiers camped on the Svir.

For two years President Risto Ryti tried to extricate his country from this war. It was a hopeless strategy. Finland was no less dependent upon Germany than before; her need for arms and supplies could only get worse as Germany began to fall apart. Russia, now sensing victory, lost interest in talking peace terms with Finland. By the summer of 1944 the Soviet armies were rolling out of the east, Normandy had been invaded, and Italy and southern France. Nazi Germany was dying, although her death throes would go on for almost another year.

In the north: retreat. Back from the Svir, back across Russian Karelia, back from Ladoga, back behind the old frontiers of Finland, back to the last frontiers, after three years of war back to the starting point. On the Isthmus alone, under a canopy of bombers, 30 new divisions and thousands of tanks rolled toward the gates of Viborg. By Mannerheim's calculation the concentration of artillery fire used on the Isthmus was nearly double that employed at Stalingrad. As in the Winter War the small Finnish army stood almost alone; the subjugation of their country again seemed but a matter of weeks. There was both expiation and self-discovery at that moment. Linna writes:

> Hietanen never exhorted. He merely slung his tommy gun over his shoulder and went on, and the others followed. But as the days passed he seemed to grow visibly older and gloomier. And with his gloominess his courage also grew. . . .
>
> His was not the care of any good officer for the morale of his men. It was the reaction of a man who in the face of defeat realizes that the patriotism he had formerly regarded so lightly was actually an integral part of his attitude toward life and that to strike at it was to strike at the very roots of his being. The man in him had let the boy be gay and carefree while everything went well, but in defeat came forth to shoulder the burden.

Yet before final collapse an ingenious scheme and an accident combined to save Finland. The scheme, which provided a kind of legalistic framework for armistice, was as simple-minded as it was unorthodox. Finland desperately needed food, troops, arms and antitank guns from Germany in order to stop Russia and force her to negotiate. Germany was unwilling to supply Finland without a clear and written guarantee that no separate peace would be made. In this impossible trap, according to the plan, President Ryti would send a personal letter to Hitler, assuring him that neither he nor his government would ever make peace with Russia; then when the shipments of arms and the soldiers were safely in Finland, when the Russian forces were momentarily halted, Ryti would resign "for reasons of health" and the new President (Mannerheim), being "not bound" by the promises of a former government, would negotiate and accept any reasonable terms.

This fantastic ruse actually worked.

And now a lucky accident played into the hands of Finnish diplomats—the accident that far to the south, across France, Allied armies were moving toward Germany with unexpected speed. (A temporary Finland, Stalin thought, was indeed too small a fish to fry.) Crack Russian troops, artillery, and armor, poised for the final dash across Finland, were suddenly pulled out and sent to Germany. According to a story told in Helsinki, when the Russian commander-in-chief on the Isthmus protested giving up so easy a victory, Stalin fixed him with his eye and said: "Berlin is important. Helsinki not."

Thus in early September, 1944, for the second time in five years, peace and a harsh armistice came to the men of the swamps.

Mess tins hung over campfires as Mielonen strode along the road shouting: "Anyone who wants can come to the Command Post to hear the broadcast. A minister'll be spouting."

The men were lying on the roadside, some asleep, others brewing ersatz coffee. "Who cares . . . When your powder's all gone it's better to keep your mouth shut . . ."

A solitary cart came along the road, the clumping of its wheels echoing among the pines. The load it bore was covered with tent canvas, but protruding from beneath it was a stiffened arm terminating in a clenched fist. The last dead were journeying homeward.

Deep in the forest Lieutenant Jalovaara sat dejectedly on a stump. . . . He buried his face in his hands . . . these were good men. The autumn sun warmed the ground and the men sleeping on it, lingonberry plants glistened in the sunlight. . . .

President Mannerheim knew that Finland's defection would not be taken magnanimously by the madman in Berlin. Yet he hoped to avoid further useless bloodshed, and so, on the eve of that still secret armistice with Russia, he wrote a personal letter to Hitler, saying what both necessity and honor required him to declare:

> . . . the salvation of my nation makes it my duty to find a means of ending the war. Germany will live on even if fate should not crown your arms with victory. Nobody could give such assurances regarding Finland. If that nation of barely four millions be militarily defeated, there can be little doubt that all will be driven into exile or exterminated.

To this appeal the Germans replied with fire.

Molotov's terms were calculated to be barely acceptable: Finland was to give up all the lands taken back and more besides, including the rich nickel mines of Petsamo and the Petsamo arm reaching to the Arctic Sea; it guaranteed to pay $300,000,000 (in goods it did not have from factories which did not exist) over a seven-year period; and it undertook to drive out or intern all German troops within two and a half months.

To supervise the carrying out of the armistice, the "Allies" (the Russians) were to maintain a large Control Commission in Helsinki. At the same time the Red Army was to take over the Porkkala peninsula on the south coast of Finland.

Mannerheim's first task therefore was to quarantine the German divisions in the north, some 200,000 seasoned and embittered veterans—yesterday's brothers in arms, today the enemy. No crazier task was ever set a defeated Hercules to perform in the stables of the great, for, according to the armistice, Mannerheim at the same time was required to demobilize and disband his army!

If President Mannerheim feared the Germans in the north, he feared as much the possibility of rebellion by his own soldiers. It was not a question of disloyalty among Finns, or of any sentimental attachment to the Germans, but just that this sudden topsy-turvy turn of events coming on top of four years of futile war and the hopelessness of the peace terms might prove too much for simple soldiers to endure.

Yet no revolt occurred. The Finnish soldier, however truculent he might be and openly scornful of officers, remains a Finn, conservative, law-abiding, and clannish. The soldiers stuck together; some instinct for survival united them, in contrast to the suicidal twilight which seemed to beckon their recent Teutonic partners. The demobilizing army turned its arms upon the enraged Germans; they brought in fresh young recruits; they made a surprise Anzio-type attack at the northern Baltic port of Tornio. In the end the Finns drove the German forces into the mountains around Norway where they remained until the end of the European conflict.

It was a short fierce campaign. Finns paid for it with 40,000 new casualties and by having to watch Lapland put systematically to the torch. Farms, villages, the city of Rovaniemi, churches, schools, hotels, bridges, hospitals, factories throughout this sparsely populated area were blown up or burned up by the Germans in their vengeful slog into Norway.

Perhaps the very excesses of the Germans were a kind of blessing, inspiring the Finns to be rid of these people as quickly as possible. Germans have claimed that their scorched-earth policy in Lapland was a military necessity: they feared attack by Russian troops. But there were no Russian troops in northern Finland. Nor was the burning of Lapland any different from what the German people themselves suffered when the fronts caved in and the Reich of a Thousand Years hastened to its inglorious *dämmerung*.

"What is going to happen to us?"
"The battalion, you mean?"
"No, all of us. The whole of Finland."
"What always happens to losers. We'll have
Ivan's fist stuffed down our throats."

—VÄINÖ LINNA

Years of Danger

Two wars with the Soviets were not the worst trials the
Finns had to endure. The immediate postwar years took more
courage, and stamina, and even more luck than the years of
war. From 1944 to 1946, war reparations were heaped on top
of domestic dislocations, Communists were riding in police
cars, and the whole foundation of Finnish independence was
shaky with repeated attempts at subversion. The enemy across
barbed wire can be seen and faced, but no one knows the
enemy within. For this period Finns reserve the special title:
the Years of Danger.

The conditions of the armistice of September, 1944, seen
against subsequent events, leave little room for doubt that they
were to be anything but temporary expedients. They would
serve to put the "Finnish Question" on ice while more important business was being settled in Germany. The provisions
of the treaty look ingenious—just soft enough for Finns to
accept, yet hard enough to be impossible.

The Kremlin, in effect, prepared three plans it could acti-
vate almost at will. If the Finns failed to keep strictly to the
agreement then a "breach of the treaty" could be claimed and
"appropriate action" taken. If by some miracle the treaty was
fulfilled, then civil strife had only to be fomented among the
impoverished and angry populace, touched off when needed
by the large and disciplined Communist party. Any effort by
the government to control the rioting would be labeled the
work of "reactionary fascist elements" and Mr. Molotov

would have to intervene, reluctantly, to "restore order." If neither of these schemes worked there was still another method: the take-over, in the style worked out for Czechoslovakia.

In 1944, '45, or '46 the surviving countries of the West, sick of wars and crawling from the rubble of their own cities, would be unlikely seriously to oppose Russia in any one of these moves. Finland was too far away and too small—a brave little country but perversely on the wrong side of victory.

Molotov had his instrument in Helsinki, a fist of a man called General Zhdanov. He with his ninety-man Russian delegation (the Control Commission) moved into the Torni Hotel to oversee the armistice. Meanwhile, Russian troops illegally occupied strategic areas inside the eastern and northern boundaries, and the principal Russian base in Finland was moved from Hanko to Porkkala, some forty miles west of Helsinki.

The first job for the Torni shadow government was to see that the right people took control of the ministries of Interior, Justice, State Police. The Finnish Communist party, underground since the thirties, was returned to legal status, and its chairman made deputy chief of the police. Political prisoners were released from jail, and many of them found their way into office or into the new mobile police. Following the first parliamentary elections, Yrjö Leino, a prominent Communist, was given the Ministry of Interior.

At the same time the Control Commission supervised the agreed dissolution of patriotic clubs and associations (any groups which might provide an organized opposition to the Communist-controlled police). Several hundred organizations, lumped together as "Fascist-type," were legally dissolved, though the purge went far beyond potential Fascists to include the Finnish Veterans' Association, and the Women's Army Auxiliary.

A public circus was also demanded—a trial to punish "war criminals," or, as the Russians preferred to call them, the "war responsibles." That is: members of the government of the defeated country. Trial and punishment had been agreed to in the articles of armistice, and yet it was plainly contrary to both the letter and the spirit of Finnish law. It was, in fact, illegal on three counts: 1) members of the government had held their offices properly according to the constitution; 2) there was no court empowered to try such defendants, and the constitution made no provision for setting up any special court for such purpose; 3) no retroactive or *ex post facto* law could legally be passed by which the defendants could be made guilty. President Mannerheim consulted the best legal mind in the country, Professor K. J. Stålberg, author of the Finnish constitution and first President of the Republic. Judge Stålberg declared that such a trial was impossible.

Since the trial was illegal, impossible, and necessary, the Finns quietly set about the business: Parliament passed a retroactive law, a special court was convened, and a three-month trial was carried out with all the mock-seriousness that the monkey court required. Twelve men, ranging from ex-President Risto Ryti on down to the Minister of Finance, Väinö Tanner, were tried and sentenced to a total of thirty-eight and a half years. The final remarks of Ryti, given ten years at hard labor, must have been a steadying force among his countrymen and a reminder to soldiers that ministers occasionally do more than spout:

"When it comes to serving the fatherland, the place is not important but the will. It can be done as well in prison as in the President's Palace."

But of all the difficult tasks expected of Finns during the Years of Danger, none took so much good sense and dogged endurance as did the work of paying the War Debt. The agreement had specified $300,000,000 worth of "goods"; later instructions defined that amount as based on 1938 values, and this provision virtually doubled the debt. Moreover the new instructions provided that 60 per cent of the goods were to be from "metal industries"—ships, machinery, wire rope, instruments, machine tools, copper products, et cetera. Some of these industries were small home industries in Finland; others did not yet exist. According to the agreement, interest at 3.5 per cent per month was to be charged for all late deliveries.

Thus all at once the country had to expand her old plants

and build new ones, buy raw materials and machinery abroad, and train a new labor force. With most of Europe still at war, loans and materials were not easy to come by. Here Sweden came generously to Finland's aid. (On top of these economic problems were the dislocations left from the war. Half a million refugees from Karelia had to be settled in new homes and jobs. Another 50,000 had been turned out and burned out by the Germans in Lapland. The country, through lands ceded and factories destroyed, had lost 13 per cent of its productive capacity; 7 per cent of the nation's manpower had been killed or permanently disabled.)

It was against this background that President Mannerheim and Prime Minister Paasikivi set to work reconstructing the country and paying the war debts. It was against this background, doubtless, that the Torni shadow government and its agents in the state police expected riots and uprisings which would justify intervention by the Red Army. Yet the disorders did not come. The work went on, not by blind faith or exhortations, but by a clear insight that there was one chance for Finns, and one chance only.

In the first year, according to Mannerheim's calculation, Finland shipped 80 per cent of her exports (roughly 10 per cent of her total productivity) directly to Russia as war reparations. Delayed deliveries cost her an additional $200,000 in goods. From then on, year by year, with growing confidence of success, the Finns made their payments and suffered without serious unrest the restrictions on housing, food, and consumer goods which the war debt imposed. Large land holdings, estates, unused properties, and government-held acreage were broken up to settle the new populations; housing was rigidly held to one room per person; hospital care and rehabilitation for wounded and disabled men was established with the help of generous gifts from abroad; and the extensive social programs pushed by the Communists and trade unionists (which would have bankrupted the country) were held in check by the Prime Minister. Though Finns suffered a 400-per-cent inflation during the next half decade, they succeeded in keeping Finland free.

Mannerheim, ailing in health, retired in March, 1946. The

great task he had set himself after the retirement of President Ryti—to take his country out of war and to guide it through the first postwar years—had been fulfilled. His Prime Minister, J. K. Paasikivi was elected to succeed him. Paasikivi had been influential in Finland since the first days of the republic and was a man with an almost uncanny skill in handling Russians.

It was inevitable, in the days when Russia was building up its satellite empire—Rumania, Bulgaria, Hungary, Poland, East Germany, Yugoslavia, Albania—that it should seek to incorporate Finland. Early in 1948, three days after the *coup d'état* which carried Czechoslovakia into the Soviet system, Premier Stalin wrote to President Paasikivi requesting talks about "a Treaty of Mutual Assistance." If the timing of this request was brutally frank, so was the suggestion that the treaties with Hungary and Rumania might serve as models.

This was a summons, 1939 all over again, and no one doubted but that, beneath the legal language, it portended the final Estoniaization of Finland. According to Austin Goodrich, in his book *Sisu*: "Anyone with a sense of the continuity of history shudders at the implications of this invitation. . . . Tension mounted, became unendurable for thousands of Finns who (considering themselves marked men) crossed the frozen Torni River under cover of darkness to seek refuge in Sweden."

Paasikivi, with the face of a poker player and the same attention to detail, sent off a delegation of five, headed by his Prime Minister. They had careful written instructions and were to go slow. However, accident once again may have intervened to save Finland: the accident this time was the violent reactions in the western world to the take-over in Czechoslovakia. (Stalin was pushing the world rapidly into the cold war, but at the time of these negotiations Russia was still six months away from exploding its first experimental atomic bomb.) In any case the demands presented by the Kremlin to the Finnish delegation were suddenly moderated and the pacts with Hungary and Rumania no longer held up as models.

In April, a pact of Friendship, Co-operation, and Mutual Assistance was signed. Contrary to fears in Finland and suspicions abroad, the pact did little more than recognize on paper the facts of the postwar world: that co-operation and development of cultural and economic relations between Finland and the Soviet Union would be mutually advantageous; that Finland would neither ally herself with, nor allow herself to be occupied by, a force hostile to the USSR; and that in return for these assurances, Russia would guarantee the integrity of Finland and pledge noninterference in Finland's internal affairs.

Geography had already said as much—geography together with the endless failures of Scandinavian countries ever to form an alliance or union stronger than belated declarations of sympathy. Finland, now, was neither of the East nor of the West, but something special, unique, and quite alone.

But there are other ways to skin a skinny lion: when open negotiation and a pact will not bring in the pelt, subversion is still good Leninist strategy.

While polite ceremonies were taking place in the Kremlin over the pact of Friendship, Co-operation, and Mutual Assistance, another scheme was under way in Helsinki, a Prague-type *coup* planned for just this period of negotiation. The time was ripe. The Finnish army was just then shifting from one conscript class to another, so the country would be virtually defenseless; the State Police were infiltrated with Communists and sympathizers; the Mobile Police were almost a law unto themselves; and the Minister of Interior, Yrjö Leino, husband of the Communist Party's most effective voice in Parliament, was one of the five men sent to Moscow for the deliberations.

Whether the Control Commission or Mr. Molotov had any part in the plot, of course, will never be documented, and Leino's subsequent autobiography has been suppressed. Yet the evidence is strong that upon a minimum of well-planned disorder, the police, heavily armed with automatic weapons, were to take over key posts and ministries, and, backed by the Red Army from Porkkala, to declare and set up a new Finnish Government.

Something went wrong. Austin Goodrich, quoting from the few documents that exist, suggests that at the last moment Yrjö Leino, the man chosen to lead the new satellite government, found he could not do it. In the quiet of his conscience he suddenly came to the realization that he was a Finn first, a Communist second. Even as a lifelong anti-Finn, he was more Finn than Soviet agent. Leino tipped off General Sihvo, Commander of the Defense Forces. Sihvo called back the reservists from terminal leave, special guards and tanks were deployed around Helsinki, the Mobile Police were denied access to weapons supplies . . . "and Police Chief Gabrielsson in a surprise move ordered the transfer of all extra police arms, including a formidable stock of machine pistols, from the vulnerable precinct stations to a huge bomb shelter vault." With the sardonic humor of a true Finn, Chief Gabrielsson chose for his cache of arms the basement of the great white church, Finland's Lutheran Cathedral. The *coup* came to nothing.

Leino escaped with his life. He was forced to resign from the government; his wife, Hertta Kuusinen (daughter of Otto Kuusinen, head of Terijoki-Finland during the Winter War) divorced him; the party expelled him. Unlike President Ryti, he had no jail to go to, nor any job—yet Leino, too, was a kind of Finnish hero at the end.

Hertta Kuusinen, born with a silver fork in her mouth, tried once more to recoup the lost plot during the July elections of that year. But her slogan "Czechoslovakia is our way" only earned the party a loss of 13 seats in Parliament, the worst reverse in any postwar election.

Still another unskillful last-ditch effort to take over Finland was attempted in August, 1948, but by now the act had become something of a musical comedy. The cool Gabrielsson knew the script and rang down the curtain. That was the end. Times were changing. After 1948, Finnish-Soviet relations steadily improved, and Mr. Molotov had to accept that the Finnish Question was one that might never be settled once and for all.

The reasons for the reversal in Kremlin policy are not clear. After the *Putsch* in Czechoslovakia, the risk of general war from the subversion of small countries certainly increased. It may be, too, that Sweden let it be known in Moscow that conquest of Finland, under whatever legal guise, would force Sweden into the developing NATO alliance. Russian scientists were preparing to test their first atomic explosion in the open.

This was bound to bring about so radical a change in the military plans of Washington that perhaps Stalin reconsidered, after the defection of Leino, and decided he did not want to risk a general war over Finland.

Or it may be that the simplest and most sensible policy finally filtered through to the consciousness of Russians: that a productive and peaceful Finland, little by little incorporated into the Soviet economic empire, was preferable both in fact and in propaganda value to a sullen and spiny satellite.

For whatever reasons, the Years of Danger were over. Russia allowed an extension of time in the payment of the war debts, and toward the end forgave some of the payments altogether. In 1952, Finland settled its accounts and turned to celebrate a long-deserved holiday by holding the Olympic Games in the beautiful stadium built for that purpose just prior to World War II. Since 1952 the Finns have built apartments, hospitals, schools, industries at such an astounding rate that people seem in some ways better off in Helsinki now than in Stockholm, Oslo, or Copenhagen.

Russia has not, of course, kept strictly to "non-intervention in internal affairs." The annual trade negotiations provide an effective lever to direct both the economic and political life of Finland. Governments have fallen in Finland because the Neighbor across the spruce wall didn't like the look of the ministers. Economic squeezes have been put on, once to the point of stopping all trade until the "reactionary elements" (*i.e.*, pro-Western Socialists) in the Finnish Government were removed. Such pressures will be used again. Finns know all this; it is a condition of life. Yet they do not consider their independence a sham merely because it is not unlimited.

Lapland

After breaking camp and leaving Suomussalmi, we continued north on roads that wound comfortably through the dales and over the sandy morains. There was little sign of the war here any more. Now and then we passed by a wide hillside that had been hastily cut over, leaving the larger trees standing about twelve feet high as a possible barrier for small tanks and other vehicles. Elsewhere, whole ridges had been cut clean, but these represented the heavy logging of the postwar debt years where many seasons of growth had had to be sacrificed. Even now these butchered hillsides were losing their raw identity under new stands of birch and pine. We were on the Juntusranta road where the 163rd Soviet division had blundered down to Suomussalmi.

The rain had passed, leaving the forest humid under an intense high sun. Water brimmed in the ditches, the air sang with insects, bugs came steaming from the moist blueberry turf as though suddenly struck with the shortness of summer. Here and there we passed hillside farms washed clean by the rain and all the laundry celebrating on a tossing line. Where the road ambled over a knoll, we could look out far to the north, east, west, upon succeeding ridges and long lakes. Only wilderness ahead. We were within a few miles of the border between Russia and Finland, but there was little to show that the line ever really existed: the trees and hills recognized no such distinctions.

After passing the village of Juntusranta we got off on a

wrong track. A narrow stony road hemmed in by deep ditches led us up over several ridges, and then suddenly we came into a clearing where the road was blocked by a simple wooden barricade. A dilapidated circular iron sign hung from the barrier proclaiming *National boundary 1 Km. Forbidden.* No guards or people were in sight.

"Is that Russia?" Ben asked. "That doesn't look like so much."

"It's over there beyond the woods, one kilometer," I said.

"What did they stick that log across for then?"

"To give Saturday night Finns time to slow down."

Nearby in the woods we discovered a group of buildings, some sort of an outpost. The place seemed to be deserted and since it was the easiest way to turn the car around we ran ahead into the square or parade ground around which the yellow wooden buildings were arranged. And then we saw that the outpost was in use. A man was sitting on the steps in front of one of the buildings, whittling on a piece of wood with his sheath knife. There was nothing military about him except his high boots. He did not raise his head as we drove in, or interrupt his methodical work with the knife. I backed the car around, feeling a little foolish to be here, and just then a young soldier appeared in one of the doors. He stepped out on the sunny wooden veranda, smiling pleasantly and buttoning up his grey battle jacket. Behind him came a buxom woman with rolled-up sleeves.

I stopped: a foreigner didn't just go joyriding into an encampment of Finnish soldiers and whiz right out the other side.

"Go and talk to him, Bronwen," I said, she being our best Finn.

"But what'll I say?"

"Just tell him something, anything, so he won't think we're crazy."

"I don't know how to say that!" she squeaked.

"Oh, I will," Ben said with masculine assurance. Ben and I got out of the car and approached the waiting soldier.

"*Terve!*" said the barefoot boy, hitching up his jeans. He used the familiar greeting, reserved for old friends.

"*Terve*," the young man grinned.

"What is heard?"

"Nothing much. . . . Germans?"

"Americans."

"Welcome," said the soldier.

"My father"—with a patronizing nod toward me—"said he wanted to see the Finnish army."

"Well . . ."—momentarily stiffening to attention—"here I am."

They had a good laugh over that. Then Ben explained that we were driving north to Lapland, had taken the wrong road and come to the border. The soldier made a sweeping gesture over the forest to the east and said it was not a good idea to go any farther. "*Russkis*," he said with a shrug, "you never know . . ."

Ben had been admiring the green lapel markings on the young man's blouse. They looked very colorful and military.

"Are you a captain or a lieutenant or what?" he asked.

"Him?" shouted the woman behind, bursting into a guffaw and belting the soldier on the back. "*Voi, voi*, that's just a plain ordinary soldier."

The young man was equal to this attack. Over his shoulder he made some satirical reference to camp girls. They both laughed, and that was the end of our interview. There was nothing militaristic about this young man. He was a conscript putting in his nine months of military service before going back to farm or job or University. (By the terms of the Peace Treaty with Russia, Finland may have only about 40,000 men under arms. Those who go on to officers' training, or those in the specialized branches have to do a few months more. But the period is not so long as to disrupt a young man's career, and all men, without exception, must serve. It seemed a very just and sensible system.)

The soldier gave us a friendly "*Näkemiin*" as we drove away, and the whittler stopped his knife work long enough to watch us go; then we were back on the road to Juntusranta, and later the road to the north.

Lapland is not a place but an environment. Its borders blend imperceptibly into the richer more populous regions to the

194

south. You don't know for sure when you arrive in Lapland, though the first herd of reindeer loping through the woods will serve for a marker better than the arctic circle or the midnight sun. In the Kuusamo area you begin to feel the change. In spite of the vacationers from the south and the visitors from many parts of central Europe, in spite of the shops, gas stations, and rooming houses of this most famous of Finland's National Parks, you sense that here nature is quietly in charge. The distractions of the human race produce only excrescences among the tremendous forces always at work here. The hills struggle into low rocky mountains where the trees thin out and leave the crests bare granite. The special name *tunturi* comes to be used in place of hill or ridge or esker. Great rivers, greater than any others in Finland, flow west and southwest to the Gulf of Bothnia, their yellow saw logs looking no larger than straws on the broad streams.

Now for the first time in Finland you can see ahead. Trees no longer hem you in. From the top of a ridge you can see the dirt road in front of you as a narrowing lavender ribbon running down into a wide forested valley. Somewhere in the distance it leads toward the blue cones of *tunturis* twenty or thirty miles away. The sweep is Lapland: in all this area, occupying the northern half of Finland, there are fewer than 200,000 people. What the ice left in rounded granite, twenty thousand summers have softened into an immense peace.

Here blueberry bushes grow in the forests as well as on the bare hillsides, the berries as big as grapes. Sometimes they grow so thick that a brilliant blue smoke seems to be rising from the leafy earth. In other places the pale green rubbery reindeer moss covers the forest floor so far and wide that you wonder whether you are walking abroad in full moonlight. In the fields cool daisies swing in the wind and beside the road the fireweed grows like hot pokers.

Gradually as you go north you see the land change: after Kuusamo with its abrupt hills, defiles, and white-water streams, the land subsides into the great valleys of the Kemi, Ounas, and Tornio Rivers; then the land climbs slowly toward the mountains that form the border between Norway and Finland. In the far north is a new lakeland, Inari's archipelago, a small Saimaa, where the water flows to the arctic sea. Some few hundred Lapp families live here the year round. Lake Inari, the midnight sun, and the salmon fishing attract tourists in summer. A few skiers come in winter. But the land looks not long from under the ice, and the threat of ice always hangs in the pale blue sky.

The trees, too, gradually change: the spruces thin out, demanding more room; they hold their branches close and dense, grow tall and spear-pointed. On rocky knolls the yellow-barked Norway pines straggle out to a few gaunt determined giants who with bent arms and bunched needles have learned to stand against the long snow. Birches even better show the slim margin of survival; dwarfed and crooked, like ancient apple trees, they climb the sides of *tunturis*, and then suddenly vanish leaving the mountain as bare as the hull of a ship above waterline.

There is little here to keep people. Though tourists annually discover Lapland, Lapland scarcely notices their presence. Farms are few, hotels but a handful. The reindeer herds are still the basis of the spare economy. There are fish in the streams, berries in the forest, and the short hot summers grow the sweetest potatoes in Finland. But there is little else. Some work on the roads and on new power plants in Russian-held Lapland; some copper and iron mining. On the Lemmenjoki a little yellow metal is still panned, not much more than on that New Hampshire farm Robert Frost described:

> But not gold in commercial quantities,
> Just enough gold to make the engagement rings
> And marriage rings of those who owned the farm.

But Lapland has scarcely changed in ten thousand years. One goes there as a guest of the summer sun with a sense of trespassing upon a form of life so slow in its rhythms, so eternal in its purposes, as to be beyond comprehension. Glacial ages are building these open walls, the spring thaws paving these wide floors. Time does not tick to days and nights but to the year-hands of the solstice.

No wonder, then, that on August evenings the Lapland man is apt to withdraw to a rocky bluff above a lake or stream to light a small fire and watch the colors change. He may fish awhile in a pale-star lake, or hang a small black pot from a forked stick over the fire and lounge and wait for the smell of simmering coffee. Darkness does not come, only a pearly twilight. At midnight the forest green is suffused with purple-black, the water quiets into lavender, the fire burns redder. Out there in the sky the color is sedimenting down into definite layers of light so pure and intense as not to be believed by eyes trained in temperate zones: a smoky crimson burning over the hills, a band of lemon yellow above it, next a band of apple green, then the whole firmament a radiant ultramarine. While the man sits on his rock, the sun circumluminates the pole, dusk blends into dawn, yesterday becomes tomorrow.

In our short time we could see but a small part of Lapland, some of the long empty gravel roads, the new city of Rovaniemi, a few wind-blown mountain tops. By day we fed upon berries, by night the mosquitos fed upon us. At Kittelä we looked across twenty miles of swamp to the arches of the Ylläs range where we had skied at Easter. Ben and Bronwen felt very much at home again, seeing Yllästunturi. To me the area looked like northern Wisconsin or Michigan or Quebec, and something of upland Colorado, too, where the pines grow cool on rocky knolls.

Often we were hailed by squads of hitchhikers—always young Germans. You could tell them half a kilometer away by their grease-proofed leather shorts and their ostentatious rucksacks. They were friendly young people. They wore sandals on their feet, and didn't intend to hike very far. Some had come to Finland to visit pen pals; some to see the places their fathers talked about; but many came, tired of the wrangle and congestion of Central Europe. Finland, they said, was one of the few wild places left in the world.

We met no Finnish hitchhikers. Young Finns were camping and tramping through Lapland, but a Finn goes light, with a small knapsack, and he goes under his own power. He will not turn to examine an approaching car. He is accustomed to going his own way, asking no help and expecting none, and he is incapable of humbling himself to his thumb.

The people of the north, living on a frontier, are generally a happy talkative democratic race, full of curiosity about other people and having none of the Helsinki inhibitions. One day we stopped at a *Kahvila* in a small border village, the only place in the area where we could obtain coffee and a bite to eat. This simple roadside establishment served as a kind of social center for the region. Several tables were occupied by sharp-faced tousled men taking their nooning over bottles of a dark liquid called Beer No. 1. They were smoking, playing cards, and joshing a prim young waitress who seemed to be running the place singlehanded.

We ordered *pihvi*, hamburgers in brown gravy. (Potatoes come without asking.) No sooner had the dishes arrived than the waitress supplied me with a large bottle of Beer No. 1.

"I did not order that," I said.

"That man over there," she replied, indicating a man at the far end of the room whose gold-toothed smile shone across to us like the beam from a lighthouse. I raised my glass to him, and he to me; then I drank the stuff, a vile prohibitionist's decoction, like crankcase oil only not so smooth. Then presently my benefactor wandered over to our table. I offered him a cigarette. He took the pack with a bow and with care and deliberation extracted one of the cigarettes. He sat down to chat, letting the smoke eddy around one squinting eye while he talked.

"Germans?"

"No, Americans. Thanks for the beer."

"It is nothing. But the *bussi*, it is German."

"Yes. We have a big family. One hundred children."

"Ohho!" He relayed this information over his shoulder to his friends across the room. In a short time they too had joined us to hear where we came from, where we lived, how we liked Finland. We spoke a mixture of German and Finnish which served well enough; they had picked up German during the war. . . . Yes, there were many Germans in Lapland during the war, they said. Up here more Germans than Finns. Good soldiers, too; very good soldiers. Tough. But in summer only; not so good in winter. Germans were not to deep snow and forests accustomed, it had to be said. But tough. Very hard men. Also like Russians who were good soldiers but afraid of the forest. . . . But, none were so good as the Finnish *poikas*, of course. That much one had to say. Finnish boys were the best . . . wasn't it true? Always. The best. . . .

And with that, laughing and shouting as though what Finnish *poikas* could do was a big joke, but also true, they slapped Ben on the back, shook hands all around, and went out the door. We could hear them bedeviling a dog in the road as they started back to work. High spirits and generous impulses seemed to bubble in these people like spring sap. Laplanders always surprised us, for they seemed so different from southern Finns.

Of the original natives, the Lapps, we saw almost nothing. They are the true recluses. Some 2,500 Lapps live in northern Finland, but all one will see are occasional families camped by the side of the road. These are the Tourist Lapps, corrupted by money, who set up their teepees and squat grinning in all their finery for photographs, and who sell trinkets of birchbark and reindeer skin for a meager living.

The true Lapp is a loner. He winters on a little farm as far away from other families as he can get; in summer he roves with his tent and his herd on the grassy fjellsides above timberline. He is a throwback to the stone age and he likes it that way. It is this race to which Tacitus refers when he speaks of the people of Fen-land. In those days the Lapps lived in the south. But when the first quarrelsome Finns came over from Estonia, the shy Lapps migrated north. The race now numbers some 30,000 in northern Norway, Sweden, Finland, and Russian Lapland. Of forests, lakes, fjells, reindeer the Lapp understands everything; only recently has he been persuaded to accept the illogic of political boundaries.

The Lapp is generally slender, short, black-haired and black-eyed—though occasionally you see one with shocking blue eyes. Often he is squat and bowlegged, perhaps the result of rickets acquired in the long nights of the north. According to a deep-rooted suspicion, as shown in western folklore and literature, Lapps are thought to be in league with the powers of magic. Knut Hamsun's northern pioneers felt that the very passing by of a smiling Lapp was an omen of evil so great that no amount of hard work and watchfulness could overcome it.

A more modern opinion would say that Lapps are the true

children of nature. Surely it is childlike to favor growing things over an accumulation of material effects, to live by preference in a teepee on the fjells, and see security a herd of reindeer. These are a different people. The excellent books about them by men like Yrjö Kokko, written without illusion or sentimentality, only make their strangeness more strange.

We didn't try to seek out the Lapps. Our time in the north was much too short to gain anything but false impressions. Besides, these people had earned their right to privacy. Who more so than a people who believe that when you break camp on a river bend or lakeside, you should leave it looking as though no one had ever been there?

The lordly sun was already two months out on its journey to the south when, at the end of August, we returned to Helsinki. Lauttasaari looked full of summer still. Barelegged children were racing on the yellow sands and the statuesque sails of sloops were gliding by on the pale blue Baltic sea. Ben and Bronwen joined their friends in games of baseball and jump rope as though only a noon hour had passed since our departure for Kaunissaari.

Yet our world had changed somewhat. Some Finn, unheard of before, had gone south and startled the newspapers by showing up as the best pole vaulter in Europe. The parks and back yards of Lauttasaari were suddenly full of leggy towheads lofting themselves like octopuses into the unfamiliar air.

And over the water from Berlin came the crash of sledges, the bark of orders, the rip of machine guns. We had no idea what all this would mean—we hadn't even heard about it in Lapland—but Germans were at it again, this time building a wall.

Part Three

ROBERT FROST: I think about you sometimes, worry about you a little—small country like that—how you're getting on, what the future's likely to be.

FINNISH FRIEND: We don't think about it. Only big nations can talk about the future. We do our work, take care of our families, but we don't worry about the future.

Indian Summer

For the children it was the beginning of another school year, one which would go quickly and even smoothly. But for Elisabeth and me the time was bound to be a sequence of last times. In nine months we would pack up our household and leave. Whatever happened—the long autumnal dragging into darkness, the denuding of the birches, the opening night at the National Theater, snow, ice, the icebreakers in the harbor, the breakup in spring—whatever happened would happen to us for the last time.

Kim was back with her class at the Zilliacus School where, she was secretly proud to note, the teachers still complained that she spoke Swedish with "a horrible Norwegian accent." Wendy was in school in Norway. Ben, his hair slicked down for the first time in three months and his feet suddenly huge with new shoes, was bussing across town to the Steiner School.

"It's a great school," Ben exulted after the first day. "No books." Questioned on this point, he clarified the matter: "Well—anyway the teacher says we're supposed to have fun in school. That's right, too. We're going to make our own books."

Bronwen was the only one of the family going to the Lauttasaari folk school. She missed the protection of her older brother on the first day of classes and asked if we would go with her. In the cool summer sunshine we walked through the woods under Windmill Hill, passed the church, then down the slope toward the mass of yelling, running figures collected outside the yellow brick buildings. Combed and curried, decked out in her best Finnish dress and mud-colored stockings, Bronwen suddenly felt embarrassed to be seen with her foreign parents. "That's far enough," she said. "G'bye."

Bron went on down the path and crossed the road—a willowy little girl who had forgotten that at this very spot a year ago some blustering protector of the public health had routed her with a broomstick and chased her into the woods. Bronwen was returning to her class under Mrs. Laitinen, for it is the sensible Finnish policy to have one teacher stay with her beginning class through the first three years. Bron slowed down as she approached the schoolyard. Headlong games of tag and soccer were in progress there, and boys and girls were lining up on logs for a game much like Indian Wrestling. Bron stopped, listening to the piercing Finnish voices from an upheaval of children. And then from the mass in the schoolyard, two little girls came skipping, each putting an arm around Bron to welcome her back.

Elisabeth wiped her nose with a handkerchief: a year ago she had sniffled because Ben "looked so lost," now she did the same because Bronwen was so found.

It may well be that no nation can be greater than its elementary school teachers, and in Finland one can only speak of them with admiration bordering on love. They seem to know by training everything that can be taught in up-to-date teachers' colleges, and they seem to know by heart all that can't be taught. Reading, writing, arithmetic are not subjects that children must learn. It is the other way around: children are the subjects. They learn by reading and writing, by measuring and figuring, by memorizing poetry, and chanting folk songs; they learn by taking parts in dramas, making scenery, giving plays, writing melodramas in class; they learn by painting, drawing, modeling, sewing, embroidering, making things of wood, drafting and designing. Discipline does not seem to be a problem. The children rise when the teacher enters the room, sit down when she bids them to; they speak respectfully. A teacher may leave the room for twenty minutes, no football game or small war gets started during her absence. We knew many children with severe home problems—the boy in one of

Ben's classes whose mother died during the school year, and the boy whose father suddenly bolted for Canada with a woman of his choice—but we never heard of an elementary teacher with discipline problems.

In the country, primary schooling is for seven years and may lead to trade schools, high schools, people's institutes and other special training programs. But more and more the formal academic curricula are being followed: four years of Primary, six years of Second School, three years of Third School, in preparation for university or the technical and business high schools.

Something happens to children after their first effervescent years in the folk schools. It is almost a metamorphosis. As the work becomes harder, as the great dividing line of the matriculation exams approaches—the only pass to higher education—the students in the "language line" or the "math line" become glum, unresponsive, and wary. The teachers of the Third Schools often seem to have been trained in a Teutonic age. They run their classes like drill sergeants. Their job is to lay siege to and conquer the citadel of higher education; failing this, at least their troops will look smart as they march off to drygoods stores and factories.

Such complex subjects as physics, chemistry and advanced algebra, which naturally bristle with questions, are taught mainly by lectures, didactically, routinely, often dully, with a minimum of laboratory work and almost no discussion. "I am the teacher here . . . I'll do all the asking of questions" seems to be a universal pedagogical motto. The student, humiliated by such a slogan, doesn't become merely a passive recording machine, he seeks self-effacement, hoping the teacher will not notice him or ask him questions which might embarrass him before his fellows.

In spite of student passivity the results of Finnish education or self-education are impressive. There is a passion for books in this land. People in middle age or beyond are constantly taking night courses. Put up a sign saying merely *"Kurssi,"* without telling what the course is all about, and you can fill an auditorium. Educated Finns know three or four languages, sometimes as many as six; mathematics and engineering are on a high level in the country; medicine is as good as any in the world.

But an even better test of education is found in a man's informal thought processes. In politics, in the army, in business and the arts, it is clear that the Finn thinks for himself, and though he may never talk, he is not afraid to act.

One day during September, Bronwen came home from school with the news that Miss Tanner, Ben's guardian teacher the year before, was sick with a kidney infection picked up during a summer vacation in Greece. Ben sat down at once at the kitchen table and began stringing wooden beads on a length of nylon fishline. Placing small black separators between the beads, and tying a clasp and ring at the ends, he soon had a handsome teak and jet necklace which he wrapped carefully in tissue and tied with a ribbon. Then he wrote on a card, in his best Finnish:

Dear Miss Tanner:
    I hope you are soon well. I go to Swedish school now but I speak Finnish anyway. You see I was not such a bad boy after all.
                    Love from
                    Ben

This note and gift he delivered at Miss Tanner's apartment in Lauttasaari. An elderly lady wearing a peasant's scarf on her head came to the door in response to his knock.

"Miss Tanner?"

"Away," the woman said.

"This is for her," Ben said, presenting the package.

"Thank you, boy."

"Is she sick?"

"Very very sick. Away, away," the woman motioned with her hand, "in the hospital. For many weeks."

Ben left the apartment sure from the way the woman had talked that Miss Tanner would soon be dead. But three months later a bunch of red roses were delivered at our door by a lady too shy to wait or ring the bell. The note read:

Dear Ben:

Thank you for the necklace. It is beautiful. But I always knew you were not a bad boy.

Time passed quickly that fall, crowding into winter. The children were happy in school and the weather often sunny. In teeming markets we hurried to collect vanishing items, for soon we would be back to buying imported lettuce, leaf by leaf, and living on such durable staples as potatoes, cabbage, and cauliflower.

One Sunday when the birches were in gold and a blue and white sky was pouring overhead, we drove out to spend the day with Dr. Sandelin on Porkkala. Much of the peninsula looked brushy and drab from years of disuse, although here and there new houses and barns had been built and new land plowed. One old farmhouse stood unoccupied in the woods near a bend in the road. The Russians had painted it blue. Russian forces had occupied Porkkala from 1944 to 1956, then suddenly abandoned it. Finns thought this unexpected evacuation probably to have been an attempt to influence a Parliamentary election, though no change in the votes had been discernible. It was true, too, that under modern circumstances, Porkkala was of no strategic value to Russians.

The dirt road wound over low hills to an arm of the sea, then took to the woods again, dividing, diminishing to little more than parallel tracks: at last we came to a sign saying *Brakkeudd* and turned in. Lars Sandelin put aside his ax as we drove up. He was a tall, youthful man, already a noted specialist in diseases of the ear, nose, and throat. He had that boundless graciousness of manner which seems to come so easily to Swedes and Swedish-Finns. "Welcome, welcome," he said, and called to his children to come and greet the visitors. Mrs. Sandelin, too, came down the rocky hill from the little house, inviting us to come and have coffee on the porch.

Brakkeudd (Breaking Point) was a smooth apron of glaciated granite and a grey sand beach facing an inshore sound and barrier of spruce-tufted islands. The sea would never break heavy here, but Swedish-Finns have salt water in their veins;

207

they like the sound of such names even if their lives are land-locked. Down on the beach was the family yacht, an old row-boat which the doctor had been painting with pine tar. In the trees were gill nets and corks, blowing and drying after a morning hawl. Nearby was the hollow of a machine-gun nest, dug under the trees.

Once the Sandelin ancestral summer home had stood on the hill, a large house of hewn logs. The enormous stone walls which had been its foundation served as a kind of patio and rock garden for the small prefab the family now occupied. The loom of that great dark home, where he had lived as a child, was still in the doctor's mind. "When the Russians came we had three days to get out. We must leave everything. People drove out from Helsinki in cars, trucks, taxis, wagons—anything—to help us bring our things away." After the Russian evacuation, Karelian refugees had taken the land, thinking to farm here, but discouraged by a few bad seasons they had sold it back to the Sandelins.

Of the great house not a timber remained, or charred log. An arboreal arch, fence, and even the flagstones of a formal garden out in back had also vanished. "I think," Sandelin said with a laugh, "one day I will go to Russia and there I will find somewhere the arbor, the stones, the house, exactly as be-fore—except of course, painted blue. I hope someone enjoys the house, it was very fine."

He had no thought of replacing the house, a prefab was all he could afford, but he took great pride in showing off a new outhouse he had just built out back. It was well constructed, painted, and screened; its odors banished by lime, and its ap-proaches brightened by flowers that Mrs. Sandelin had planted.

Dr. Sandelin was better off than most Finns, yet he would not have thought that modern plumbing, electricity, and re-frigeration were essential to a summer home. Summers were for sunshine, bare skins, family reunions, and outings in "The Nature." You didn't have to be rich for that; you were rich already.

There was one edifice in the back yard which Lars Sandelin said he would always preserve as a monument to the Neighbor: a potato cellar where four men had lived during their tenure at *Brakkeudd*. Only the slanting boards of the roof showed above ground, looking like the top of a small pump-house. Beneath this cover a space had been hollowed into the ground, perhaps five by five across and four feet deep. Four bunks had been cramped into this room, beds of boards and leaves only, and in the remaining space a column of stones had been balanced which, without help of mortar, had to serve as a fireplace, cookstove, and chimney. Tins and bottles still littered the tiny floor; heaps of refuse outside (now cleared away) had convinced our host that the digs had been used for many seasons, winter and summer. An officer, he supposed, had occupied the big house, but the men, certainly, had lived in the potato cellar.

Stooped down in order to see in at the small aperture, Dr. Sandelin shook his head and grimaced: "You know, sometimes it is very difficult to understand Russians."

Early in October, Helsinki celebrates the harvest festival of offshore people. Islanders come from all along the southern coast, from as far east as Kotka, and as far west as the Åland Islands, almost to Sweden. Fishermen bring their prime fall catches, tubbed in wine and spice, and the ladies have baked loaves of whole dark meal in old-fashioned ovens, such breads as only the islanders know how to make any more. One morning the word goes around Helsinki—"The boats are in"—and the whole town moves down to the great market square to greet old friends.

There, Elisabeth and I found Aarne Kantola. His double-ended fishing boat was moored stern first at the stone quay, bobbing among scores of others. Aarne, wearing his eternal beret, was standing among a cargo of barrels and kegs. He'd rigged a canvas tent over the open cockpit; with only a blanket for a bunk, he had planned to stay and see the sights of the big city. Over the tent on a temporary short mast he had nailed up a placard and lettered it big: Kaunissaari—The Best.

"Aarne, welcome, welcome."

He looked up quickly, with that boyish smile, then shoved out his paw. This was followed at once by a small keg:

"I saved one for you."

"Thank you, what is it?"

"*Silakkaa.*"

"How do we eat them?"

Aarne made a motion in the air as though forking something into his mouth, then laughed.

"Good then," I said. "We will have them tonight. You are coming to supper, remember?"

"*Ei, ei,*" he replied quickly, "look at me."

"When do you finish here?"

"We never finish until the boat is empty. Perhaps three days."

"Then we will come for you at six o'clock." I said.

"But it is impossible. I smell like a fish."

"Where is Mrs. Kantola?"

"Home. This is *my* vacation."

"Good. Do you like beer?"

"Too much. Too much," he said, shaking his head contritely. "Three bottles set my head spinning and last night some of the boys had a party . . . oh, and I finished seventeen."

"Then we will have Finnish beer and Italian spaghetti for you," I shouted. "Six o'clock."

"No, no," he protested again. "It is impossible."

When we arrived at the quay that evening, Aarne Kantola was spruced up and ready to go on the town. Somewhere in the cramped cuddy of his boat he'd kept a dark suit, white shirt, and necktie. Except for his scarred hard hands he might have been the finest dude in town. Some men in a neighboring boat, gathered around a loaf of bread and a wedge of cheese, promised to keep an eye on Aarne's vessel and see that he got aboard without falling in when we brought him back.

Kantola had never been in the cockpit of a VW bus before. The motorcycles scooting in front, almost under his feet, and the swaying blue buses towering on all sides unnerved him. With one hand he gripped the door, with the other the dashboard. "*Varokaa!* Watch out. Here one comes!" he kept shouting. After the tide rip of traffic over the railroad tracks, and the headstones of the National Cemetery, after the great avenue where four lanes of rushing buses fuse into two on the Lauttasaari bridge, he took slaughter to be a certainty.

"*Voi, voi*, tonight it is sure we will all lie out on the dunghill of the world."

But there was no collision. We came in time to the quiet cove of Ducks' Slope No. 2 and ushered him to the place of honor at the table.

That party will long be remembered by the children. There was none of the formal dining ceremonies we had thought were typical of Finnish parties, the bowing, the toasts, the measured conversation. Aarne Kantola pulled his chair up to the table and sat solidly in it, expecting action. First came the *silakkaa* from the keg—silvery fingerlings packed in layers and bathed in spicy purple sauce. Aarne forked out a heaping plateful, covered it with sugar and set to work, washing the fish down with gulps of Lahti beer. Boiled potatoes next. After that, spaghetti. Three platefuls he went through to our one. Propping his elbows firmly on the table and hunching over so that no time would be wasted, he shoveled down the spaghetti with one hand and crammed home pieces of bread with the other whenever the swallowing mechanism seemed to be clogged. If there was something across the table, he didn't ask for it—he couldn't have uttered a word—but reached over the plates, over the heads of the children, to get it for himself. Then, finishing as abruptly as he started, he pushed back his chair, eased himself, slapped his stomach, and gave a great smiling sigh.

"Aaaaah. That was good. Much thanks."

"Is there anything more you'd like, Aarne?"

"Yes. Two more bottles of beer. *Silakkaa* is salty."

There was nothing uncouth about Aarne Kantola. He was a good man who liked food and no nonsense. It was a pleasure to see him eat. Though the children would never think of mentioning it, this was a miracle of a man; a man so free that he could eat just the way children wanted to. Ben hinted his admiration when he whispered confidentially: "Man, can this guy slug it in!"

It was very dark when we took Aarne back to the harbor,

the tides of traffic had fully ebbed and the fishing boats bobbed on a black sea beside the wharf. Aarne's friends were still there, smoking and talking in the cockpit. They were surprised to see the rake home so early.

That was the last time we saw Aarne Kantola. Two days later when we returned to the marketplace his boat was gone. One of his friends said he had sold all his fish, loaded the vessel with potatoes, and set out for Kaunissaari.

"*Pois, pois,*" the fisherman said, motioning with his hand across the bay, over the islands. "Long trip, long trip."

"If no one speaks it is also possible someone is thinking."

—Finnish student

A University Education

One night, before the opening of classes at the University, Professor Reuter telephoned from his summer home.

"Look here," he said, sounding rested and ready for the year's work, "I am trying to organize this a little bit—what about these lectures in modern American poetry? I want you to do them."

"There is a fair amount of modern poetry I don't care about," I said. "You should know that."

"You don't understand it?" he asked.

"I can read the words . . ."

"Well, I don't understand it either. Naturally it is up to you to teach the course the way you think best. What do you say, now?"

"I say, Ole, that it looks like you're down to the last herring in the barrel."

"Hmmm, yes, well, it does rather, doesn't it?" He laughed. "All right, that's settled then."

Professor Reuter was no admiral, but he ran a loose and happy ship. In addition to himself there was one other full-time English professor, Tauno Mustanoja. Both were fine scholars, with a wide range of knowledge in English literature, and Tauno was already an English philologist of international reputation. I suppose they were rivals. They disagreed on everything; the curriculum, which Ole thought one of variety and excellence, Tauno openly characterized as "putting one patch upon another patch." But they were good friends, and both were much too busy to spend more than passing thoughts on ideal organizations.

Between the two, and with the help of seven British instructors and four American Fulbright teachers, they were responsible for some 1,900 students. No one knew exactly how many, for lectures were open to the public and students came and went according to their majors and the examinations passed. As head of perhaps the largest English Department of any University on the continent of Europe, Ole Reuter was one kind of genius at organization: he trusted people, not committees. In two years he held only one departmental meeting and that turned into an all-night party. He selected his staff and planned the work on two assumptions: that his people knew what they were teaching, and that they liked to teach. Morale was the least problem in that department. When the Americans came in with their Fulbright professorships, they were not relegated to an occasional public lecture or an out-of-the-way voluntary course given mainly for academic courtesy; Professor Reuter incorporated the Fulbrighters into an expanded curriculum which included even a concurrent study of American history.

The British instructors, however, carried the main load of instruction. They were more or less permanent. Opportunities for teaching were better in Finland than in the British Isles. Two of the seven had married Finns and settled down, and the other five had only to take a summer holiday in the clamor of mid-Europe to be convinced that they wanted to return to Helsinki.

They were a high-spirited group, those British instructors. Two had already published books of poetry, another had a musical comedy currently playing at the National Theater, and still another occupied his spare time translating Greek comedy into modern verse.

Professor Reuter was fortunate to have such assistants; between them they could cover the whole range of English literature, if not philology, where he and Professor Mustanoja were the authorities. Professor Reuter had long hoped to add one other person to the faculty of English. This was Irma Rantavaara, who was teaching at the University as well as at the KKK. But Irma's true field and real love was comparative literature and she already had a promising position in the Department of Aesthetics. This brilliant woman, blessed with Finnish passion and British wit, was a born scholar and teacher. She was as much at home with Dostoevski or medieval German as she was with Middle English and the stylistic qualities of William Faulkner.

By any sensible academic system Irma should already have been a professor at the University. She would have graced the faculty of any English or American institution. But there was no professorship "open" to her at the time. True to the medieval government of European universities, each department was a kingdom of its own, ruled by the Professor. The system has some advantages. It frees a good professor to do his work; it also frees an inferior one for sleep. Certainly the system does not reduce academic politics. On the contrary, it makes politics the daily study of all ambitious young scholars.

No one had any doubt that Irma would one day become a full professor, but it might still be a five-year ordeal as well as a foolish diversion of her talents. When an "opening" appeared, she would have to apply for it and submit all her work and publications to an examining board which would decide whether she were "qualified" and in which order to rate the many applicants. The full faculty of the University would then have to review the judgment of the panel and recommend an order of preference. This would be studied by a committee of the Parliament; next it would be sent on to the President of the Republic, who alone could make the appointment. Politics inevitably played a part in every step of the way.

On the whole, however, the University bothered very little about organization, politics or committees. The work of the departments was divided into three progressive levels of specialization; at the end of each, comprehensive examinations were given. The student might take one year, or two or three, to pass the first level, depending on his ability and whether he had to work outside to support himself. When he felt he was ready he took the examinations, which were given frequently throughout the year, and then went on to the next level. It might take six or seven years for a student to finish all the work and begin on his doctoral thesis.

In the English faculty the first stage was primarily grammar, spoken English, and translations. After passing these the student took up more detailed work—Chaucer, Shakespeare, Milton, the novelists, English poets, American Literature, philology, and seminars in essay writing. As most of our students were going to be secondary-school teachers, or were seeking jobs in business or in the foreign office, few went beyond the second level of academic work.

One of the blessings of this system was the impersonality and objectivity with which examinations could be conducted. Teachers did not examine their students on their courses the moment their lectures were done. They did not have to play the roles of mentor, friend, and executioner.

We British and American teachers did most of our work in the first two levels of the curriculum, in the translation exercises, the essay instruction, and the lecture courses. To my surprise, I found I did my best teaching in classes in translation. Here the student was involved directly and personally with putting ideas into English words. Most of the students came up to the University with the notion, acquired in secondary school, that there was one and only one right translation for a given set of Finnish words. They clung to dictionary equivalents and even tried to follow the original Finnish word order. A simple newspaper article in Finnish would come out this way in English:

> Sometime in the future . . . perhaps already in the next summer . . . because the water is not so deep to take modern ships . . . and the port constructions are not . . . according to the government officers who have studied conditions for more than a year . . . the water must be made deeper . . . and new constructions made in the port of Kotka.

It shocked students to learn that an idea could be translated several different ways and that a single sentence in "government Finnish" might best be turned into three English sentences. But this was excellent training for them. They were

216

face to face with the choices of words, with idiom, style, and tone. I have often wished we had some device as good as translation to use in teaching English to Americans.

I found the students at the University very like those of the KKK, reluctant to commit themselves to words. Seminar sessions tended to be question-and-answer periods conducted by the teacher upon himself. I called the students my cigar-store Indians. They snickered a little, enjoying the notion of being likened to redskins, Apaches perhaps, and waited for me to get on with the performance. There was no help for it, class discussion had been forbidden them during their earlier schooling and now the habit of seeking safety in self-effacement was too strong to break. I thought it a shame that they had been taught never to question anything the teacher might say, at least not in public, but seminars were something each of us had to survive. The students were very polite, though: they could see that it must be lonesome up there in front with no one to talk to but old Whitman, roaring in the pines.

However, I learned in time that reticence was no criterion by which to judge a student's ability. Unusual written work began to appear. Because it was English processed through foreign minds, it had a strange, fresh reality all its own. Essays, short stories, poems—many were laborious and dull, but some took you by the lapels and said: Stop, Look. This is the way it is for Finns.

A poem, for example, with

What is Europe
jumps the frog its nose under a stone . . .

Or a short story which began:

At half past nine she began slowly gathering the pale blue reins of her mind together and with gentle jerks at the airy cords she brought it hovering down nearer and nearer to her body. . . . She wanted to look at her watch but could not move a finger. Today's separation was unusually long. It must have been unusually late last night. What HAD happened. She had the suspicion that she ought not to work it out; that she ought to fall asleep again. Then her mind sol-

emnly began to descend on her . . . The clouds were drifting away. YES. He had been drunk. YES. And those other
things. Oh. The snake inside her writhed.

This story, written by a shy young lady, fulfilled all its promises with instinctive directness and was an unabashed revelation
of the turbulent secrets of young people. The British instructors said such writing was not commonplace, but neither was it
exceptional. Finnish students might be unresponsive in class,
but that was only the blank face they kept for strangers. Alone
with a sheet of paper, anything might happen.

Some of the work seemed good enough to publish. Therefore we canvassed the classes, raised money, set up an informal
editorial board of students and teachers, and put out an edition
called *"First*—prose and poetry by Finnish students." The edition sold out in the bookstores almost overnight. In the second
year, a new *First* was printed, this time with student editorship
and sketches by a student artist. The stories and poems in *First*
were in original English, not translated from Finnish. A long
ground swell from Ezra Pound and T. S. Eliot was running on
Finland at the time, as well as angry young winds blowing
from the west, so that we (the conservative, probably dense)
teachers often found ourselves struggling with incomprehen-
sibles, but many of the pieces were pellucid and sharp-edged,
like fragments from a shattered illusion:

The Traitor
I was eight years old.
Before Christmas I remembered little Jesus.
I wept my eyes sore, wanted to be good,
and already I was afraid of Good Friday.
But alas,
just as I was kneeling and praying
behind a little bush
there came a big boy of the house nearby
sliding in a sleigh—just then—and
　　　shouted
that he had a Christmas card for me.

218

I crept on my hands and knees
through the snow like a mole, took the card
between my teeth
to make him believe
that I was just a baby and playing.
— LEENA MÄKELÄ

Anselm Hollo, a student working for a time in London, sent
in a poem dedicated to a priest who had been sentenced to
prison in Algeria for having helped the Freedom Fighters:

Stopping a man with a gun
stopping a man with a wall—
these methods
we have approved.
But stopping a man with love, try
that, and they'll stop you
with a gun, or a
wall, four
walls, a cell, three
years, three years for stopping to love
a man
many men, men on the run
from guns, men on the run
from walls, or trying
to vault them:
three years, father, three years
in a cell, three years
they have stolen
from you—for us all
three years in a cell
chalked up on what wall
in our minds
that we do not
cry out
do not fall on that ground
where stone
is said to have sprouted with voice?

They still seem remarkable to me, those stories and poems of the magazine *First*. Perhaps I should not have been surprised. Writing and drama run strong through Finnish natures. It is a shame so much has to lie out of reach behind the barriers of translation. In any case, *First* helped to stimulate student writing and this was part of the disorderly magic of Ole Reuter's department.

It didn't, however, affect the student-teacher relationships in the seminars. We carried on the monologue in the old polite way. One day in a jocose mood, stimulated by an hour or two of talking to "my murals," I stepped over to the nearest boy and pointed a finger at his head:

"Suppose this were a pistol, a great big Luger, aimed straight at your head, and I said, 'Say something, Olavi, or I pull the trigger.' What would you do?"

Olavi regarded me a long time, blandly, curiously, blinking his blue eyes. Finally, trying to suppress a smile, he said in a gentle baritone: "I would say . . . 'Pull the trigger.' "

Technology and a Bridge

The faculty room on the third floor of the old Tech School building, down at the end of Bulevardi, was quite unlike the lounges at KKK and the University. No one ever came there. There was scarcely a magazine or paper to read. One journal in English was kept—*Time*—and the issues were two years out of date. Nevertheless when I had an hour to spare between classes with engineers and chemists, I often went up to the room just to keep an eye on things, to see what new ships were in West Harbor and how the work was coming on Russia's atomic-powered icebreaker.

This end of town was a vigorous grimy place, constantly shaken by trucks and stabbed by the whistles of the switching engines. Children had to play ball in the alleys. Old women in shawls scrambled in front of buses and streetcars. Men out of work sat on the stone steps of apartments, smoking, and payday drunks lurched on the sidewalks. Here you could get a haircut for fifty cents; for another fifty, the barber, a woman member of the Olympic wrestling team, would scrub the roots of your hair with a wire brush and slosh you down with alcohol.

I was glad to be working here instead of at the plush new institutes going up at Otaniemi. The past of Finland was here as well as its future, and the old yellow buildings of the Tech School presided over the surrounding industrial area with a calm scarred dignity. They were chipped and drilled and stained by steel mementos of the recent wars. The shipyards had been a prime target, although the first load of bombs had missed the mark by miles and smashed the Soviet Embassy. Later, however, the chemistry building had taken a bomb through the roof. The building had been repaired after the war, but then, with the projected move of the school outside Helsinki, everything had been let go. We worked in a penumbra behind windows encrusted with dirt and nailed shut. Heat was an optional item in the budget and plumbing in winter a matter of conjecture.

My part in the workings of this institution were never clear to me, even after a year of teaching there. I doubt if anyone save my transient students knew I was there. The faculty ignored me as they seemed to ignore each other. I met no one. If I had a boss, he never came out into the open to tell me what my duties were. Instead, classes were organized by one of the students, calling on the telephone; we arranged the entire schedule in five minutes.

The students, too, were entirely different from those of the KKK and the University. These wore jeans and scuffers and sweaters; they shaved when they remembered and had their hair cut when they got around to it; they walked with coat collars turned up at the neck and pork-pie hats tipped forward on their noses. They were intelligent, humorous, demanding, and entirely uninhibited by language.

"What should we study?" I asked my first class.

"Anything," one volunteered.

"Nothing," laughed a second. "Just talk."

"Anything except not grammar," said a third.

"Cuba," shouted a fourth, passing over a grimy copy of *Newsweek*. "What do you like about Cuba?" And so the class went all year. The students did not want lectures, or formal work, or technical English. They wanted practice in the spoken language and a chance to look at the world outside Finland. We read some stories, discussed the mining of coal in Pennsylvania, imperialism, communism, and the sex life of students in America; but over and over the boys came back to challenge me on American policies, or lack of policies, in the cold war.

Over and over they faced me with the impression that America was a skittish nation belligerently waving her standard of living with one hand and her sky full of bombs with the other. These were good tough minds, wanting facts not evasions. I found myself saying things I had never thought of before. I found myself having to defend America against the very things I most criticized in her. One's country looks different from the outside, not so much because she may be wrong, but because even the wrongs are misunderstood. Criticism, however, must be met; problems can't be blamed on Congress or left to the President to take care of.

Why did Americans feel it necessary to experiment with their atomic bombs on Japanese people?

Why did the U.S. Army have to fight a war with Orville Faubus so that a few small black children could go to school?

Monstrosities of this kind are not defensible, but I had to defend, or at least explain, them. These young Finns were not accusing America of anything in particular—we stood self-condemned—but they wanted to know why such things could happen. I was accountable to the students, the more so since they were generally friendly to America.

It seemed to me that here in the Tech School I was looking into a new era. This was not the old Finland, determined to apologize for its backward ways. Rather it was a country now confirmed in independence and confident in itself. It lay, by an accident of geography, exactly between East and West; trade and culture tied it to both. Whatever might be thought about Finland abroad, it was truly neutral, neither cringing in one direction nor conniving in another.

One group at the Tech School was entirely different from the rest, the chemistry teachers. They wanted literature. After a lifetime spent in the sciences, they came to literature with a fresh delight and surprise. We read many books that year. In discussing them around a long table in the chemistry library, I could see how each person began to understand something new about America. The country they had heard about from our magazines and our political pronouncements was a very different land from the America of her writers.

I enjoyed this class with chemistry teachers more than any other, for, as is often the case, people outside of literature get the most excitement from it. They have not been chastened by too much study.

We read Hemingway's Caribbean fable, *The Old Man and the Sea*. They had expected a prize-winning tough guy, and they found instead the compassionate soft voice of one who venerated life in its simple dignity. Then we turned to James Thurber's descriptions of the nightmare he had lived, in living with himself. But of all the books we read, the one that made the greatest impression on them was Thornton Wilder's *Bridge of San Luis Ray*. Trained by *Time* and Tennessee Williams, these people had never heard English like that, cultivated, calm, rich with harmonic meanings.

Wilder had discovered into words an ancient Andean myth of a vine bridge that breaks, sending five people tumbling antlike into a canyon, and of a humble priest who sets out to prove to himself what he already knows: that God's will and purpose is manifest in the death of the five. The magic of the book is both in the quest and the irony, woven so carefully in flesh-colored yarn. Its long phrases gave a grace to a world almost forgotten, where beliefs fade in the high air and love pursues its needs over devious and frustrating mountain paths. In the end all that is certain of God's will is that there is a bridge—call it love—which hangs on a charm of air linking the living with the dead; there is no other bridge and it can be made no stronger.

Sometimes when the morning work was done, I took my lunch in the cafeteria in the cellar, which had been a bomb shelter during the war. A buxom lady and her husband served the food, which was very plain. Here I noticed that the usually argumentative and loquacious students were subdued and seemed to prefer eating alone. But there was a large round table reserved for teachers; often I took my cabbage soup or macaroni and sat down at the table to eat. Sometimes other

224

teachers were there engrossed in talk. I was prepared with my best Finnish "Good day," but no notice was taken of my arrival. It was a strange sensation, sitting there with my colleagues, yet feeling like a hole in the air.

After this formality had continued for a few weeks I began to wonder whether I had committed some breach of etiquette sitting down like that in the only place for teachers. Weeks later I still did not know. Should I wait—and perhaps seem standoffish? Should I speak up? Would I then intrude? I began to be intrigued by the game, wondering how long it could go on, and deciding to eat my soup there as often as possible, just to see. I should have known better. Finns were simply behaving like Finns, world champions at playing a silent waiting game. They won completely. Impossible as it may seem, not a single member of the faculty said a word to me during the entire year.

It didn't matter. Everyone was busy. Most of the professors were carrying outside jobs in industry or consulting for the government. Technology is the key to Finland's future survival. That much was fairly clear to me.

Prior to the war Finland had built its prosperity out of shipments of paper, pulp, and lumber to Europe and America. That export trade had been regained after the war, but as cuttings were approaching the annual growth of timber, it could not be greatly expanded. However, specialized wood products were becoming important—processed wood in the form of cardboard, wallboard, plywood, and the prefabricated houses. These would open up wholly new markets abroad and provide new jobs at home. Manufactured forest products were perhaps the most promising recent development in Finnish industry.

But the war had radically changed the country's economic base. The demands laid down by the Soviets as payment of war reparations ran heavily to metal products. Finns had had to build up an entire industrial complex which never existed before. After the debt to Russia had been paid off, the metal industries continued to prosper, owing to orders from Russia and the satellite countries. The metal engineering indus-

225

tries now employ a sizable proportion of the labor force, produce half the country's wealth, and account for more than 20 per cent of its exports.

For all the instinctive desire of Finns to be left alone, out of big power politics, this is not possible. Though few Finns realize it, a quarter of each man's pay check is earned abroad. England, West Germany, and Russia are Finland's best customers. Since her exports are strictly divided—metals to the East, wood products to the West—Finland has no choice but to go with both East and West.

More and more this paradox becomes the dominating economic force, but all Finland's industries will have to be rapidly expanded if she is to find new jobs for the postwar "bulge" of babies now coming to maturity. New markets outside Europe will have to be discovered and built up. Far from being cloistered and forgotten among her swamps and spruces, Finland finds herself caught in a new East-West dilemma: she cannot join the emerging economic groups of Europe (EFTA and the Common Market) owing to her commitments to Russia; and she cannot neglect them owing to her dependence on Western trade. Her young technologists, economists, businessmen, and linguists, now in training, will have roles to play which few can yet imagine.

I often wished, watching from the windows of the Tech School faculty room, that I could foresee a little of the future. The cranes moving over the holds of the freighters, the acres of spools of wire rope and cubic miles of lumber that passed over the docks, Russia's great gaunt icebreaker, unlovely in her lines but powerful—all these spoke of a prosperous present in Finland. Perhaps if I had been able to read the smoke signals of the switching engines and the eery blue semaphores flashed day and night by the arc welders in the Wärtsilä shipworks, I could have learned something of the future.

It seemed to me that Finland was ahead of both Russia and America in its preparation for the future. The cold war might suit American and Russian politics for a time, but it made no sense for either side in the long run. Meanwhile, Finland had made a separate peace: once a battleground for Swedish and Russian imperialists, once a bridgehead for Nazi and Soviet armies, Finland was now becoming a bridge to unite East and West.

In the course of that year I watched many red sunsets burn down over West Harbor, many shades of blue twilight supervene, many flurries of snow come, or the black enameling of rain. Always the work went on. It didn't matter if the students asked questions impossible to answer. It didn't matter if the faculty failed to notice the comings and goings of one disembodied English teacher. Finns were Finns and they had other work to attend to.

I had a dream
about two children in a dangerless house
under the birds' heaven . . .

        —LEENA MÄKELÄ

⫸omestic Problems

That fall was full of domestic questions for Finns. It was to be a long season of politics, for they were girding themselves for two major elections in the coming year: the choice of a President in midwinter, followed by Parliamentary elections in early summer. Either one would bring on savage fighting among the parties; Finns have long memories and the wounds of previous decades never really heal down to the heroism of scars.

One might think from the outside that an election in Finland is a sedate and gentlemanly affair. There is little electioneering and almost no canvassing for votes, no rallies, no torchlight parades, handouts, or other forms of hoopla. No person would think of asking another how he will vote. But the fact seems to be that when Finns cannot find an outside menace to rally against they gratefully turn to fighting among themselves. Politics is a hard-fisted business. Governments rise and fall on such issues as the price of butter; sometimes there are two or three changes of government in a year; sometimes no coalition government has enough votes to please the Parliament, so that a minority government has to carry on; sometimes for weeks at a time no official government exists. Scandals are commonplace. The newspapers, organs of political parties, spare no effort to delight their followers with the deviltries that other parties are up to.

The apparent stability of political parties in Finland does not come from any bovine contentment, but from the unforgiving

228

nature of the Finns. Thus, no amount of socialistic programs—excellent programs, too—seems to have made any dent upon the strength of the Communist party. Unlike Sweden and Norway, where communism has withered away to negligible minorities, the Communists in Finland maintain the largest, most active, and best-organized political body in the country. They have a budget of more than $800,000 a month to spend, derived from captured German enterprises, and probably augmented from the outside. They operate two newspapers whose immoderate statements, however wrong, cannot be curtailed by the Government for fear of antagonizing Russia. They can count on almost exactly 24 per cent of the votes in any Parliamentary election, and the only influence in recent times that has succeeded in trimming this figure was overt Soviet pressure to increase it. Since the sorry days of Yrjö Leino, and the attempted coups of 1948, no Communist has been given a ministry in the government. The Party therefore has a ready-made election platform: how can it be that a quarter of the Finns must remain outside their government. Other Finns don't attempt to answer this charge on any theoretical grounds; it would just be too dangerous, they say.

The Agrarian Party, led by the able and canny President Kekkonen, has become the party of most power. Unlike the farm vote in many countries, the Agrarians of Finland are not an ultraconservative group of small holders determined to keep their power from slipping away to the cities. Theirs is a center and generally liberal party. Their principal strength, however, comes from the weakness of the formerly dominant Social Democratic Party. The Social Democrats are perhaps the only group in Finland having the potential to replace the Communists. Though not a radical group, the Social Democrats are certainly socialistic. Their programs do not differ greatly from those demanded by Finnish Communists, though, of course, their social and political objectives are entirely different.

Since the war this party has been split into factions warring against each other. Doubtless the situation delights both the Agrarians and the Kremlin, for the division guarantees to the former their continued success at the polls, and for the latter it helps maintain tht wide Communist bridgehead in Finland.

Though we, as outsiders, knew very little of the details of Finnish political life, we could see the main divisions fairly well and it was easy to mark the updrafts of hot air collecting into thunderheads over the land.

The President, Mr. Kekkonen, at first seemed quite invulnerable as the candidate for a second six-year term. He was not revered by Finns the way the prewar Presidents had been—Stålberg, Relander, Svinhufud, Kallio, Ryti, Mannerheim—but he was popular with his followers and even people who distrusted him said he was the best man to manage relations with Russia. However, a new force had recently come onto the political scene, or rather an old one back from retirement. This was Väinö Tanner, one of the great men of Finland. Tanner had come the long way up from most humble beginnings to the managership of one of the country's two great co-operatives. Before the war, and during it, he had served in many posts, including that of Minister of Finance under President Risto Ryti, where he had earned such high respect from General Mannerheim. Of course he had served his time as a "War Criminal," and the Russians paid him the compliment of believing he had "masterminded from jail" the overthrow of their planned coup in 1948. He was one of the tough, upright, uncompromising men of the past.

Väinö Tanner himself could not run for office; he was hated and distrusted in Russia. Pravda called him a "reactionary" and a "Fascist"—Stone Age epithets applied to such a man. But he returned from jail to take up the work of the Social Democratic Party. Now, as its head, he backed the good if colorless Judge Olavi Honka for the presidency and then set about welding the factions of the party into a solid organization again.

While Mr. Kekkonen was certainly running far in front, during the fall Mr. Honka seemed clearly to be gaining public interest. The incumbent President however had a full hand of face cards to play: he had recently welcomed Mr. Khrushchev to a cordial visit in Finland; now he went off at the invitation of Canada and United States to pay state visits there. Although the campaign issues at the time seemed to be entirely domestic—no word ever being mentioned of a foreign policy other than the Paasikivi-Kekkonen line—such evidence of Finland's statesmanship abroad was the best kind of electioneering.

President Kekkonen made an impressive tour, particularly in Washington where he handled himself before a barrage of questions at a Press Club evening with wit and honesty. I heard reports of the session from friends at the KKK. Some of them did not personally like the President but they were proud of his showing in Washington, particularly since the strict lines of Finnish neutrality are often hard for Americans to comprehend. It was obvious, too, to the Finns that President Kennedy had welcomed the Finnish leader with more than cordiality, with a thorough understanding of the conditions of Finnish independence.

After a highly successful visit, President Kekkonen and his wife and entourage flew on to Hawaii to spend a sunny vacation in the wholly unfamiliar tropics. I could not help but feel uneasy about this expedition to America. The President was a long way from home and virtually in forbidden territory. The time seemed ill-chosen. Although the reception in Washington might favorably influence the pro-Western vote in Finland, one could not foresee what outburst it might arouse in Moscow. Moscow was in fact preparing for another Communist Party Congress, one that was bound to be more than routine, for China was growing difficult and the final disposal of Mr. Stalin had yet to be attended to.

One day I chanced to meet Rector Kalle Kauppi in the cafeteria of the KKK. He invited me to come and eat with him and I was glad for the opportunity to talk with him again. I told him of my worries over Mr. Kekkonen's trip, but he smiled and shook his head.

"Why should he not go? This is a free country."

"When things are going well here," I said, "I always have the feeling there is someone looking over my shoulder."

"But someone is always looking over our shoulder!"

Rector Kauppi said he could see no harm in the visit; Mr. Kekkonen had made many trips to Russia, it was time he became acquainted in other parts of the world, including America. There was, after all, much that he might be able to do to stimulate trade. For example, Finns found it very difficult to understand why America gave away money to many countries, even to former enemies, and yet made so little effort to promote trade with a friendly country like Finland. The Rector knew some of the reasons, of course; they were complicated economic reasons; nevertheless he thought President Kekkonen might be able to improve the situation.

After a while Rector Kauppi stopped eating and looked at me very sharply:

"Suppose you are right. Suppose Russia threatens us in some way . . . What will America do?"

"I don't know, sir," I said.

"Finland is so little known . . ."

"Finland is not well known but much admired."

"And very far away."

"Americans have strong feelings about Finland," I reminded him.

"Thank you," he replied. "But America could do very little to help us."

"I hope that by now my country realizes—as in Greece and Turkey—that we must stand together."

The Rector smiled. "You hope?" he said softly.

"I hope Mr. Kennedy would say, 'Hold on, Russia. If you go into Finland, that's the big one.' "

"You hope, but do you think that would happen?"

"No," I said.

"No," the Rector laughed. "Nor I. As a practical matter, no."

I found it hard to accept this sense of absolute isolation in Finland. Yet Finns have for years accepted it, realizing that the friendship and admiration of other peoples play no part in their future. What they have to do they have to do alone. So I gave up thinking about Russia and the interest it was bound to take in the affairs of its little neighbor.

Moreover we had our own domestic problems that fall. Elisabeth had to go into the hospital for some surgical repairs. Dr. Sandelin arranged for her to see a gynecologist; he examined her and then said he would arrange to operate on her at 7:30 the following morning at the Eira hospital, which was near to where we lived. In the morning the doctor apologized for having suggested the Eira, as it was a private hospital:

232

"You could as well go to the Women's Clinic," he explained. "Then it would cost you almost nothing . . . and in any case I would probably do the work."

But Elisabeth wanted to get the job over with, so Eira was the hospital. I went over in the afternoon to see her, but she was still groggy from the operation and scarcely seemed to know what had happened to her. Everything was fine. No nurses were around, but flowers had been put in the room to make things cheery.

During the next five days Elisabeth was cared for by old-fashioned nurses who knew their work and carried it out without any nonsense. Certainly they did not pamper the patients. Elisabeth suffered, but mainly from loneliness. The nurses came for business, not visiting. The doctor never came at all. Once, after three days had passed, I questioned the Head Nurse about this, wondering whether the doctor had forgotten my wife altogether; she shook her head and gently pushed me aside:

"No, no. It is not necessary for him to see her. He is very busy. Your wife is doing very well. I will call to the doctor if there comes something important, but everything is fine now."

That was the end of the interview. Later Elisabeth was discharged, healed and well, without ever seeing the doctor again.

Save for the middle-ear infections which Steve had and which Dr. Sandelin had twice to lance and drain, this was our only personal experience with Finnish medicine. It was, so far as we could tell, of the highest order. Finnish medicine has an excellent reputation. The training period for young doctors is seven to eight years, and many, following their specialties, go on to further study in England or America. Though a bedside manner seems not to be cultivated, there is no question of the skill of Finnish doctors.

All this was a little surprising to us, for Americans are never allowed to forget the boogy man of socialized medicine, and Finnish medicine is primarily socialized. Indeed, adequate medical protection as well as public health are provided for in the Constitution. Except for one or two, hospitals are maintained by the cities and the towns, and most doctors work in both the state clinics and in private practice.

As the gynecologist said, Elisabeth could have received exactly the same surgery and hospitalization at the Women's Clinic. Surgery and drugs would then have cost her nothing, and hospital care between $1 and $3 a day.

The time may come when Americans will cease to believe their feudal system to be the best and only medicine. They would be wise to study Finland's, for it is technically as good and more humane. The success of Finnish medicine, as is true of other socialist programs, lies in a practical combination of both state and private enterprise. (In Housing, it is the vigorous *competition* between public, private, institutional, and co-operative building which probably accounts for both the availability of apartments and the excellence of design.) Finns are not doctrinaire people, but pragmatists. Theory is not important, only what works reasonably well. Not wholly one system, not wholly another, but the best of each, with only a minimal bureaucracy—that seems to be the Finnish philosophy, and I think it is a good one.

After Elisabeth came home from the hospital, a new and exciting development overtook our family: Tytti blandly announced one evening that she was going to have a baby.

"Why, Tytti . . . !" Elisabeth exclaimed, unable to continue.

Kim blushed.

"Yaay Tytti," shouted Ben. "Ya made it! But you're not married!"

"But someday I will," Tytti said.

Bronnie hugged her. "Oh, Tytti. How neat."

It wasn't altogether neat, however. Tytti was uncertain when she could be married. William, the father of the baby, worked in the Palace Hotel too, and both of them needed to go on working. Moreover William would soon be called up for military service, which is required of all young men, married or otherwise. To make matters more complicated, William was a Swedish-Finn, and William's father, because of some personal trouble forty years earlier, had an abiding distaste for Finnish-Finns.

Tytti, however, looked very pretty and happy. She could even joke about taking the name Johanson. It was a good thing, she said, that she had taken care of Steven over the

234

summer, he had taught her more than she had taught him. If she was embarrassed at being unmarried, she did not show it. Nor do I think she was. She treated the whole matter as being entirely normal; so therefore did the children.

"Is this the way of things in Finland?" I asked her. "Babies first, marriage after?"

"Well," she allowed, smiling, "sometimes . . . it can happen . . ."

There were other matters besides Tytti's baby and Mr. Kekkonen's re-election to occupy Finland that fall. One morning in late October the papers carried photographs taken in Lapland of a great white flare seen in the northeast sky, a light as large as a small dawn over that country which had gone into its winter night. The explanation came from Mr. Khrushchev, exulting to the Party Congress in Moscow: Russian scientists had just set off in the island of Novaya Zemlya the largest nuclear explosion ever attempted. "It was expected to be about forty-five megatons," he said modestly, "but it proved better than that—more than fifty megatons."

I suppose I should have known. There was too great a conjunction of stars in the autumn of 1961 for our little cosmos not to be shaken. Fifty megatons. The equivalent of 50,000,000 tons of TNT. Numbers get away from you. This single explosion incorporated in itself a power equal to twenty times all the bombs dropped on Germany in the five years of the last war. It was the equal of 2,500 Hiroshima bombs. What then might the potential target be?

My friends at the KKK, imperturbable as ever, had no certain explanation. Surely the target was not Finland: nothing in that little country would require so massive an explosion. Perhaps China. (Stalin was just now being ceremoniously exhumed and sent to liquidation.) Perhaps Mr. Khrushchev was saying to the Chinese: "Look, go easy. We are much tougher than you imagine." Or perhaps the explosive was directed toward America, in hopes that its baleful light would reach there with a warning not to push the little tanks and riflemen too far against the wall in Berlin.

Another of my colleagues had a quite different theory: this was the Russian way of hastening the negotiations over Finland's lease of the old Saimaa Canal and the port facilities of Viborg. A year before, Russia had made the bland suggestion that it would be economically beneficial for Finland to reconstruct the abandoned canal and rent the excellent port of Viborg for export of pulp and lumber. Finns had instantly recognized the friendly offer for what it was—a scheme to bring the country into further economic dependence upon the Neighbor. Nor was the scheme considered economically sound. Finland had built up new outlets for her wood exports; the old canal was much too small and in a state of dilapidation; a wholly new canal, running from Lake Saimaa through Finnish territory to Kotka, would probably be cheaper to build. Yet . . . as my friends pointed out, one does not easily turn down a gift offer from the Soviet Union. A technical committee had been appointed to study the matter, though few people in the KKK doubted but that Finland would ultimately have to accept the offer and make the best of it.

One morning a few days later the telephone rang at breakfast time and out of the earpiece rattled the agitated voice of a British friend:

"Hello, hello. Are you there? Hello, Alan here. What are you going to do about it?"

"What?"

"Wrap it up? Go home?"

"What?"

"Some of your countrymen have already shoved off. They think it's serious. What about your bus?"

Alan was a genius at teaching English to Finns, and an inspired if somewhat unreliable prophet of coming events. Normally I could grasp a little of what he was driving at, but now his words poured from the phone like broken glass: "Sonsobitches. Where can you go any more without them coming after you?"

"Who, Alan?" I shouted.

"What?" he bellowed.

"Who's after you?"

"Christ, they may be here with their bloody tanks tomorrow. Bloody fools. You could send it to Sweden, you know. What about the kids? We've had it here, though. My two kids . . . I'm getting bloody sick of being pushed around all over the globe . . ."

I waited for him to stop yelling at himself, then asked what on earth he was so worked up about. This brought on another convulsion: "Don't you read the papers?"

"I can't read the papers."

"The Note, the Note, what do you think?"

"What Note?"

"The bloody Russian Note, that's what. They say there's danger of war in the Baltic. Look, chum, don't try to be funny. Those devils mean business. This is 1939 all over again!"

I had a couple of hours before class at the University and I told him I'd meet him at the bar of the Helsinki Hotel. He said "Good-o" and hung up. Elisabeth asked what all the trouble was about. I told her what little I'd been able to gather from Alan. None of our neighbors had spoken about any Russian Note, and the children had not been told anything in school. Yet Alan knew Finland very well, since his business was here, and he had a normal Anglo-Saxon nervous system: I was bound to think that something serious had happened.

On the way downtown I studied the people in the bus but could detect no change in them: they were the same stolid people who rode glumly into the city every morning. If a threatening message had come from Russia, my companions appeared to be unmoved by it. Moreover, I could discover no cause for such an action on the part of the Kremlin. Nothing had changed; Finland was still disarmed; Germany was still divided and disarmed; Sweden was not going to attack anyone.

Alan was already at a table in the Helsinki bar, hunched over three empty beer glasses. He was a bear of a man, heavy-shouldered, with a thick shock of dark hair, glittering eyes, and a fine dark beard.

"Waiter, another beer please. Make it four beers, thank you very much."

"What's up?" I said.

Alan looked around at the people in the bar and shook his bushy head: "Look at them! Standing around with blank faces. Why don't they do something? What's their President doing sitting on a Pacific Island? These Russians are tough. Christ, I'm tired. Look at them. Sheep to the slaughter."

A radio was going in the hotel lobby and a number of people had stopped to listen to a news broadcast. This was quite unusual; for a moment the sounds of the Winter War, those calamitous broadcasts spoken in so calm a voice, filled the lobby for me. A disgruntled hat-check man was walking around reciting that all persons were supposed to check their hats and coats, it was the rule of the hotel, but the listeners stared him down and finally he went away.

"Somebody from the government talking," Alan explained, moodily wiping beer from his beard. "He says the President says there is no need for alarm. Like hell there isn't! Consultations . . . on matters of defense are asked for, and all that you know what . . ."

The Note, Alan went on, after the newscast, was a typical Soviet missive, full of sound and fury and aimed somewhere else. Nine-tenths of the Note had been spent upon Norway and Denmark, excoriating them for alleged provocative actions; the rest had been a proposal for immediate consultations with the Finnish Government on defense and mutual assistance.

"It doesn't make sense," I said to Alan, thinking of the improbability of Norway and Denmark setting out to attack Russia.

"Of course it makes sense," snapped Alan. "With a quarter of the people in this country Communists? This is the takeover. I don't want to be around when that civil war starts. Finns have an awful streak of cruelty in them when they get going. Murder, chum, they love it."

"What's Kekkonen going to do?"

"He doesn't say, naturally."

After an hour another news broadcast came on the air. One could feel the Finns beginning to hum like high-tension lines. Mr. Karjalainen, the Foreign Minister, was going to take up discussions with the Russians.

Alan ordered up some more beer and sat there punching cigarettes into an ash tray. "I'd get out if I could," he said. "You don't have to stay here. Don't be a fool."

"What would they want Finland for?" I wondered.

"Missile bases. Swedish steel. Norwegian ports, Norway's a NATO country and all that."

"They've had twenty-four per cent Communists around here since before the Civil War. Nobody takes them very seriously. . . ."

"I take them seriously," Alan roared. "Bloody seriously. Give them a chance, they're all ready. A little civil disorder, stir up a riot, bring in the tanks . . . you know . . . poof, just like that. . . . And nobody takes it seriously!"

"Well, what are you going to do—get your gun and white pants and join the ski troops?"

"I don't know," Alan said, "but I'm not going to sit around like a rat in a trap."

Alan could well be right and I knew it. Few people had understood the Notes of 1939 which, in similar words, had been a diplomatic prelude to the Winter War. Russian officials had a way of hiding their meaning, but showing their teeth, and it was evident that they were very angry about something. Though their anger might really be directed over the Atlantic, or across their continent to China, somehow Finland seemed always to be in the way. I left Alan to bubble with his beer and went off up the hill to the University, wondering what I might say that the students didn't already know about *The Red Badge of Courage*.

Bringing a stone grasped firmly by the top
In each hand, like an old-stone savage armed.
He moves in darkness . . .

ROBERT FROST

November

From abroad messages poured in to people in Finland offering asylum, sympathy, and advice. Some Finns, sure that they would be *persona non grata* in Sovietized Finland, slipped away over the border to Sweden. More megatonnage was going up over Novaya Zemlya. It was hard to believe that these nuclear demonstrations, coming at the same time as the Note to Finland and the vanishment of Stalin, were not somehow related, but no one I knew could suggest the connection. With the President away in Hawaii, the Finnish government, unable to discover the alleged "danger in the Baltic," warily procrastinated.

Some people seemed to think that the whole elaborate scare was set up to ensure the re-election of President Kekkonen. Others thought that the Note was a diplomatic rap across the knuckles for Mr. Kekkonen, a way of telling him to come home and stop flirting with Western countries. These people were grimly proud when their President did not hasten home but decided to stay and finish out his vacation.

"Don't worry," one said to me with a knowing smile, "Kekkonen was a champion high jumper. Already he has jumped over higher things than this."

My friends at the Business School had other guesses about the crisis. Between classes I tried to understand what they were saying, though they were talking rapidly and often jesting. One professor of economics said that the Note and the explosions were intended to soften up the Finns for new trade negotiations with Moscow. Another thought the pressure was entirely political, to control the elections and force the coming government to give the Communist party a share of the cabinet positions.

Another idea was that Russia, after stabilizing the East-West wall in Berlin, would next seek full recognition of the puppet East German Republic; Finland was to play the cat's paw. In spite of constant pressure from Russia, Finland had managed to maintain neutrality toward the Germans: she had not officially recognized either German government, although she traded actively with both. If Finland could now be persuaded to recognize the East German Republic, then the way might be eased for other Western countries to do the same.

It was pretty clear to me, after listening to these many suggestions, all reasonable and all different, that the best minds in the country had no clear idea of what the Kremlin was after in its demand to discuss mutual defense measures. Nor did the Mutual Assistance Treaty of 1948 provide any clue:

Article 1   In the eventuality of Finland, or the Soviet Union through Finnish Territory, becoming the object of armed attack by Germany or any state allied with the latter, Finland will . . . fight to repel the attack . . . if necessary with the assistance of, or jointly with, the Soviet Union.

NATO countries, including Denmark and Norway, could be considered allies of Germany, but to think they were contemplating using Finland as a base for an armed attack on Russia could only be a hallucination.

That the Kremlin should try to influence an election in Finland, or interfere with her policies in any way, was equally forbidden by the treaty:

Article 6   The High Contracting Parties pledge themselves to observe the principles of mutual respect of sovereignty and integrity and that of non-interference in the internal affairs of the other state.

But a treaty is no more than a treaty and this provision had already suffered many Soviet interpretations.

One prediction by a student of Russia at the University was

especially interesting: the Note, he said, was really aimed at neutralizing the entire Scandinavian area. Denmark and Norway must first be frightened out of NATO; then economic inducements would be given them to trade with the East; finally, with Finland leading the way, and Sweden following her traditional mercantile neutrality, little by little the whole Scandinavian peninsula would be brought into the Soviet economic empire. This was a long-range policy, he admitted, but he believed that the Kremlin, much more than the Western democracies, was able to plan a long way ahead.

The fascination of playing games with geography is a disease of fanatics—everything looks so neat and logical, for maps do not show people, cultures, homes, children. But it is a grim game; that kind of tidy world is possible only in an empty world. Tacitus had said something about it when the Romans were trying to straighten things up in Caledonia: "They make a desert and call it peace." Going home on the bus I tried to force myself to think clearly about this crisis. Logic would say that Finns were faced either with a wholly illogical war scare, or with a plan that was the product of the Kremlin minds brooding over their maps and their messianic obsessions. In either case there was little anyone here could do. Whatever the problem was it was too big for a disarmed Finland to manage. As in 1939 and 1941, Finns were caught in the web of geography and economics.

But so were we all in the west. Living in Finland, we Americans were probably in no greater danger than our countrymen back home, though comforted by fewer illusions of invulnerability.

Reindeer meat was going unsold in the markets because scientists had discovered high concentrations of radio-strontium in Lapland. The new bombs would shower their poisonous load on all people alike, whatever their cultures or military pretensions. Sweden was building underground caves to house factories and cities; some of these were reputed to be quite large and ready for operation. Lauttasaari people, like many others in the world, were talking about bomb shelters. One shelter was being blasted out of granite, capable, it was said, of holding 500 people. Lauttasaari already had more than 23,000 inhabitants. If a take-over came in Finland, we Americans might be shipped home on the next passage of the *Gripsholm*, or we might be shipped anywhere, according to recent civilized practices in the West. If the big test came, here or elsewhere, no neolithic caverns would help us much. Food, fire, shelter, clothing would be the sum of our needs—an ax, matches, and seed for the spring.

I realized that I could not think logically or sensibly about this crisis. Like the Finns, I would have to wait and see.

Home had a special bright look that evening. The fragrance of cooking and the sounds of laughter filled the white echoing place. Steven had somehow worked the back loose from the high chair and was remodeling it with a hammer and fork; Bronwen, chinning herself on some book shelves for the junk piled on top, had pulled everything down from the wall and now stood in tears among the alien plaster. But aside from such minor incidents, home was still standing, a haven against darkness. Somewhere in Finland, somewhere in Russia, somewhere, everywhere for that matter, other families were working out small destinies among such problems as these.

At supper I asked the children if they had heard anything about the trouble with Russia. Kim said something had been mentioned about it, but she had not understood what it was all about. Both Ben and Bron had heard nothing, although the school had had an air-raid drill.

"We could drop that bomb," Ben reminded me.

"What bomb, Ben?"

"Down the chimney of those Russians. You know."

"I don't know any Russians."

"Those guys in the next apartment."

"They're not Russians, they're East Germans. Wrong guys."

"The teacher said there's a crazy man in the woods," Bron said very seriously, "and he chases kids."

"That's right," Ben agreed. "I heard that long ago."

"And he's got a knife."

"Why don't the police come and get him?" I asked. "Somebody's trying to scare you."

"No they're not!" Bron was sure the man existed.

243

"Well, don't go in the woods any more," Elisabeth said.

"The police don't know who he is," Ben went on. "Most of the time he's okay. They said maybe he got hurt in the head in the war."

"What would you do if you saw a crazy man?" Elisabeth asked.

"I'd run," Bronwen replied. "But what does he look like? Just any old man?"

We didn't really believe the story of this mysterious man, thinking him but a local spook, until we saw him under a street lamp down by the shore one snowy dark evening. He looked both angry and frightened, moving backward in jumps and making threatening knife gestures at three young dudes, who were pestering him but keeping out of range. The man's face was a turbulent black shadow. Suddenly he fled, running and stumbling off through the reeds at the end of the bay.

Even with this immediate lead the police were unable to locate the man. He came out of the darkness with a knife, his head in a storm of danger, and vanished again, a pathetic throwback to the caves, or a wounded creature who trusted no one and whom no one could find or help.

For a week or more after the Note, Russia kept its grudging peace. In due time President Kekkonen flew back to Helsinki to face a real if imaginary crisis that had only been kept in suspension until his return. Most of my friends found the Kremlin's silences no easier to endure than its outbursts. And Alan, though he had pondered the matter over many beers, had not yet read his fortune in the bubbles.

The President took to the radio soon after his return. In a nationwide broadcast he told the people that no threat to Finnish independence was involved or implied in the Note. The world was a dangerous place to live in and it was entirely proper for Finland and Russia, according to their treaties, to consult on matters of defense. Mr. Kekkonen spoke in a calm reassuring manner. He went on to suggest that the management of the country should not be entrusted to "dilettantes" in politics, but added that he had no doubt that all misunderstanding could be cleared up.

It was a strange speech. For the nation at large—a nation

under apparent threat to its very existence—the talk must have been a steadying force. But it was also a very political speech: the reference to "dilettantes" could only refer to Judge Honka. On the one hand the President was saying, "There is no danger; go home to your beds" and on the other he was saying, "Only a great man can save Finland."

The President dispatched his Foreign Minister to Moscow for talks with Mr. Gromyko. Mr. Karjalainen soon returned without any new demands to report (an unexpected blessing) —but without any clarification of the trouble either. Norway and Denmark were said to be playing a cosy game with re-surgent Nazis and great danger existed now in the Baltic.

One morning President Kekkonen suddenly dissolved the Parliament and sent the members home. That morning I decided the end had really come. Somewhere back in my memory I thought I could recall a similar maneuver by Napoleon, and all too well I could remember the burning of the German Reichstag. However, friends at the KKK were not alarmed by this development: the idea of one-man rule in Finland was ridiculous. The President had acted entirely according to the Constitution; it was a clever move on his part, for now the Parliamentary elections had to be held within three months. If there was to be trouble with Russia, it was best that the country be finished with all campaigns and elections as soon as possible. The supporters of Judge Honka, of course, were incensed and claimed that speeding up the elections was nothing but a tactic to short-circuit their campaign. Social Democrats stepped up their activity. For a few days Notes and international problems were forgotten in the smoke of local politics.

It was only a lull. On the seventeenth of November a new and more belligerent Note was presented to the Government: there were, it declared, "alarming new developments" and "danger of immediate attack" through the Baltic. The Kremlin demanded consultations at once, "perhaps military concessions."

These were almost the exact words of the communications of 1939, received in the same dark month, in the same isolation, the same horror of the irrational. Radios went on again in all the hotels, people collected in silent knots to listen, and the blue and white flags began flying daily from apartment houses. Then came the harbingers, winging from all over Europe, the special correspondents and cameramen, to fill up the Kämp Hotel again and watch for the kill over their glasses of whiskey. Nothing could have foretold disaster more clearly than the coming of the world's press. Marked men, who had returned during the three-week lull, slipped back across the border to Sweden. They met Swedish camera experts coming north with instructions to "shoot the Russians as they moved in."

Two British TV teams showed up in Helsinki to line up interviews with English-speaking Finns. Finland would be "on the air" in London Saturday night at eight o'clock, a toothy minion promised. (I wondered if Finland would be off the air permanently at the same time.)

Marja Binham was caught by the TV gangs down at the water-front market. Were the Russians after the Åland Islands or Lapland? Did she think the demands might possibly lead, perhaps, to war? If the Russians came would Finland fight? Marja, worried, plagued, embarrassed finally burst out wrathfully: "Fight, fight, of course, to the last drop! What are you thinking of?"

But the suave man smiled away from the question and went on to the next victim, Tauno Mustanoja, Professor of English.

"And now, Professor, would you say that Finland will fight?"

"I . . . hm . . . couldn't say."

"Why not, Professor? What about yourself, personally?"

"I . . . well . . . expect . . . as an officer in the reserve . . . to carry out my orders."

"But if the Russians are planning to take over . . . ?"

"That probably would not happen without . . . hm . . . a little bloodshed."

It didn't seem to occur to the job-doers of the BBC that all questions were much too relevant, and all answers potentially dangerous. The Saturday night show must go on; it had been promised. The interviewer wanted some local color, for the fall sunshine and the activity around the market place inspired the artist in him. His cameramen trained their lenses on one of

246

the fish vendors, an apple-cheeked apple-shaped woman who was scooping silvery Baltic herring into the kilo weighing boxes.

"Fish, young fellow?" she asked in Swedish.

"No, Madam. I want to put you on television."

"Go away then. Be so good."

"But the people in London are interested in Finland."

"What for?"

"Because of the crisis."

"What crisis?"

"The crisis with Russia, Madam."

"Oh, look, I haven't time for that . . ." and with that she returned to her fish boxes and customers.

Watching these queer presumptuous interviews, I was reminded once again of the old map of Finland, that outline of a man teetering but erect on his misshapen world, seeming to shout, with one arm raised to the West. The picture had changed before: first the cry was a glad one, of jubilation over his independence; then a cry of "Hurry" during the Winter War. Now the man seemed to be raising his hand in a warning to the West: "Hold on. Don't crowd me too hard. I'm alone up here, don't expect too much of me."

The dissolution of Parliament did not placate the Kremlin in any way. New threatening rumors filtered over the border and the sense of crisis deepened. After several days of silence, President Kekkonen abruptly decided to go and see the Soviet Premier personally. He was coolly informed at the Embassy that if he wished to see Mr. Khrushchev he would have to go all the way to Novosibirsk; the boss was a busy man. Mr. Kekkonen wanted no demonstrations at the railway station; instead he drove to Kotka to visit his brother, blinded in the past war, and then took the train to Leningrad and Novosibirsk. He had to travel clear across Russia into western Siberia. What weapons he had for argument, conciliation, or bargaining, no one but his closest associates knew. It would be hard to negotiate about a danger that didn't seem to exist, but the Soviet Note was clearly a summons.

Killing a nation takes a certain ceremony, and thinking that the time had not yet come, Elisabeth and I drove out with some friends to spend the night in their summer cottage. Their place was but a small piece of shoreline, facing out to sea, which they, because the man was a disabled veteran, had been permitted to buy from a Karelian refugee couple. In the early dark we followed the narrow road over rocky hills and beside swamps. The headlights of the car, moving to one side and the other, revealed a few small fields encumbered with brush, some haycocks gone brown with rain, and a forest dense and untrimmed. It was poor land, like many of the marginal farms one sees in the back country of New England.

When we reached the end of the road, we were in the muddy yard of a farm. The Karelians lived here, our friends said; they always stopped to see how the old couple was getting on. A barn loomed on one side of us and a small frame house on the other. Both looked dark until we switched off our lights, then we could see a glimmer from one of the windows of the house. Suddenly a door opened and a large man, silhouetted holding a paper, hailed us to come in.

"*Mitä kuulu?*" That expression so turgid with Finnish history. "What is heard?"

"Nothing much," our friend answered.

We followed the big man into the kitchen. Newspapers were spread upon the plain wood floor. An old-fashioned brick stove, oven and fireplace occupied one corner of the room and near it was a primitive sink and counter where the farmer's short, grey-haired wife was cleaning up the supper dishes. She came at once to greet us, wiping her hands on her apron.

"Welcome. Welcome." Then she set about making coffee.

Those two old people had the weather-beaten look of sixty or seventy years of farming, and a certain slow moving weariness of life. The summer had been a bad one, the old man mentioned, the rain had always come at the wrong time for the hay, and barley and wheat had not fared much better. He would have to log pulp in the winter, which, he wryly added, was no longer as easy as it used to be. After much talking of other things, the old man finally asked what was heard around the Capitol: did Honka have any chance to defeat Kekkonen? Not now, probably. What of this trouble with Russia? What was it all about?

248

"Difficult to say," our friend admitted. "But serious."

"Who can tell," the old Karelian sighed, "what Ivan is thinking about when he takes a notion in his head?"

The mistress of the house came with hot coffee and cups. She poured out coffee and motioned to us to sit down at the oilcloth-covered table. Then she brought some bread and cinnamon cake.

"If the Russians want to come here, let them come," she said emphatically.

Her husband smiled. "I don't know that I'd say that."

"We were chased out three times in the last war," she said. "This time I'm not going to budge."

For a while we ate cake and drank coffee in silence. Then the old farmer said, "She's right. We're too old. It is of no consequence what happens to us, although I can still use a gun . . . pretty well, too . . . But the young ones, it is a hard thing they face now."

"Let them come, I say," his wife said again, with a shrug. "If there is anything of value around here, I'd be glad to know."

ʝꝟureaucracy without Paper

November the dark month was three weeks deep when President Kekkonen journeyed across Russia to sit down with Premier Khrushchev around a bottle of vodka in a room in smoky Novosibirsk. He arrived just at nightfall, and at that critical moment he received word from Helsinki that Judge Olavi Honka had withdrawn his candidacy "for the sake of national unity." What happened that night in Novosibirsk was never made public in Finland, but by the following morning the "danger of attack in the Baltic" had apparently evaporated, formal discussions concerning military concessions were postponed indefinitely, and, according to Mr. Kekkonen, he and Mr. Khrushchev were in "complete agreement" on all questions.

The crisis passed. The absurdity of its inception was only emphasized by the speed of its resolution. Judge Honka, a minor martyr to pacts of nonintervention, retired from politics. The Social Democratic Party tried for a while to find another candidate, but the campaigns were in effect over. After a few days President Kekkonen returned and was acclaimed in the capital. In due time he was re-elected. The only visible effect of the crisis on the Parliamentary elections, held a month later, was that the Communists lost three seats.

Speculation concerning the resolution of the crisis ran to almost as many possibilities as the theories about its cause. The most interesting (though, I think, unlikely) suggestion was that "military concessions" *i.e.,* Russian bases in Finland, were

250

to have been demanded, but that at the last moment Swedish diplomats dropped a hint that such a move by Russia might force Sweden into the NATO organization.

In any case, President Kekkonen never explained what there had been "complete agreement" about, and the newspapers let the matter pass. Finnish politicians are a tight-lipped breed who believe that success should not be unsettled by too many facts, and that the better part of discretion is the wastebasket. The only clear statement of foreign policy to come out of the crisis was left to a young Helsinki poetess, Sirja Kumo:

> ... light green
> people
> musn't
> be oppressed
> we come
> from
> Persica
> in the
> far east
> and
> demand
> that
> our country
> has to be
> moved
> a few
> inches
> to the West.

The simplest explanation is probably the likeliest: that all this megaton diplomacy was blown up merely to ensure the re-election of President Kekkonen. He at least was a known quantity to the Russians, while behind Mr. Honka's back loomed not only that hated statesman, Väinö Tanner, but, what was worse, the probability of a rejuvenated Social Democratic Party. Not that Mr. Kekkonen and his Agrarian Party were particularly agreeable to the Kremlin, but the Social Democrats were a positive menace; they were the only party which, unified and back in power again, might ultimately cause the Finnish Communists to wither away.

Helsinki turned with gladness to Little Christmas, Independence Day, Lucia, the end of school, then Christmas. Prof. Kivimaa wrote one of those queer footnotes to civilization in the cold war, when he took a National Theater group to Berlin: on the west side of the new wall, barely out of earshot of the machine guns, they played Chekov's *Seagull* in Finnish to a packed German house and were acclaimed by forty-three curtain calls.

Time hurried by. We seemed to have much less time the second year in Finland. Marja Binham's father died—old Väinö Sola, one of the last of Sibelius' generation. Rector Kalle Kauppi died suddenly, three months after retiring from the KKK. Elisabeth's father was taken seriously ill and she flew home for three weeks in January to be with him. ("Hallelujah," I could hear the Judge singing, after his return from Leningrad. "Hallelujah," we echoed, after Novosibirsk.)

The only one of us who seemed not to bother about time was Tytti, she who was most pressed. As her Swedo-Finno-Karelian baby grew inside her, Tytti seemed to grow in spirits. Her mother had changed with the announcement of the baby. No longer did Mrs. Kaija demand that Tytti bring all her money home; instead the good lady began laying away clothes and sheets in readiness for the wedding. But the wedding was on no schedule. William said nothing about it. The kitchen staff of the Palace Hotel were joyfully collecting a sweepstakes—whether Tytti's offspring would be single or twins— but no one seemed to worry about a wedding. Tytti brushed the matter aside as unimportant. William's father, after all, was a strong-minded Swedish-Finn and it would take time for him to come around. Meanwhile, any pressure would only make him more stubborn. Tytti continued to come to our home twice a week—a fascinating changing figure for Ben and Bronwen to wonder about; she sang Karelian songs with Bronwen, romped with Steve, and murdered carpets with her bat. Tytti and William had recently been looking for an apartment, but only for the fun of looking, for William said he would be called to military service in the spring. However, such was Tytti's happiness at having a baby that even this she regarded as a minor detail.

In mid-February winter came. A few Siberian nights set the ice solid all along the coast and out several kilometers beyond the islands. Soon after, the snow came, and the mists vanished, leaving a pale blue sky overhead and a creamy soft light on the snow. For six weeks the weather hung steady, the temperature rarely going below 25° F. during the short day or below 15° at night. Icebreakers came out from the harbor to plow lanes through the islands to open water. Then the stately freighters began to pass, moving magically without a sound over a white desert.

We got out our birch touring skis, burned pine tar into the bottoms, waxed them for cold snow, and joined the travelers on the sea. Skiing is so simple, the Scandinavian way. The light equipment makes motion easy and a good track in cold snow naturally turns walking into a run. Old and young move with that effortless long stride which makes a 10-kilometer trip commonplace for grandmothers and 40 kilometers (25 miles) nothing for hardy men. Skiing is no fashion show or cocktail sport in Finland. It is a way of traveling and exploring in winter, of passing a day out of doors, alone or with friends, stopping, perhaps, to brew a cup of coffee by a ledge, sheltered from the piney wind.

One snowy night in March, as I was driving home alone after a ski jaunt with the Binhams, enjoying the lassitude of a long day in the woods, a sauna, and a good meal, I was hailed to the side of the road from an ancient black sedan. Two policemen in blue coats stepped out of the car, one a tall fellow, the other short and stocky. They sauntered up in a friendly manner and then the tall one said in German: "Your papers, please, mein Herr." I got out a wad of documents and passed them over. The two men read them, form by form, growing more and more puzzled. They seemed unaware, standing in the falling snow, of the rumbling traffic of Mannerheim Avenue brushing past their coats.

Shifting to English the tall man said: "Your plates? What is Skenic New Hampshire? No country has that name."

253

"It is a state—Scenic New Hampshire—in America, where I live."

"But the papers show," said the short man, in the tone of one who instinctively distrusts all paper, "that this car came from Germany more than a year ago." According to law, he went on, no foreign car could stay in Finland for more than a year without the owner having to pay the usual state excise tax. I explained that I had known this, but that the VW salesman in Helsinki had said everything would be all right if, at the end of the year, I had the car registered and insured as American.

At this, the two men shrugged their shoulders: "Salesmen tell many things . . ." They asked me to report in the morning to the chief of police and, after writing down my name and address, wished me good night.

My two friends—they had been so courteous I could think of them only as friends—were waiting for me at the office of the chief when I came in next morning. The deep grooving of the wooden floors and the stains on the corridor walls of the old building on Alexander's Square reminded me that the police in Finland had at times been as important as the government and the army; thinking of Chief Gabrielsson, who twice in 1948 had blocked a Soviet coup, I was a little ashamed to be bothering the police with so minor a matter, yet at the same time intrigued by the idea of seeing the workings of Finnish bureaucracy.

By daylight the two policemen seemed even more agreeable than they had the night before. The tall one had the lean sharp face and halting speech of a small-town Vermont cop; the same sad, friendly expression, too. He seemed uneasy in a tight blue uniform. The other man was the opposite, a chubby, happy, talkative extrovert, dressed as a plain-clothes detective.

When the chief was free to see us, the two men conducted me into an inner office. They took all the documents including my passport, work permit, and University appointment, and laid out the case before him. The chief however was unimpressed. He kept shaking his head saying, "It is impossible, the law is quite clear," and "It is a matter for the customs inspector." When the session was over, the chief apologized, but said he had no authority to make an exception to the law. I didn't quite know what he meant, but I could see the case was going badly.

My two friends ushered me out of the office and then in the corridor outside the tall one said, "I am sorry, but we must take the car to customs."

"He can take it home and take everything out," interceded the stocky one. "We will come for it in the evening."

"Will I be able to get it back?" I asked.

"Perhaps. . . . But I am not so sure."

For a fleeting moment, driving home, I thought that the best thing would be to load up the car and drive it immediately to Sweden. Once over the border nothing could happen to it and we would be able to pick it up on our way to Norway and England. But then I reflected that Finns had always treated me squarely. Something would happen, some reasonable way would be found out of this legal dilemma.

With true consideration the two policemen did not call to take the car until well after dark. No one but our children saw the red bus driving off, and they were excited by the idea that "Daddy almost was thrown in jail!"

Two interviews with a customs inspector (a janitor who had once been a sailor acting as interpreter) convinced me that I had been far too optimistic about the reasonableness of Finnish law. The inspector said I must either pay the Finnish excise tax (about $1,800, 80 per cent of the purchase price) or I must ship the car at once back to Germany. Later, as an extreme concession, he agreed to impound the car for the next three months in a state warehouse and then see that it was delivered aboard the ship *Bore* on our day of departure. The trouble, he said, was not that we had done anything very wrong—although the advice from the VW salesman had been entirely contrary to Finnish law—but that the law was very simple, and made no provision whatsoever for any exceptions.

Elisabeth, who has a practical mind, got in touch with a lawyer, but he, after reading the law aloud to us, thought we were lucky that customs had not confiscated the car altogether.

"You could, of course, call your Ambassador," he suggested.

But we were opposed to asking such a favor. Finns might give in to an Ambassador, but they would resent that kind of pressure; they had had enough of outside pressures.

Fortunately the spring thaw had set in and we had little need of a car. During the "sports vacation" from school Ben went off with a busload of Finnish boys and two trip leaders to a Sports Institute in central Finland. The boys skied all day, going on cross-country tours or running races. Ben returned full of praise for the Finnish school system, especially the vacations, and for the teachers, who, it seemed, had let them drink coffee and stay up half the night playing poker. But that was the end of the skiing in Finland for us.

Meanwhile Bronwen had acquired, according to all rumors, "a boy friend." She fiercely denied the fact, said he was the worst boy in the class, always jumping out on her from the bushes to chase her and pull her hair. Once Bronnie complained so bitterly to her teacher about this ruffian that Mrs. Laitinen asked young Risto why he wanted to hurt Bronwen. "But I *love* Bronwen," wailed the honest Finn, full of a lonely passion.

When the ice broke up out on the sea, young Finns came to the shore with another passion. From all over Lauttasaari they came, to jump onto the floes and pole and paddle them out to sea, two or three urchins to a cake of ice as big as the wall of a house. When the floes split, there was a hectic scramble to get aboard the largest fragments. We saw one boy stranded with his bicycle on a slab of ice in the middle of the bay. A shift of wind was driving him steadily offshore; many watched, but no one thought of launching a boat. As the boy passed an edge of solid ice making out from the gulls' island, he gave the bicycle a mighty heave toward safety, but the machine went down in deep water with its wheels spinning. Then the boy fell in, swam to the ice and clambered out to dance and wait for rescue.

On another day two young seafarers in Bronwen's school had the bad luck to put to sea in a skiff with little more than a lattice for a bottom. When the boys were picked up, hanging to the gunwales in a mash of ice, both were too cold to speak or move and one spent the rest of the spring convalescing from pneumonia.

These reckless acts always horrified me, but had long since ceased to surprise me. Some lemming instinct seizes young Finns in the spring and they board a chunk of ice or driftwood raft and go down to the sea. Neither parents nor police interfere.

Spring weather and the long soft evenings of May once again brought up the question of the VW bus, impounded by customs and awaiting our departure. To make a small frustration matter more acute, we had been offered a chance to cruise in June among the western islands of Finland, and would need the bus to get out to the rather remote starting point. Elisabeth had worn out her patience anyway. Daughter of a lawyer, she felt sure that no law could be written, in Finland or anywhere else, that a good man couldn't find a way around. If worst came to worst, we should ask the Ambassador for help; arguments against using his good offices daily became more academic, she thought. An economist at the KKK, who said he knew someone high up in customs, volunteered to take up the case again, but he came back downcast at having to report that there was absolutely no loophole in the law.

Another friend, a man in the export-import business, tried to persuade the Department of Transport to issue a special temporary bus license; this ingenious scheme came to nothing. Very sadly he said, "There is only one way I can think of . . . that is, I can try to get the chief customs inspector to change the date on the importation slip . . . write a later date . . ."

I believe the good man would have attempted even that, but I refused. Everyone had treated us courteously and with great honesty in Finland and I couldn't stomach the idea of asking such a grotesque favor. Instead I went back to the customs officer whom I had originally interviewed. I understood about the bus, I said, and was sorry for the trouble it had caused; I only wanted permission to have the car taken to a garage where the winter salt might be washed off and the oil drained and changed, so that all would be ready when, on a Sunday, we disembarked in Stockholm.

The officer agreed at once, called in an assistant, gave me back all the papers and documents he had kept, and sent us off to get the bus and take it to a garage. Two days later, the bus oiled, washed and polished, I drove back to the warehouse where it had been stored. The attendant at the door seemed surprised to see the car again and the officer to whom I handed the papers refused to accept them, saying, "We are finished with that car. You are free to take it."

Mystified by this turn of events, and certain that if I drove the car away the police would only pick me up again, I asked to see the chief of the customs depot. This man, a handsome man of Swedish extraction, assured me that what I had learned was true, I could take the car and go.

"But I don't understand," I said. "Who has cleared the car?"

"One of the men called on the telephone. A big boss."

"I will need some paper, or statement, to show if the police—"

"No paper is necessary. All is quite in order."

"Then could I have the man's name?" I asked. "I'd like to thank him for his kindness."

The officer smiled across the desk and shook his head.

"No thanks are necessary."

So, feeling like a felon turned loose by some mistake, feeling even that the car was not ours but something I had stolen, I took the car and drove back to Lauttasaari. Well, I thought, here is a car thrown into hock because of an inadequate law and released again because someone wanted to wash salt off and change the oil. . . . That's a queer way to run a government, but who am I to complain?

Weeks later, when no police came to inquire about Skenic New Hampshire, it slowly filtered into my head what had happened. All along, Customs had wanted to find some pretext by which to accommodate us; since the law did not provide for an exception, the case must somehow be made to disappear. Unwittingly I had given customs that opportunity by asking to take the car out; the file on the case could then be disposed of and a few telephone calls would take care of the rest.

I don't know that this is what happened; I never tried to find out, for I, too, am nervous about getting things down on paper. But to make sure that the police would not confiscate the car on the day of our departure, I went down to see my two friends at headquarters. They were much amused by what had happened, but would not commit themselves as to how it came about.

"I never heard of this way"—the short man grinned—"but if it works, why not?"

We do not know
how long
the sea has washed
our bones.
—Timo Elo

A Passage of Shores

What the lakes are in the east of Finland, islands are in the west, the one a fair after-image of the other. Where chains of lakes, countless in number, run down like fragments of sky to the great Saimaa waterway, in the west the land makes off in constellations of islands, skerries, reefs, many unnamed and unsounded, more than a hundred miles before coalescing into the land mass of the Åland Islands. Geologists say that the granite bed of Finland is the oldest rock on the continent and that it is slowly rising. Little by little the archipelago grows seaward as the bones of the Baltic rise and weather in the wind.

With the luck of a good boat, and a willing sailor, we cruised for seven days and saw one configuration of islands. Of course we should have been packing up, making ready to go—we had but two weeks left; already I had begun to have that tumbrel feeling, but Elisabeth, with a sure instinct for the important, simply said, "I don't care if we never pack—just throw the junk in a box—but let's go sailing in the Ålands."

Arndt was our skipper, the *Freya* his father's sloop. Arndt had received a grant to study agricultural economics at the University of Wisconsin; he was glad for a crew and a chance to practice his English. Moreover these were his waters. With his father and mother he had twice made the passage to Stockholm. Arndt wanted a week in The Nature before exiling himself to America. Thus the cruise had been arranged.

Even the excellent charts did not prepare us for the island

nebulae we would sail through. For two days out of Turku we sailed embedded in forests, reaching west and southwest as the waterways allowed. On our first day's run we saw many summer cottages scattered along the bluffs of the larger islands, each with its flagpole and its sauna down by the water, but after that the habitations disappeared except for an occasional farm holding back the spruce with emerald fields. Sometimes the channels opened out to a fair reach and then the *Freya*, with a good northwester over her quarter, picked up her skirts and ran. But soon after we were back, tacking through narrows where the sun beat on deck and the wind brushed fitfully past from any point of the compass. In two days we saw no other people and only three other sails. They crossed briefly, miles away, between the islands.

"There exists no archipelago like this anywhere in the world," Arndt claimed.

"Not the Aegean?" I countered.

"Oh, no, steep rocky cliffs, open seas, dangerous seas . . ."

I thought of the San Juan islands and of Penobscot Bay, but Finland's western archipelago could give them ten islands to one and still have enough left over to stock Long Island Sound and San Francisco Bay.

We towed no dinghy, and I felt rather reckless without one. But a Finnish skipper at night moors his vessel to a tree on some bold shore and sets an anchor out astern. In storm he does the same. If the wind should shift at night and expose the anchorage, there is light enough in the summer, even at midnight, to sail out to a better shelter.

On the evening of the second night we finally left the domesticated waters of the coast behind for the open water and scattered small islands that are the best sailing grounds. At once the heat of the inner archipelago left us, the west wind turned raw. One by one the layers of clothes went on, until under eight layers, we were reasonably comfortable. We beat to the west; though we passed many good anchorages that evening, Arndt wanted to make one of his father's favorite coves. After passing a lighthouse and coastguard station, Arndt slacked the sheets and let the *Freya* run to the south, away from the main channel, until he reached his cherished harbor.

261

He brought the *Freya* between lumpy low islets into a small landlocked basin. But there, to his disgust, were two other sailboats, tied up snug to a steep bluff. Without a second thought he put the boat about and headed out.

"Hey. What's going on?" Ben wailed. His belly had been clamoring for hours.

"That place wasn't very nice . . ." Arndt replied, surprised that anyone would want to tie up there. "It is too crowded. Already there are people . . ."

Instead, we spent the night snugged up to a smooth apron of reddish granite in a tiny cove surrounded by spruce. We pitched the tent for Kim and Elisabeth on a shelf of blueberry bushes and then built a fire of driftwood. For supper we had chunks of sauna sausage grilled on sticks over a sputtering fire. Grease and charcoal collected around our lips, and on our hands. The expedition began to look like a minstrel show. Day dwindled into evening and evening into a pearly twilight. Midnight came with pale stars overhead. We sang a few songs. Arndt taught us some sea songs from the Åland Islands, and one haunting melody about a girl whose love has been taken to a castle in the service of the king. No one could think of any good reason to go to bed except that the June dawn would be upon us in two hours.

We thought we were miles from other people that night, but in the morning we were wakened by the intermittent running of a motorboat engine, as though some fisherman were hauling traps. Then while we were at breakfast two small blonde girls came atop the rock slope, staring down at us with steadfast gazes until our notice and a question put them to flight. Even on this remote island there must be a salt-water farm. Hoping to replenish our water supply, we took a jug and started over the rocks to a wood. Soon we came to a trail, and this led to a stretch of open pasture, a bay, and a small wooden house. A plump wife met us at the door; yes of course we could have water, but where did we come from, where were we going?

On hearing from Arndt that we were Americans the woman laughed and said, "The girls said you spoke a strange language.

They thought you must be Russians." She spoke a pure lilting Swedish.

Nothing would do but we must come in and have some coffee. In a tiny room whose windows were bright with flowers the woman sat us down, called her husband, and plied us with coffee. These people had never seen Americans, but they had relatives in Minnesota . . . did we by chance know them? What was it like in Minnesota? The man had always hoped one day to travel there, but now he thought he would never be able to go; half of his living he made by the sea, the other half cutting pulpwood in winter.

"We don't get rich. But we like it, don't we, girls?" he said to the two pixies munching cake by the window.

Elisabeth asked the farmer what the girls would do when they had to go to school. Reading and writing and numbering they could learn at home—but then would they have to go to the mainland? The man put out his brown hand and touched one of the blonde heads: "We haven't decided that yet, have we?"

The little one scowled and shook her head. School, like Minnesota, was one of those irrevocable separations.

Our friends came down to the rock to see us off, the fisherman bringing a two-foot pike-perch he'd caught that morning, and the little girls arriving each with a fistful of lilies of the valley which they had run to pick for us. The lady hoped we would visit their relatives in Minnesota, and of course, someday, "Welcome to come back."

We will, we promised, believing the promise though knowing it was unlikely. They stood on the rock—a lean blue-eyed farmer, his wife, and two girls with corn-silk hair blowing across their faces—waving us off, their four blue shadows slanting down to the water.

"*Farväl.*" They called to us as the *Freya* began to feel the wind. *Farväl*, good friends, once seen. For winds change and courses alter. It is a great sea, the world—we occupy but a little stretch of island shore, and only chance winds and lucky courses hold us together.

These people of the western islands are Swedes, original and

263

undiluted. They have been here at least as long as the Finns, who preferred the mainland. Swedish is their only language; they have a regional government of their own; and but for a decision by the League of Nations after the first World War, the people of this western archipelago would now be Swedes. Arndt, a mainlander, was more truly a Swedish-Finn. Tall, handsome, soft-spoken, he had all the outgoing ways and natural courtesies of that aristocratic race. At one time his family had been landlords over a considerable tract of farms and thousands of acres of woodland in southwestern Finland. But the wars, land redistribution, the settlement of refugees, high taxes, and the penury of academic life had trimmed those acres to two small plots where the family still comes in the summer. We had visited Arndt's family once before the cruise—coming down to caulk and paint the *Freya* and get her ready for the sea. (In Finland every yachtsman does his own yard work.) The family estate had gone to weeds and vines, paint scaling, ridgepoles sagging. Yet at mealtimes when the aunts, cousins, and grandchildren collected in one tall gold and white room and sat in stiff chairs around tables covered with white linen, they brought the Victorian age back with them. I had the odd sensation of looking at a reversal of the norm of life: here in Finland the people never changed; it was the buildings that grew old and crumbled.

I think Arndt was glad to get offshore with us who brought along neither past nor future. We had no traditions to follow, were anchored to no weed-grown estate which had once been a civilization and which still bloomed each spring with frail sweet ladies. Arndt's love of the land was at least as much poetic and mystical as it was agricultural. He would probably not be a farmer; he might become a professor of farming.

All that day we beat to the westward against a steady breeze. The islands withdrew toward the horizon and left us in unbuoyed deep water. The *Freya* was a smart little sloop, one of those lapstreak Folkboats popular in Scandinavia. In twelve hours we made about thirty-five miles. That evening we anchored completely alone in a compound of low glaciated islands called Kråkskär. Sea gulls blackguarded us with epithets from the safe currents of air, and a flock of black ducks lumbered off the water at our approach, skimming the ledges and vanishing. But then with the furling of our sail everything subsided into peace, broken only by the steady sound of surf outside Kråkskär.

Arndt treated us to a supper of pike-perch baked in juniper: he wrapped the fish, buttered and salted, in eight layers of newspaper, soaking each one in sea water; then in the bed of a good fire he buried the corpus delecti, covered with juniper branches, and over this he put more coals and more wood. After exactly half an hour he dug our charred supper from the fire, peeled away the black crusty skin and laid the pale pink meat open, steaming and aromatic, on its tray of bones. The fish and our small supply of beer made up the whole meal; to wash dishes we had only to lick our fingers. Day drifted into evening, the sun had to make its trip under the northern pole and we had to think about the return leg of the cruise.

Next day, on to Utö, the Out-Island. Utö would be our farthest point, then we would have to turn back. Rain caught us, sweeping out of the south, before we had made good our passage across an unmarked stretch of water to the main inshore ship's channel. After that it was tack and tack, working from headland to island, ledge to reef or pile of stones, hour after hour in a steep sea. Sometimes a thin fog shut us in, so that we had to navigate by feel. The waters had been charted by air photographs, but soundings were incomplete. I was reminded of that blind offshore feeling Philip Booth once set down in a Penobscot poem. I had taught the poem in Helsinki, now it was teaching me:

> Whoever works a storm to windward, sails
> in rain, or navigates in inland fog,
> must reckon from slow swung lead, from squalls
>
> on cheek; must bear by compass, chart, and log.
> Parallels are ruled from compass rose
> to known red nun: but the landfall leg
>
> risks set of tide, lost buoys, and the breakers' noise
> on shore where no shore was. . . .

We risked no set of tide in the Baltic, only a keel and a spruce-planked bottom over the sudden ledges, but Arndt was not worried. We could work the *Freya* through the rocks somehow. If a storm came we could run to some island, sound our way in, and tie up for the night. It wasn't necessary to get anywhere, the important thing was to be somewhere.

Along about eight P.M. the clouds began to lift and the wind to increase. We raised the massive block tower that is Utö's famous lighthouse and radar station. Beyond Utö was the open Gulf of Finland and the main sea lanes to the east; beyond these at some unspecified distance the waters of Russian Estonia. Perhaps even Arndt was glad that evening to see the lighthouse, and the cottages and fish shacks surrounding a secure harbor. Weary but thankful we felt the *Freya* escape from the surge at the harbor mouth and slip between a bare black shore and a green-and-white reef that stood licked by long waves almost midway in the channel. On top of the stone lighthouse was a kind of walkway, above which was the glass cage of the light. Two soldiers came out on the walkway to watch us through field glasses as we beat in, and a soldier, carrying a rifle, was waiting on the government wharf to meet us.

Arndt brought the *Freya* smartly in. Inside the L of the wharf he dropped the sails and let her drift up easy. Two military boats were tied along the other side, and on the L was a two-masted schooner loaded to the booms with split birch firelogs. As we drifted up to the dock, Arndt hailed the soldier in Finnish and asked if we could tie up for the night.

"Why not?" the man said, putting down his rifle and taking the bow line. "But there is one thing, you cannot take pictures on the island. To the land you must not bring cameras."

"Good," replied Arndt. "Can we walk around?"

"Yes, except where the guns are. You must not try to look at the guns."

"What about the tent?"

"It is forbidden to stay on the land . . . but after all you could put up the tent on the wharf."

"On the wharf?" Arndt laughed.

"The wharf looks on the water to me."

So it was agreed that Elisabeth and Kim would sleep at the end of the pier next to the lumber schooner. The soldier seemed much amused by these novel arrangements and helped us unload the tent and sleeping bags. He and Arndt talked with complete amity in Finnish. Arndt spoke the language with a trace of Swedish accent, but with Finnish frankness and Finnish humor. One could see that here at least, among the younger people, the centuries of hostility between Swede and Finn had no place.

We asked the young man if he wanted to come aboard but he, suddenly remembering and picking up his rifle, said he was supposed to be on duty. As he prepared to leave he grinned and said confidentially, "About the cameras, it is forbidden, to take pictures *on the land*. . . . But if you are *on the boat* you are not on land. Who's to stop you taking pictures from the boat?"

After getting settled for the night, we went ashore to stretch our legs and see the tiny village of Utö. The rain had stopped and a lightening of the sky seemed to promise better weather. Though we had been told not to look at the guns, on that small flat island it was impossible not to see the emplacements, the trenches, even the muzzles projecting over sandbags and revetments of broken rock. As the path to the lighthouse was unbarred we climbed the hill and entered the massive stone tower. Inside were wooden steps leading to a landing some thirty feet up where two soldiers met us and conducted us to a small office that looked out over the harbor. We could not go higher on the tower, one soldier said, unless the Lieutenant gave his permission. Still, it was becoming a fine evening, the other one said, and a shame not to see all the islands from the top. The first sat down and reached for the telephone.

"It is nine thirty," Elisabeth interposed. "The Lieutenant would not want to be called so late."

"It is all right," the soldier shrugged. "He has nothing to do."

He called, but after a rapid exchange in Finnish, he said, "*Hyvää Hyvää*," and put down the telephone with a sigh.

"It is impossible to go up. I am sorry."

However from the window in the tower we could see 180°

267

to the north: sunset in a great flood of warm light was pouring in across the water under a compact ceiling of clouds, the sea was all alight except for the black islands—from which we had come, to which we would go. It was one of those evenings so intense in color, so languid in change, that even nature seems to stop and marvel at her skill.

When we were ready to go down, we thanked the soldiers and shook hands.

"I'm very sorry," the first one said again. "Perhaps next time, when you come back, you can go up there."

"The Lieutenant is new," explained the other man.

"That's it. He is only three days on Utö. . . . After a while he will know something."

We went aboard the *Freya* with the sunset still drenching the harbor. Two small boys came by sculling a heavy rowboat into the purple shadows of a boathouse. Ben went fishing, and the girls decided to prepare a hot meal. Kim set up the alcohol stove outside and when the pan of water was hot, dumped in an envelope of dried pea soup. After a while I noticed our two friends on the walkway of the tower. One had his field glasses trained on us.

"Kim, your boy friend wants to come to supper . . ."

"What?"

"He's smelled that pea soup."

"What *are* you talking about?"

"Look at the tower."

Kim looked up and at once blushed. "Me? He's not looking at me."

"Give him a wave and see."

Kim laughed, giving just the slightest wave with her fingers. At once the soldier with the glasses waved back. It must have been an instinctive reaction, for then we saw the man turn to the other, laughing, and both waved again and disappeared. But from time to time after that we caught sight of them watching us from the windows.

Sunset cooled slowly around us, the colors deepened to pools of purple light flexing to the rhythms of the harbor, pure blue night flooded in. Time to sleep.

Early in the morning the captain of the coasting schooner,

268

his cheeks bristling with grey stubble, came on deck to begin unloading his cargo of birch firelogs. There before him on the wharf was an orange mushroom-shaped tent. He hesitated, scratching his white thatch with a hooked finger, then he tapped gently on the tent with his cap: "Please—now comes a tractor for the wood."

In a moment the people of Utö were treated to the sight of two barefooted women in pink nighties striking their tent at the end of the wharf amid a shower of birch logs.

Between loads by the tractor cart the old captain had time to visit with us. An American Victory ship was wrecked here, he recalled, just after the war. It was Christmas Eve and a heavy storm going, thick snow, when she struck on a ledge just east of the island. We would see her masts still, he said, if we were going east. The people on Utö knew nothing of the disaster until red flares went up, an awful sight way off there in a storm. The flares kept going up and fading away. There was no coast guard here, but the fishermen of Utö went out in their powerboats while the women set about arranging a hot meal and bedding for the survivors in an old barracks building. The fishermen managed to bring back most of the crew of the ship, managed to bring themselves back too, which was a long chance, considering, the old seaman said. The American Government out of gratitude to the fishermen of Utö sent them money and a silver candle-tree for the chapel, one candle for each man lost.

The thing that everyone remembers best was a Negro seaman. People on Utö had never seen a Negro before. This one was a giant, black as a December night, with white all around his eyes and a big white smile. When he first shouldered through the door of the hut into the light, all wet, his face and arms shining, the women didn't know whether they were seeing a god or a cannibal. "Umm umm. Thank you Baby Jesus," he rumbled from the depths of a chest as big as an oil drum. Utö girls thought he was the handsomest man they had ever seen. They still think so.

Utö was special, one of those ports that every sailor marks with a star on his secret chart. We couldn't bring ourselves to hoist sail. Even Arndt wanted to stay. We walked around the

269

unfenced area, bought provisions and postcards at the Kiosk, visited the small wooden chapel, watched a detachment of recruits ostensibly marching. Some beardless corporal was trying to keep them in order.

"Come on. Come on. Try to look like something. You're Finnish heroes now." But they straggled and talked and smirked at the girls as they went by.

Later, as we were starting down the harbor, coiling up the halyards and getting things stowed away, I said to Kim, "What about your boyfriend, Kim?"

"What?"

"Your Finnish soldier boy. I bet he has glasses on you right now?"

"Daddy! Don't be so romantic."

"Then stand up and wave him good-by."

Kim stood on the top of the cabin and waved at the square tower now nearly half a mile away; almost at once two small black figures appeared up on the walkway, waving back.

Näkemiin

After the cruise, we said *Farväl* to Arndt and started back to Helsinki. The sea breezes vanished over the moist land and we were back in summer where we could almost feel the growing power of the sun. This southern land looked as rich as it was peaceful, stretching away in broad fields on either side and populated with barns and well-kept houses. There was a long white road running from the islands, with the chimneys of a cement factory showing over hills—a straight road where, while still at a great distance, we made out the figure of a man limping. He was carrying a black suitcase, walking like an awkward marionette, alone and miles from any town or bus station.

"Want a ride?" Ben hailed him as we pulled up alongside.

"Excuse me," the man replied.

"Want a ride?"

"Is there some trouble?" he inquired, looking at the tires.

"No. Get in. We'll take you."

The small wiry man, astonishment written on his face, pushed his suitcase through the door and clambered in after it. He was wearing a dark threadbare jacket, and a clean white shirt. He had no necktie, but the shirt was carefully buttoned at his throat. For a while he said nothing. He was looking at the passing fields and houses with a great smile. The fields were spread with yellow just now, the warm golden yellow of dandelions standing head to head over acres of coming hay.

"These are good farms," the man volunteered, nodding with

pleasure. "Anyone can see that." He told us he had come from the east to find work among the sugar beets. That job was done now and he was going to Hämeenlinna where he had heard he might find other farm work. There wasn't much else he knew how to do, he said, but it was good to get out and work on the land.

After some urging he told us about his leg. He had been wounded seven times during the past war. "There's enough steel in there to start a factory." The government had given him full disability and he now received a pension amounting to about $7 a month. That was a generous thing, he said, for after all he was not totally disabled. He could still do some work, mainly farming.

"Finland is a good country," he meditated. "Imagine, with all the wounded they had, they could still look after me."

When the way to Hämeenlinna branched off from our Helsinki road, our companion stepped out, thanked us and wished us luck. He was the last stranger we met in Finland and the impression he left was a kind of summary of our years there. Finns were strange people, just as the Russians had discovered twenty-five hundred years ago. Their simple honesty, their plain blunt peasant honesty seemed to belong to another century altogether, to the age of Jefferson and Tom Paine. It had probably gotten them into trouble, trying to manage the double-talk of modern politics, but it had also given them the strength to keep going, a spiritual second-wind. Their whole remarkable history had been one of turning impossible barriers into bare possibilities.

Three, two, one—our last days passed on Lauttasaari and abstracted us into elsewhere. I was surprised to notice how my own feelings changed. When an interlude is done it is done and everything seems to know it; immediate surroundings seem to be pulling away toward the horizon. Even the strange and beautiful language began to slip from my grasp. I began to feel dissociated, a stranger again in the place that had been our home for two years. Recent events, the cruise, the crisis, began to lose the sharp edges of detail, while things of the moment struck my consciousness with the old original shock of surprise and half-belief.

272

Bronwen had a birthday, an ecstasy of taffeta and skip ropes conducted all in Finnish. Finns had a birthday too; they call it Midsummer. The sun over Yllästunturi, in its six weeks' day, would be starting its voyage south; Aarne Kantola, having scythed his field and stacked the warm hay on spiked poles to dry, would be steaming in his sauna; and out on Utö the sweating corporal would still be exhorting his grinning recruits: "Come on. Try to look like something. You're Finland's heroes now."

Our apartment reverted to its original state, all furniture, books, dishes, pictures, lamps, clothing, skis, and many farewell gifts being in the hands of movers for crating and stowage on a ship. Once again we found ourselves making supper of bread and milk, and camping in a basketball court.

That evening Kim filled our empty bottles with candles and decorated the bare walls with murals cut from pieces of leftover wrapping paper. The Nordgrens and other neighbors dropped in to drink beer and toast the summer night with the strong but delicate Koskenkorva. From the big window we could see the bonfire growing out on the point of the beach. As the East Germans could not mix in such a party, Elisabeth and I went next door to say good-by. Only the *Hausfrau* was at home, as pretty and plump as ever. Rather timidly, she begged us to come in and have coffee with her, a strange sort of visit in a well-furnished room behind Venetian blinds that were always down. There was nothing political in her talk; she seemed not the least interested in politics—that was for her husband. In the end she held out her hand and said, "I hope all goes well for your country."

"And I for yours," I said. Neither of us knew exactly what we meant, but that did not make the wish untrue.

Later on in the evening Tytti breezed in from work at the Palace Hotel, bringing William and the good news that they were going to be married. When? "Oh sometime. Soon." William's father, after months of resistance, had given the young couple not only his consent but his blessing. Tytti looked beautiful. Her funny animated face glowed and her eyes sparkled in the candlelight. Bronnie danced around in front of her chanting, "Tytti's getting married. Tytti's getting married

273

. . ." and then she shouted those awful words: "to a *Ruotsi-lainen* . . . A SWEDE!"

William Johanson, who up to that point had hung back looking rather like a trapped male, laughed outright and shouted back, "Yes, and WHAT'S SO BAD about Swedes!"

William, a slender black-haired young man, explained in a matter-of-fact way why his father had been so slow to accept this marriage. His father had been the son of a wealthy land owner whose name and estate dated back before the Russian conquest, one on whom wealth and position had been conferred almost as a right. But one thing and another—strikes, poor investments, the wars—had divested him of his property. Piece by piece, the estate had been sold, and the man who patiently bought it up was one of the former Finnish tenant farmers.

Finally to the elder Johanson, William's grandfather, there remained only one small house in a corner lot. When the grandfather died, the house was left to William's father. One day the Finn drove a manure wagon over to the Johanson's place and, without even getting down from the seat, told them they would have to get out.

"I own this place," William's father stated.

"Where is the deed?"

"There is no deed. There is your letter to my father."

"The letter states the house is his. Nothing is mentioned about the land. . . . Take the shack then and get out."

William's father vowed he would never speak to a Finn again. He had kept the vow as best he could until this Karelian daughter came along, bright as a broadaxe and twice as sharp.

"You see"—William smiled—"now the Finns have even gotten me away."

"Perhaps, now, you can get your shack back, William," Tytti suggested.

"Tytti, you ruined my chance for an education," William said in mock sorrow.

"That's nothing. Look what you did to my Baseball!"

Tytti's marriage had been made in a bed, without a great deal of forethought (so she had admitted), but already the relationship was molding the two people and their parents into

274

a good-humored realism that should make it a success. I thought of the months the girl had spent as the child grew in her belly and began kicking, how she continued her work at the Palace Hotel and refused to be upset by the Johansons or to put any pressure on them. How wise her patience had been! Now, not the least bit abashed by her condition, nor conceding anything to the grudges of the ancients, she would go down the aisle in church to complete the ceremony. She would go down the aisle like a cup defender flying a spinnaker.

The words of the old General, written for another time, proved right for all times:

> Let us forget division and distrust and no longer dissipate the nation's power on secondary matters. We shall all need each other; God grant that shoulder to shoulder we will be strong enough.

The marriage seemed a good omen, and, in a sense, the end of things we must oversee in Finland. Tytti had brought Steve a pair of long pants and a jacket and cap; if he was to leave Finland he would leave looking like a proper Finn. From the window of our apartment we could look out upon the crowd on the beach where the Midsummer fire was vaunting its small giddy sparks into the sky. All over Finland the fires would be burning, on the sunlit hills of Lapland, along the green-backed lakes, on the skerries of the Baltic, over Sweden too, and Norway, and Denmark—this celebration of the sun who from one sky gives us all the accident of life.

When the time came for Tytti to go, she wept, kissed us all, asked to be forgiven for not coming to see us off (the Kaijas and the Johansons were having a day-long picnic on an island), hugged Steve again, then ran off up the road with William.

We blew out Kim's candelabra and lay down on the floor of Kuikkarinne 2 under our raincoats. The sky was already lightening.

Departure was almost too simple to be real: load up the VW bus at noon, pile in children and suitcases, check all the empty rooms and drawers for a last time, drive to south Harbor an hour early so the car could be hoisted onto the *Bore*'s foredeck, watch the changing colors of the light breeze on the harbor, enclosed in the arms of the city.

Only the *Bore*, of all the ships in the harbor, had steam up; the rest had been tied up and abandoned, though all of them—tugboats, liners, freighters—carried the flag of the day, young birch trees tied to the foremasts. Scarcely a person was to be seen on the waterfront of the white-walled town.

And then, unexpectedly, a delegation appeared: Maila of the solemn brown eyes, and her older blonde-haired sister. They had made the trip alone by bus from Lauttasaari to see Bronwen off; now they came up shyly and thrust a rose into the hands of Elisabeth and Bron. We bought them ice cream; soon they were jabbering away with Bron and Ben as though time did not exist, only the wonderful things there were to think about now that it was summer.

Then: a movement of people toward the gates, farewells, inspectors, passports, tickets, a gangplank, a small steel cabin and the windy sound of blowers, the pulse of engines, the first burst out on a deck filled with machinery and people, the long look down to the never-quiet water.

I think Bronwen had not thought about leaving until now. She suddenly stopped on the foredeck, stopped her running exploration of the ship, and stood like a small old woman in a blue coat. She could make out Maila and her sister by the rail fence up on the street, two tiny figures waving but much too far away to call to.

The hawsers slacked and splashed in the water, a rumble and surge came from the stern, the town began to move. To Bron no ocean would ever again seem such a gulf as this one, widening between the ship and the quay where the refuse of the harbor spun aimlessly in the eddies. She stood by herself, leaking tears, holding a sagging rose. Then as the ship began to push ahead, swinging by the Palace Hotel, the market place, the University and government buildings, as the wind of our forward motion began to be felt, Bron bolted along the deck.

"Where are you going, Little One?"

"Down."

"Don't you want to see the castle?"

"No."

276

"Or Lauttasaari? We'll go right past it."

"NO!"

The ship took the inshore passage and for a while we could make out pieces of familiar landscape, the black spires of two old churches, the Tech buildings, the Lauttasaari bridge and Windmill Hill, the water tower, our bay and its tiny boats. Then spruce islands closed them off.

Much later, after supper, the *Bore* lay over in two grinding right-angle turns that sent us all to the decks; there was a harbor and a village, many bare islands, a lighthouse. Someone said it was Hanko, near which we had cruised. After Hanko the ship headed west again where there were only islands under a low sunset.

Finland had been kind to us. She had treated us with hospitality and the courtesy of neglect; she had given us a job and a home and then gone about her business. We had seen something of the brilliance of her arts and the strength of her families. We had admired her common-sense socialism as well as her unorganizable individuals. We had shared a bad time, and the freedom kept by her uncowed, unpanicky ways.

Thinking back on the strange business of trying to teach Finns anything, I wondered after all who had been teacher and who student. It seemed likely that in years to come we would need their example more than they had needed us.

About eleven o'clock that night while the *Bore* steamed steadily to the west, Ben came running along the deck: "There it is. That's the tree. See it? Our island. Where we stayed that night. Remember? *Wine Glass Island*. Right there."

Sure enough, it was the cluster of rock where we had anchored the *Freya* on the night after leaving Utö. The island had emerged from a foggy evening drizzle, two stark bluffs of granite and a saddle of blueberry bushes in between. Midway in the saddle stood a solitary spruce trimmed by the wind to exactly the shape of a wine glass. The island was unnamed on the chart; we had called it Wine Glass Island, and on the lee side found a harbor nearly enclosed by granite islets.

From the deck of our passenger ship the island looked small and undistinguished, hardly a place where anyone would think to anchor, although we'd been glad enough for its wild rocky

277

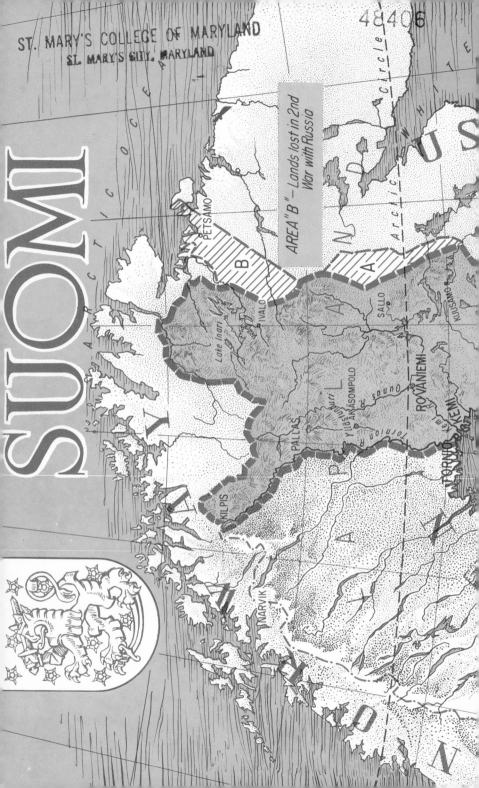

48406

SUOMI

PETSAMO

AREA "B" — Lands lost in 2nd War with Russia

B

A

IVALO

Late Inari

SALLO

PALLAS

KILPIS

ROVANIEMI

KUUSAMO

YLI\[a\]SKASOMPOLO

NARVIK

TORNIO

KEMI